CONTRACTING with UNCLE SAM

CONTRACTING with UNCLE SAM

The Essential Guide for Federal Buyers and Sellers

BILL C. GIALLOURAKIS

NAVAL INSTITUTE PRESS
Annapolis, Maryland

Naval Institute Press
291 Wood Road
Annapolis, MD 21402

Library of Congress Cataloging-in-Publication Data
Giallourakis, Bill C.
  Contracting with Uncle Sam : the essential guide for federal buyers and sellers / Bill C.
Giallourakis.
    p. cm.
  Includes bibliographical references and index.
  ISBN 978-1-59114-315-4 (alk. paper)
  1. Public contracts—United States—Handbooks, manuals, etc. 2. Government purchas-
ing—United States—Handbooks, manuals, etc. 3. Small business—United States—Hand-
books, manuals, etc. I. Title.
  HD3861.U6G53 2008
  658.8'04—dc22
                                                    2008015589

Printed in the United States of America on acid-free paper

14 13 12 11 10 09 08   9 8 7 6 5 4 3 2
First printing

Dedication

This text is dedicated to the memory of Antonia J. Giallourakis, March 17, 1944–April 12, 2004. Born to Greek immigrants in Nebraska, she was an art teacher, language arts teacher, teacher of the K–8 gifted and talented, beloved sister to her fallen Air Force fighter pilot brother of the West Point Class of 1957, mother of three children, cancer fighter, Russian Orthodox icon writer/artist, founder and inspirer of Children's Art for Children's Cancer Foundation, Inc., a nonprofit, and beloved Army–West Pointer's wife who supported unselfishly and inspired the author's military and legal careers. To the end Antonia encouraged the writing of this book from her bedside, where its outline was first drafted by the author.

Contents

Illustrations

Preface

For some years I have taught federal contracting to small groups of students, civil servants, and military and industry personnel with varying degrees of acquisition backgrounds at the invitation of the Armed Forces Communications Electronics Association in Fairfax, Virginia. This text builds on that experience; it is current and Internet-referenced so that it mirrors the federal government's move to a "paperless" procurement system. This condensed procurement book is born out of my crucible of experience in the Army as one of its warfighters, out of service on the Army General Staff, and out of my experience as a program manager.

The United States is in a global war against terrorists and at the same time needs to respond to both natural (hurricanes, earthquakes, fires, etc.) and manmade emergencies (chemical, biological, and nuclear incidents). The nation needs responsible traders to support emergency/contingency planners. Such trading should lead to the award of responsive contracts for the logistics (goods, services, construction) essential not only to winning a protracted war but also for efficiently operating our government at home and abroad and helping states recover and reconstruct after disasters and emergencies. Procurement in government, as well as in industry, is undergoing a transformation as a result of globalization, technological breakthroughs, and the surge in outsourcing. The government is using its computer systems to record purchasing transactions across its agencies, leading to more centralized purchasing (government-wide acquisition contracts, or GWACs), especially of commercial items, and cost cutting. Moreover, the United States is entering an era of scarce commodities (steel, copper, and oil, for example) when the risk of disruptions to its supply lines by terrorists and natural disasters is increasing. Hence procurement managers more than ever need to manage a worldwide network of reliable supplier relationships and be thoroughly knowledgeable not only of what is to be purchased but also of the processes necessary to manufacture a satisfactory product.

There is nothing worse for a buyer's reputation than throwing business in a reverse auction to the lowball supplier who then has trouble delivering. The prime contractors that assemble warfighters' equipment, whether armored vehicles, fighter aircraft, ships, heavy lift cranes, machine guns, or missiles, have to be good purchasers since they invariably have to purchase large quantities of raw material, supplies, and components worldwide outside of their corporations. The performance grade of the contractor and, eventually, the United States' mission will depend on how well the contractor handles this outsourcing.

This book was written to provide the fundamentals to those traders and their government counterparts who bid on, award, execute, or administer contracts so that what they read in the Federal Acquisition Regulation (FAR) on the Internet makes sense in the broad picture and under other federal procurement laws. With the plethora of government databases available on the Internet it is easy to become confused and overwhelmed, to say the least. Contracting with Uncle Sam can alleviate some of that stress.

I have written this book for the beginner—new, small businesses that need a good client, one that pays and has a need for goods and services, one that allows you to grow, and one that provides sufficient progress payments to cover your expenses while you move ahead to increase commercial sales and profitability. The federal government is that good client. This has been the case even in bad economic times.

The Global War on Terror (GWOT), the wars in Iraq and Afghanistan and the related reconstruction there, and hurricanes Katrina and Rita have highlighted the importance of this special customer. Government spending for defense and homeland security has been the most important source for growth in the economy since 1992, and projections say this trend will continue unabated.

Contracting with Uncle Sam also serves as an excellent primer for qualified companies located in countries outside the United States (e.g., in NATO, non-NATO, and other countries with U.S. free trade agreements approved by Congress) that may bid on work funded by the U.S. government. This text is intended to give a readable account of the U.S. procurement system and allows one to obtain a sense of what is expected when dealing with the government. The text is intended to remove the complexity and mystery from federal contracting in both source selection and contract administration once the contract is awarded. It covers the acquisition basics from the perspectives of both buyer and vendor.

This book is not a dry restatement of federal regulations and statutes, nor is it a step-by-step marketing text. It can serve the buyer, engineer, business developer, logistics planner, entrepreneur, disadvantaged business, disabled veteran, sole proprietor, or small business (for-profit or nonprofit) as presented through the experiences of a lawyer-engineer practitioner. Detailed resource notes for each chapter are included at the end of the book, along with an index for expanded quick reference.

This book applies to suppliers, equipment manufacturers, and industrial firms such as Raytheon, Lockheed Martin, General Dynamics, United Technologies, and Boeing, but also to a multitude of medium and small businesses, including construction firms. Any firm whose business involves public-work contracts is especially invited to use this book. Such firms include those in contracts for improvements or for any other project, fixed or not, for the public use of the United States involving construction, alteration, removal, repair, reconstruction, and maintenance, including projects or operations under service contracts for work in connection with national defense or war activities, dredging, harbor improvements, dams, roadways, water systems, bridges, pipelines, electrical power infrastructure, and housing, as well as preparatory and ancillary work in connection with that at the site or on the project. New hires in contracting and estimating departments will be able to use this book. It even suits foreign businesses that want to compete with U.S. firms for projects on a global basis in such sensitive areas as Iraq and Afghanistan. Traders and their procurement officials in countries in the Middle East, such as Israel, Kuwait, Jordan, Dubai, Iraq, and Afghanistan, not to mention acquisition professionals at the state and federal levels, should include this book in their continuing-education libraries as a reference for the pursuit, planning, and management of U.S.-funded contracts.

Every year the federal acquisition budget programs funds for products, services, research, and grants required by the executive department for the states, industry, academia, and federally funded research institutes and for any contingencies that may arise. In addition the programs and budgets fund the operations and maintenance of the government's civilian and military manpower, including maintaining readiness and sustaining combat operations globally. Congress reviews the budget and adjusts it as reflected in the annual appropriations. Unfunded requirements often arise that require special appropriations by Congress. Examples include the recovery and reconstruction of the U.S. Gulf Coast states, maintenance of U.S. armed forces in Iraq and Afghanistan, and the costs of the reconstruction of Iraq.

The totality of this budget is defined in this book as the "acquisition pie." That pie encompasses the sum of the annual budget for projected purchases by the various departments and branches of the government. A percentage of this budget by department is set aside for the competitive award of contracts to small businesses, including disadvantaged, women-owned, and service-disabled veteran-owned enterprises. As a beginner you too can get a piece of the federal acquisition pie.

There are numerous Web sites that promote the marketing of government sales, both federal and state. For a fee they can provide a weekly "culling" of business opportunities in a particular area of government procurement. The current popular business niches are the Department of Homeland Security (DHS) and the Department of Defense (DoD), the latter with its military service departments: the Army, Air Force, Navy, and Marine Corps.

In addition there are many books with titles such as Doing Business with the Government or XYZ Agency. There are for-profit and nonprofit firms that offer to identify business opportunities in your line of interest for a monthly fee. There are Internet home pages where one can ask questions and receive answers from the procurement agency. Or one may contact the National Center for Small Business and locate the nearest Small Business Administration (SBA) office (www.sba.gov) or participating educational institution that will provide procurement technical assistance at no charge or for a nominal fee. This program, known as the DoD Procurement Technical Assistance Program (PTAP), is administered by the Defense Logistics Agency on behalf of the secretary of defense. Multiple PTAP centers may be located in your state near your home.

What is not available is a procurement book that is easy to read, applies a minimum of government jargon, integrates the essential e-government Web sites in its text, and allows the reader to obtain a sense for the federal procurement process. In other words, anyone trading with the government or working for the government needs this book as a desk reference. My intent is to provide the reader with a set of actionable concepts referenced to relevant government Web sites whose useful "decay time" is slow, thus surviving the test of time. Armed with this text the reader may use the Internet, read the relevant parts and clauses of the FAR, and examine a solicitation efficiently. One can dissect a solicitation with some confidence and explore with knowledge the substantive source selection process involved, the risks, and what lies ahead in trading with Uncle Sam. Moreover, with this text a procurement professional, from his or her terminal or laptop worldwide, may use the Procurement Desktop-Defense (PD2) software, provided under the DoD's Standard Procurement System (SPS), with a better understanding of the solicitations and purchase orders generated during normal and contingency/deployment operations.

Owing to travel restrictions because of budget constraints or increased fuel costs, fewer personnel attend meetings and trade professional association conferences, which in turn results in fewer opportunities for meetings between industry and government officials in order to discuss projections and marketing opportunities. Hence the procurement process must be learned before one may enter a company into play through the Internet using the designated government points of entry (GPE) at www.fedbizopps.gov. This text does just that. In summary, this book gives insight into the U.S. procurement system through the eyes of its author—a former trader, military program manager, combat artillery officer, and procurement lawyer. The reader will judge the effectiveness of making a complex subject interesting and current.

After reading the book and using it as a desk reference, you will better understand how the system works and will be able to undertake your own adventures in contracting with Uncle Sam.

Trading Tips

FOR THE BUYER-TRADER

1. Exercise source selection, purchase authority, and contract administration ethically and with openness. Ensure that your standards of conduct in procurement matters are beyond reproach.
2. Be sensitive to war profiteering and other contractor crimes committed worldwide where U.S. operations are ongoing. Cooperate with the National Procurement Fraud Task Force under the U.S. Department of Justice in investigating and vigorously prosecuting those few.
3. Market research is a must if you are a government buyer. Based on your agency's mission, know your needs (services, products, and equipment) well, as well as the vendors in the various geographical areas in which you operate or plan to operate. There can be no sustained logistics without contracting reliable, worldwide primary sources with a proven record of managing the outsourcing of parts that go into manufacturing the deliverables under the contract.
4. Know your contract types so you can fit the acquisition, whether a commercial item or developmental item, with the right type or hybrid version before choosing a source selection procedure, whether it be simplified acquisition, sealed bidding, or negotiation procedures.
5. Find an existing contract vehicle onto which you may piggyback your requirement, if allowed by your agency, to cut down on your acquisition cycle time. Someone else has already done the paperwork and the price has been predetermined as reasonable. What a great way to have the item delivered promptly with minimum hassle. You can even request quotations from more than one scheduled vendor, thus making them compete to meet your need.
6. Do not rest until you have done your emergency and contingency contract

planning in support of what the planners and operations team foresee for possible scenarios (natural and manmade disasters, terrorist events, military operations).

7. Government credits cards for micropurchases and simplified acquisition procedures (SAPs) have expandable thresholds during a crisis. You can buy more, quickly, but only at retail prices. Put oversight procedures in place in advance (e.g., enter purchases into a bar-coded property tracking system, etc.). Rescind the increase threshold as soon as possible after the peak of the crisis in order to stop paying retail prices and return to volume discounts based on negotiations or bidding.

8. Do not forget that the acquisition team needs to be integrated—and that includes the vendor-traders. Exercise innovative contracting: If the procurement action is not precluded by the FAR then try it. You have the authority under the FAR.

9. Remember that you cannot support America's warfighters without the cooperation, innovation, and capacity of your industry counterparts. In essence it is a partnership. Industry responded in World War I, World War II, Korea, Vietnam, the 1991 Persian Gulf War, and the current war in Iraq. It is responding as you read. Just give it a chance.

FOR THE VENDOR–TRADER

1. Trade with integrity at all levels of your business. Do not tolerate fraud or defective pricing. Ethics are a must. Develop, train, and exercise a code of business conduct that includes strict compliance with the law throughout your firm. Maintain an internal control system to detect, prevent, and report on fraud. Your past performance follows you. Fight to see your performance evaluation on all projects.

2. Decide what services and products you can provide based upon your competence and resources. Do not forget that the government may be able to furnish the jigs and fixtures (government-furnished equipment and material) and may even provide a plant for a work site, especially if you are a small business.

3. Maintain a reliable worldwide network of responsible sources for materials and parts suppliers to provide confidence in meeting the quality and the schedule requirements set forth in the contract. Pay higher prices to ensure that your outsourced materials and parts arrive on time and are within quality.

4. Study the needs of the government. The government buys to meet requirements. Get the General Services Administration (GSA) to approve your schedule as a supplier of commercial items or services so you can market to the various departments whose government buyers have needs to fill and money to pay.

5. Target your market for your product and services using all media: the Internet, face-to-face visits, symposiums, demonstrations, and so on. Start with your back door. Attend trade shows and government- and industry-sponsored meetings and conferences. Be patient and persistent.

6. Market research is a must for you too. Find out who has the contracts in your North American Industry Classification System (NAICS) code using the Web site www.defenselink.mil (which lists the homepages of DoD purchasing activities).

7. Enter into alliances or coalitions with other small or large businesses. Contractor team arrangements (CTAs), such as joint ventures, are looked upon favorably by buyers. But get it down in writing from the prime contractor since you are going to be paraded around when your firm gets into the big guy's small business subcontracting plan.

8. Price estimation, including price analysis and cost analysis, is a must. Learn how to perform such analyses using proven software. Then guard your cost data and estimation techniques and tools.

9. Value your firm's technology—your business jewels—by seeking protection and value for your ideas, innovative work products, and technical data. Patents, copyrights, and technical data rights are valuable properties that allow you to leverage value through royalties or outright sale.

10. To the extent that you qualify, seek out government set-asides as a small business. If you are not a small business but operate in a designated local area affected by a manmade emergency or natural disaster, you are eligible for set-asides too.

11. Diversify as soon as possible to wean your firm from government business dependence. Adapt and transfer the technology into global commercial markets.

Acknowledgments

Aside from the Internet and open government sources, materials from this book have been gathered from several libraries, including Seton Hall Law School Library in Newark, New Jersey; the Cadet Library at the United States Military Academy in West Point, New York; the Public Library of Tarpon Springs, Florida; and the Monmouth County, Eastern Branch Library in Shrewsbury, New Jersey. The research staffs within these libraries are important to whatever success this book attains.

In addition the support and technical advice provided by the staff of the U.S. Naval Institute Press—in particular, Thomas Cutler, Susan Corrado, Marla Traweek, and Chris Onrubia—were invaluable in preparing this text for publication. Moreover, I am indebted to Karin Kaufman, my copy editor, for her extraordinary supporting efforts. I would be remiss in not acknowledging the support by Fred Rainbow and Ann Beckham of the Professional Development Center of the Armed Forces Communications Electronics Association (AFCEA). The AFCEA sponsored my teaching over a decade providing the crucible for effectively teaching federal procurement, making it interesting and dynamic to the attending professional students from government and industry.

I also acknowledge all the support by my family, particularly Cosmas, Stamie, Aris, Aakash, and Christina.

Lastly, I want to thank the constructive comments, cheerleading, and encouragement by Nick Chergotis, Helen Katsourides, Charlie Pappas, Gil Messina, Alan Salisbury, and other friends too numerous to name.

Introduction
The Factual Background

We have come a long way from the first federal procurement system developed by John Adams during the War of Independence. Today he would be dual-titled as the first U.S. contracting officer and secretary of defense. The railroads would not have been built without government land grants. Vaccinations as we know them would not have controlled disease but for the government's willingness to purchase vaccines in large numbers while indemnifying drug companies from liability. We are indemnifying industry today for qualified antiterrorism technologies.

Raytheon, which in the 1970s was a small Massachusetts engineering-manufacturing firm, would not have grown and diversified into commercial fields had it not been for its radar technology, which when placed in missiles' nose cones allowed missiles to guide on reflected signals off airborne targets with the help of a ground-to-target illuminating radar system.

During the Cold War Uncle Sam needed close-in air defense systems against the Soviet bomber, thus the HAWK Air Defense Program was born. Raytheon built the HAWK radar tracking and guidance systems and the radar homing missile in the 1960s. The company's learning curve improved, allowing it to propose the SAM-D missile system with a phased array radar, high-speed reprogrammable computer, and new missiles to provide a shield against not only manned aircraft but also incoming guided missiles and free rockets. The system became known as the PATRIOT Air Defense Missile System in the 1970s, and it was deployed in the Middle East in the 1990s. From this system sprung the Patriot Advanced Capability–3 (PAC-3) able to handle not only aircraft and cruise missiles but also tactical ballistic missiles.

Neither Boeing nor Lockheed Martin would be commercial aerospace giants had it not been for Air Force and NASA contracts. Electronic Data Systems Corporation would not have grown without the outsourcing services involving information technology and business processes (payment service, etc.) established from contracts awarded by agencies such as the Veterans Administration and Social Security Administration. Without Defense Advanced Research Project Agency (DARPA) funding of various researchers at laboratories and universities, the Internet may not have matured.

With grants from the National Science Foundation and National Institutes of Health, the large medical research centers and medical teaching colleges, with their research departments and venture company spin-offs, blossomed. The $40 million eight-year contract grant to Harvard University from the National Institutes of Health in March 2002 to establish the Molecular Target Laboratory (renamed the Initiative for Chemical Genetics) allows the laboratory to identify molecules and substances that affect cancer-causing proteins. Its work, which is catalogued in a publicly accessible data bank, is just one example of the importance of government funding. Thus your business model should include the motto "Don't start your enterprise without a public contract." In many cases, from the laser-guided munitions to the Internet, the public contract has served as the vehicle to create technology and wealth for the innovator while serving the economic well-being of the American public. Once the government has paid for the sunk costs of a military product or weapon, it is available for commercialization or foreign military sales to our allies. Such sales have been a great bonus to U.S. defense firms' profits and to the United States' trade balance sheet.

The U.S. military services comprise the Army, Navy, Marine Corps, Air Force, and Coast Guard. All of the services are under the management of the DoD, except the Coast Guard, which is managed by the Department of Homeland Security. These organizations maintain procurement commands that conduct research and development and supply, equip, train, and deploy operational warfighters using regular forces, reserves, and National Guard units under the operational commands of the Joint Chiefs of Staff. These joint or combined operational commands are positioned in various parts of the world. They are themselves buyers of transportation, supplies, equipment, and services from U.S. as well as indigenous local or international vendors. The DoD also includes agencies such as DARPA, the Defense Logistics Agency, and the Defense Intelligence Agency, the latter including combat support agencies such as the National Geospatial-Intelligence Agency, to mention only a few. All of them operate procurement management offices.

These acquisition organizations are under cost and regulatory pressure to maximize sourcing and management. Hence federal procurement since World War II has evolved into a world-class sourcing and contract administration system. By standardizing and streamlining the procurement processes, productivity has improved over the years. This process could be labeled a "contract-centric" approach to procurement. Remember that the acquisition procedures are both regulation and compliance driven.

The U.S. acquisition system is codified by the Armed Services Procurement Act (applicable to the Army, Navy, Marine Corps, Air Force, Coast Guard, and NASA) and the Federal Property and Administrative Services Act (applicable to the General Services Administration and other government agencies). These statutes have been translated for execution in the FAR as of 1984 and supplemental agency regulations. The hallmark of the current system is that the process promotes standardization for efficiency and fairness and minimizes favoritism.

The U.S. system evolved through lessons learned from arming the United States in two world wars and reached its maturity in Operation Overlord during World War II as the Allies stormed the Normandy beaches in France. Despite its current critics the system's resiliency in procuring supplies, adapting weapons to evolving threats, and pushing a logistics pipeline thousands of miles in support of a half million soldiers and allies was demonstrated again in 1991 during Desert Storm, in 2003 during Operation Iraqi Freedom, and in 2001 and later in Afghanistan.

For the foreseeable future, acquisitions policy and procedures will continue to be refined and used in the worldwide fight against terrorism in which lighter and swifter forces are being designed, equipped, and trained for deployment in a variety of theaters of operation. The same procedures are being used to equip and train forces to fight conventional and/or nuclear heavy warfare against foes with armor and fighter aircraft. They were key to the reconstruction of Western Europe after World War II and now serve in the Global War on Terror, the related wars in Iraq and Afghanistan, and the reconstruction of the two countries. You too can participate in this endeavor.

No procurement system is perfect. It needs constant refinement. Recently there has been justified criticism at the lack of providing our warfighters with timely body armor and fielding defenses, such as the Marine's Mine Resistant Ambush Protection Vehicle for use against improvised explosive devices in Iraq. The federal buyer and the U.S. prime contractor need to realize that manufacturing in a responsive manner for defense equipment can no longer be accomplished within costs and in a timely manner with only raw materials and parts from within the United States. Prime contractors need worldwide, multiple sources for parts and supplies. Still, the procurement system in place in the United States is the best overall in the world, despite its shortcomings.

Operated by a professional cadre of procurement specialists, our procurement system remains the envy of many countries, as evidenced by the delegations of procurement authorities from many countries sent to U.S. foreign military sales programs. The United States continues to serve as the agent for the procurement management of supplies and defense warfighting equipment, from air defense systems to diagnostic maintenance systems and software, not to mention fighters and airlift jet transports.

One may ask why commit valuable resources to chase government opportunities whose profit margin historically is low? The answer to that depends on your pipeline's backlog, how hungry you are for work, and project risk. More important, commercialization and global marketing may make it worthwhile, as Raytheon found by selling its U.S. air defense systems to countries in the Middle East. Such international sales allow a U.S.-based firm to recover its one-time developmental costs from military equipment and software sales after first supplying the U.S. force, thus reaping substantial profits.

No one is saying that it is easy to win a government contract, especially for a start-up without venture capital. But you have to start somewhere. Why not the federal government? That is our target. All we need is our slice of the federal procurement pie. Let's get started.

Abbreviations

ACO	Administrative contracting officer
ANSI/EIA	American National Standards Institute and Electronics Industries Alliance
ASSIST	Acquisition Streamlining and Standardization Information System
B&P	Bid and proposal
BAA	Broad Agency Announcement
BCA	Board of Contract Appeals
BPA	Blanket Purchase Agreement
BPN	Business Partner Network
CAGE	Commercial and Government Entity
CAO	Contract administration office
CAS	Cost accounting standards
CCL	Commerce Control List
CCO	Contingency contracting officer
CCR	Central Contractor Registration
CDA	Contract Disputes Act
CDRL	Contract Data Requirements Lists
CI	Commercial item
CICA	Competition in Contracting Act
CLIN	Contract Line Item Number
CMO	Contract management office
COC	Certificate of Competency
COFC	Court of Federal Claims
COR	Contracting officer's representative
COTR	Contracting officer's technical representative
CPIF	Cost-Plus-Incentive-Fee (Contract)

CTA	Contractor team arrangement
DBA	Davis-Bacon Act
D&B	Dun and Bradstreet
DARPA	Defense Advanced Research Project Agency
DCAA	Defense Contract Audit Agency
DCMA	Defense Contract Management Agency
DEC	Digital Equipment Corporation
DFARS	Defense Federal Acquisition Regulation Supplement
DHS	Department of Homeland Security
DO	Delivery order
DoD	Department of Defense
DOE	Department of Energy
DPAS	Defense Priorities and Allocation System
DTIC	Defense Technical Information Center
DUNS	Data Universal Numbering System
EAR	Export Administration Regulations
ECCN	Export Control Classification Number
EFT	Electronic Funds Transfer
eSRS	Electronic Subcontractor Reporting System
EVMS	Earned value management system
FADAC	Field artillery digital automatic computer
FAR	Federal Acquisition Regulation
FBO	Federal Business Opportunities
FEMA	Federal Emergency Management Agency
FFP	Firm-Fixed-Price (Contract)
FOIA	Freedom of Information Act
FPDS-NG	Federal Procurement Data System–Next Generation
FPI	Fixed-Price-Incentive (Contract)
FPR	Final Proposal Revision
FSC	Federal Supply Classification
FSS	Federal Supply Service
GAO	Government Accountability Office
GE	General Electric
GOF	Government-owned facilities
GPE	Government point of entry
GSA	General Services Administration
GWAC	Government-wide Acquisition Contract

GWOT	Global War on Terror
HDL	Harry Diamond Laboratories
HUBZone	Historically Underutilized Business Zone
IAE	Integrated Acquisition Environment
IBR	Integrated Baseline Review
IDDQ	Indefinite-Delivery/Definite-Quantity (Contract)
IDIQ	Indefinite-Delivery/Indefinite-Quantity (Contract)
IDIR	Indefinite-Delivery/Indefinite-Requirements (Contract)
IFB	Invitation for Bids
IFN	Item for negotiation
IGCE	Independent government cost estimate
IPT	Integrated procurement team
IR&D	Independent research and development
IT	Information technology
J&A	Justification and approval
MAC	Multiple-Agency Contract
MAS	Multiple Award Schedules
MPIN	Marketing Partner Identification Number
NAFTA	North American Free Trade Agreement
NAICS	North American Industry Classification System
NBC	Nuclear, biological, chemical
NCP	National Checklist Program
NIST	National Institute of Standards and Technology
NSN	National Stock Number
NVD	National Vulnerability Database
OFPP	Office of Federal Procurement Policy
ORCA	Online Representations and Certifications Application
PBA	Performance-based acquisition
PBC	Performance-based contracting
PD2	Procurement Desktop-Defense
PDP	Programmed Data Processor computer series
PNM	Price negotiation memorandum
PPIRS	Past Performance Information Retrieval System
PTA	Point of Total Assumption
PTAC	Procurement Technical Assistance Centers
PTAP	Procurement Technical Assistance Program
PWS	Performance Work Statement

QASP	Quality Assurance Surveillance Plan
QATT	Qualified anti-terror technology
QBL	Qualified Bidder's List
QML	Qualified Manufacturer's List
QPL	Qualified Products List
R&D	Research and development
RFI	Request for Information
RFP	Request for Proposal
RFQ	Request for Quotation
RFR	Request for Revisions
RIE	Range of incentive effectiveness
RTEP	Request for Task Execution Plan
SADBU	Small and Disadvantaged Business Utilization
SAP	Simplified acquisition procedures
SAT	Simplified acquisition threshold
SBA	Small Business Administration
SBIR	Small Business Innovation Research
SBU	Sensitive But Unclassified
SCA	Service Contract Act
SCAP	Security Content Automation Protocol
SDB	Small disadvantaged business
SDVOSB	Service-disabled veteran-owned small business
SF	Standard Form
SINCGARS	Single channel ground and airborne radio system
SOO	Statement of Objectives
SPS	Standard Procurement System
SSA	Source Selection Authority
SSAC	Source Selection Advisory Council
SSEB	Source Selection Evaluation Board
SSP	Source Selection Plan
STTR	Small Business Technology Transfer Research
TDP	Technical Data Package
TEP	Task Execution Plan
TIN	Taxpayer Identification Number
TO	Tasking order
TPIN	Trading Partner Identification Number
TPP	Trading Partner Profile

TRFP	Task Request for Proposal
TSA	Transportation Security Administration
USPTO	U.S. Patent and Trademark Office
USTR	U.S. Trade Representative
V&V	Verification and validation
VAX	Virtual Address Extension computer series
VECP	Value Engineering Change Proposal
VIQ	Variation in estimated quantities
VMS	Virtual memory system
WBS	Work breakdown structure
WDOL	Department of Labor Wage Determinations Online
WOSB	Women-owned small business
WTO GPA	World Trade Organization Government Procurement Agreement

CHAPTER 1

Winning the First Job
A Small Business Innovation Research Grant

I t was a chilly February day in 1983. The snow had just started, and the projection was for four to six inches. I was at Bolling Air Force Base in Maryland, just outside Washington, D.C., having a hot breakfast in the Officers' Club near the Bachelor Officers' Quarters, which was to be my temporary home for five days. As a retired "bird" colonel, I was allowed to use the quarters on a space-available basis—one of the coveted benefits of twenty-plus years in the Army.

My primary concern that day was not the road conditions but my ability or inability to master from scratch how to program on a 32-bit platform "super-minicomputer" using FORTRAN IV, a computer-programming language. The computer was a VAX (Virtual Address Extension) 11/780 manufactured by the Digital Equipment Corporation (DEC) of Maynard, Massachusetts. In 1976 DEC decided to move to an entirely new platform with 32 bits. The company released the VAX 11/780 in 1978 and immediately took over the vast majority of the minicomputer market. The VAX series had an instruction set rich even by today's standards (as well as an abundance of addressing modes). In addition to the paging and memory protection features of the earlier Programmed Data Processor (PDP) series, the VAX supported virtual memory. The VAX could use both the Unix operating system and DEC's own virtual memory system (VMS) operating system.

At its peak in the late 1980s DEC was the second largest computer company in the world, with more than one hundred thousand employees. Its systems were used to control and monitor factories, transportation systems, and nuclear plants and were found throughout various branches and agencies of the Department of Defense (DoD). The company was an early champion of time-sharing systems and one of the first commercial businesses connected to the Internet, so Digital.com became one of the first of the dot-com domains. Hewlett-Packard purchased DEC and produced its product line under the Hewlett-Packard name.

In 1983 I was enrolled in a crash programming course at a DEC commercial teaching center just outside the gates of Bolling Air Force Base. The course would teach me how to transport my programming skills in FORTRAN IV to a desktop PC. Several weeks earlier I had been informed that my one-man company had been awarded a DoD Small Business Innovation Research (SBIR) contract by the Air Force for a fixed sum of $42,782. The SBIR program was at that time and continues to be part of the DoD's effort, mandated by the Small Business Administration (SBA), to promote innovative research by small businesses for the fulfillment of various needs within the department. At the same time the program is intended to encourage young firms to take their products or services to the commercial marketplace. Eleven federal agencies participate in the SBIR program, and Congress reauthorizes it annually. The program's official Web site, www.sbir.gov, is administered by the National Science Foundation.

The SBIR program consists of three stages. Phase I provides for six months' time and funds of up to $100,000 for the feasibility study of an announced agency need. Phase II allows federal funds of up to $750,000 over a period of two years for the development and prototyping of the concept defined in Phase I. And finally, in Phase III, the agency expects the small business to obtain funding from the private sector or non-SBIR government sources to develop the concept into a product for sale in the private sector or military market. The terms of each phase and the government funds to be provided will vary from agency to agency and as a function of the need being studied or developed.

Related to this program is the Small Business Technology Transfer Research (STTR) program, initiated in 1992, which currently may provide up to $850,000 in early-stage research and development (R&D) funding (Phases I and II) to a small business to do cooperative R&D with researchers at universities, federally funded R&D centers, or nonprofit research institutions. The purpose of STTR is to provide an effective vehicle for moving ideas from our nation's research institutions to the marketplace, where they can benefit both private-sector and military customers. The same eleven agencies that take part in the SBIR program also participate in the STTR program.

In the past the Department of Defense's SBIR and STTR programs together have funded a billion dollars each year in early-stage R&D projects at small technology companies for projects that serve a DoD need and have commercial applications. Companies generally retain the intellectual property rights to the technologies they develop under these programs. Funding is awarded competitively, but the process is streamlined by the electronic submission of technical proposals, which are limited to twenty-five pages. The Web site for the programs (www.acq.osd.mil/sadbu/sbir) is user friendly.

The SBIR program fit my business model because, having recently retired from the Army, I had just opened a law office. My law degree from Seton Hall was paid for by the GI education bill. However, my new office's one-time start-up costs and monthly overhead were not covered. The Air Force contract was the answer to my money problems. True, it was not the practice of law, but I had decided to use my prior analytic and higher-order mathematics background as an electrical engineer and planning skills as an assistant project manager for the U.S. Army's Communications–Electronics Command (now known as the Communications–Electronics Life Cycle Management Command) to fulfill the Air Force's need.

The name of the new firm was Bill C. Giallourakis, P.C., and the New Jersey Business Corporation Act under which the firm was incorporated allowed me to conduct any legitimate business. Today I would form a registered limited liability company instead, because of its tax advantages, its treatment as a partnership, and its superior liability protection. I had never bid on a project, although I had managed many other contracts worth millions of dollars. This was to become a real personal challenge. I checked the laws on conflicts of interests for former government employees and found that none applied to me in this situation. Moreover, I had a written opinion from the government's ethics officer. (Chapter 10 covers the details about ethics and standards of conduct for employees.) Doing business with the federal government was perfectly legal. The way was clear. I noted that the Air Force was interested in research related to predicting the costs of new jet engines and decided to accept the challenge to see if I could win an SBIR contract.

At that time military jet engines were being manufactured by both General Electric (GE) in Cincinnati and Boston and Pratt & Whitney in Connecticut. They still are. The procedure for awarding contracts is the same now as it was then. In the "annual call for improvements process" between GE and Pratt & Whitney—in essence a perpetual competition using a split-award technique decided by the secretary of the Air Force—each contractor's originally submitted certified cost or pricing data is subjected to a call for improvements letter requesting improvements in price as well as terms and conditions over the years.

The Air Force wanted cost-estimating research done to assist it in award-ing the next round of jet engine contracts. The $42,782 SBIR grant to my firm was to be my dollar share of the DoD's small business. My slice of the research "pie" was to adopt nonlinear regression modeling using FORTRAN on an IBM PC platform to predict production cost. I had recently purchased the tenth IBM PC sold by Computerland in Monmouth County—a fact that made me so proud that it was part of my cocktail-hour bragging. Little did I realize the role that desktop PC would play in making my one-man firm highly efficient and productive in comparison to a much larger firm without this tool. Its use on behalf of the Air Force set the stage for catapulting my business to high profitability.

I felt serious trepidation about being able to handle such a project by myself, but I had nothing to lose. After all, I had served on the Army General Staff in the Pentagon doing missile R&D. Later I was reassigned as the military assistant to the Army's chief scientist. More important, I had taught "juice" at West Point some twenty years earlier. "Juice" was the slang term for the academy's mandatory course in electricity, the course most feared by all the "cows," as cadet juniors were called, and an obstacle to graduation. It was considered by most cadets a "mystery." (The course is not mandatory now, but it remains in the West Point curriculum as taught by the Department of Electrical Engineering and Computer Science.)

Moreover, I recalled the arrival at West Point of five field artillery digital automatic computers (FADACs) in 1964. These were the first ruggedized PCs to be used by artillery fire direction officers to electronically solve the gunnery trajectory equations in computing the range to the target for a howitzer (155 mm), an artillery gun (8 inch), and even rockets and missiles. It could com-pute the elevation and azimuth settings based on the projectile type to hit a target. The FADAC's versatility also enabled the solution of field artillery sup-port computations related to surveying, counterbattery, fire planning, flash and sound ranging, reduction of meteorological data, and master control and programming for the automatic checkout of missiles.

The mechanization of FADAC is based on solving the differential equations of projectile motion from firing to impact. Necessary data such as target location, powder temperature, gun location, and meteorological data (inserted manually or by tape reader) are entered by means of a simplified keyboard. When all data are entered the depression of a button initiates computation: Gun orders comprising deflection, quadrant elevation, fuse time, and charge are displayed in decimal form. As a trained fire direction officer I had used a series of artillery slide rules to determine trajectory. When the FADACs arrived I was assigned the task of training the cadets on their use. The wooden artillery slide rules were discarded. As a result of the revolution in microcomputing, a handheld calculator version could suffice today.

My graduate work in Lafayette, Indiana, while a student at Purdue University in 1962, stood me well for the computer challenge. It was in Lafayette that I taught myself to use programming to design the electrical communications networks the professors assigned graduate students. I could not help but reflect on the stack of punch cards I dropped off every day at the computer center. Then I would go back again in the late evening to see how my program had faired. Did it work? Usually it did not on the first try. Then I would work all night to deliver another stack of computer punch cards the next morning before going to class. Punch cards are now gone. Writing software code has become friendlier; however, one still is left with a labor-intensive product that requires much testing and validation.

I had spent eight years as a quality-control and test manager. This led me first to camping out for extended periods of time on the assembly line for the HAWK missile production at Raytheon's Andover plant and later to designing the testing for the SINCGARS (single channel ground and airborne) VHF radio system with Cincinnati Electronics (a subsidiary of British-owned Marconi Electronics). There seemed to be respect and even relief from the two vendors for a quality-control manager who wore a warrior's uniform and was competent technically off the battlefield. The design of a test program whose execution would have an impact on their bottom line was found to be fair and ensured a combat-fit missile and radio for the Army. If I could do it with missiles and radios, why not with the production of jet engines?

I prepared a proposal, including a bibliography based on the technical documentation of prior contractors' research sent to me from the Defense Technical Information Center (DTIC) of the DoD. Figure 1-1 depicts to a prospective researcher and proposal writer the scientific and technical databases available at the DTIC. It provides e-mail addresses for queries and the Web site to access reported scientific and technical information. The abstracts from the DTIC, which also stocks hard copies of research papers and maintains a database of similar ongoing and completed works, was a big help. It allowed me to cull what research was relevant and to pinpoint the state of the art in nonlinear regression for supporting "should-cost" studies. The DTIC provided me with the technical printed knowledge base that allowed me to decide whether or not to bid for the project. The technical information also served as an aid in writing the proposal I submitted to the Air Force. It prevented me from proposing research that rediscovered or retraced known "art." If you are not allowed access or are not eligible to register on DTIC, then search DTIC's unclassified collection and order documents through the National Technical Information Center at www.ntis.gov. The center provides a supplementary, broader database search.

To my surprise I was selected for contract award. Some time later I found out that 2,902 proposals had been submitted, 283 of which had been selected for awards on various topics. Out of the 283 selected firms, only 2 were in my topic area—my one-man firm and Computer Sciences Corporation, a firm that now has more than eighty thousand employees worldwide providing services in information technology.

FIGURE 1–1. Defense Technical Information Center (DTIC)

Scientific and Technical Information (STINFO)
STINET MultiSearch provides alphabetical database descriptions (http://multisearch.dtic.mil/descriptions.html).

Types of Accessible Databases
Tech Reports
Standards and Specifications
R&D Descriptive Summaries
IR&D Database

DTIC Registration Web site for access
(www.dtic.mil/dtic/registration/index.html)

Written queries by users to DTIC
(Email: online@dtic.mil; stinfo@dtic.mil)

Perhaps my resume, with its bachelor of science, master's in electrical engineering, master's in business administration, and doctor of law degrees, was too heavy to ignore, or perhaps the Air Force checked my flight record as a jumpmaster with the 82nd Airborne Division from Fort Bragg and 173rd Airborne out of Okinawa and was satisfied with my past performance. Seriously, my earlier teaching of electrical engineering with its mathematical base and more recent project management experiences contributed to my selection for an award by the Air Force's evaluation team. Moreover, I was a veteran small business owner whose award by the Air Force balanced its award to a large business. My award furthered the Air Force's goal for the number of awards given to small businesses.

As a matter of normal practice depending on the overall evaluation criteria, a purchasing agency can rate a newly formed company with no past performance history on similar contracts as "neutral." Alternatively, the agency's evaluation scheme may allow offerors to meet experience requirements using the experience of properly committed key employees or subcontractors. This was my case. I was able to jump over the hurdle poised by the lack of past performance. Although my firm was newly formed, my personal resumé and stated written commitment to the SBIR project made the jump. The Air Force valued and found credible my proposal to accomplish the research as the main researcher. The risk of default had been reduced to a competitive, acceptable level.

An offeror's past performance on similar projects is a key criterion in the assessment of risk as to whether or not a new project will be completed on time and within budgeted costs. Its weight in a competitive negotiated proposal evaluation may be worth more than the technical and cost factors combined. Congress, through reports rendered by the General Accountability Office, has noted repeatedly the numerous cost overruns and delivery delays on DoD weapons systems and other service projects. These reports have caused legislation and regulations to be passed that require past performance to be evaluated on every contract awarded in excess of one hundred thousand dollars.

A government database of offerors' past performance reports, known as the Past Performance Information Retrieval System (PPIRS), has been established. A source selection official can access it (at www.ppirs.gov) and assess the past in an effort to evaluate future performance risk. A contractor must be registered in the Central Contractor Registration (CCR) database and have a marketing partner identification number (MPIN) to access the database's confidential information (see chapter 2).

It was certainly surprising that I was awarded this contract, since I had never performed a project that required the development of a set of computer software specifications and the follow-up prototyping of a working software model with substantial lines of human-written code and its translation into related machine code. After the jubilation passed, anxiety set in because performance on the contract was required to commence within thirty days and be completed within six months.

The trek over to the DEC school for FORTRAN was indeed with purpose. My incentive to comprehend and learn had never before risen to such a tense level, except perhaps for my first day in calculus class as a cadet plebe at West Point. I had learned basic FORTRAN while at Purdue in 1963 and taught the "cows" at West Point, but it was now more than fifteen years later and I had forgotten the details of all that I had learned. But I was amazed at my recall, and my new teachers were astounded at my interest and attention to master FORTRAN IV. Although my project was not a secret, I hesitated to disclose the basis for my intense, if not fanatic, interest.

I thought seriously of hiring a part-time consultant to assist me with the project but hesitated because those I had found to be qualified had either a temporary visa status for professionals (H-1 type visa) or had just attained permanent residency in the United States—and neither status was sufficient to allow them to work on any classified project (which is still true today). In addition, employees with such a status do not have the authorization to enter a military base such as Wright-Patterson Air Force Base to consult with the Air Force, much less the Naval Submarine Base at Groton, Connecticut. The need for security was not lost on me. Today security considerations are even more restrictive and important. With the recent government policy allowing employees to telecommute, security considerations are even more heightened.

When I returned late that evening on the first day to the Bachelor Officers' Quarters, I was exhausted. The wet snow made the ride back to the air base treacherous. It snowed all week. In the evenings I would dredge over to the Officer's Club for a late snack. There I realized that the contract work I had won was not a piece of cake but would require enormous effort. The working software model I had proposed to demonstrate at the end of the contract would require numerous hours of tedious coding and testing. Today that would lead one to team up with an offshore software development firm to do the detail software code creation work. For security reasons that offshore firm could be located in Australia, Canada, or the United Kingdom, if relatively quick approval was a criterion for a teammate.

I realized that I was stuck with what I had proposed. The Air Force had accepted my proposal and its associated schedules without change. The award was based upon my "initial" proposal. There were no requested discussions or negotiations prior to the award. The Air Force had gone strictly with my written work plan and my biography. This is not uncommon today; hence the big push in good proposal writing. Better make sure your initial cost proposal covers all the work. If you expect to have the opportunity to negotiate with the government, you may be surprised or even disappointed when your proposal is accepted "as is." Do not hold back your "best and final" cost offer. Give the government your best prices on the initial submission, for you may not have a chance to drop them. You may never enter negotiations and be invited to revise your initial proposal. Writing software code in FORTRAN IV for an IBM PC in 1982 was laborious and exhausting. One had to master FORTRAN IV and then apply it to the nonlinear regression math model, plus adapt the software to the peculiarities of the computer machine to ensure that the object code was converted to machine language—something a good compiler can do effortlessly today. My contract required me to deliver a demonstration model of the software in human readable format.

Yet even today, despite efficient computer compilers and use of higher-order languages, the process remains labor intensive and requires the use of talented professionals. No wonder the software firms and financial houses have outsourced their software houses and back rooms to India, Ireland, Eastern Europe, China, and other overseas locations where cheap computer science–educated labor is plentiful in comparison to the United States. This trend will continue and poses serious security problems for defense contractors whose contracts require the programming of security-sensitive material and software embedded in weapons systems or part of military Internet-centric intelligence fusion systems.

At the end of the computer course I left Bolling, recognizing that I had only scratched the surface on being a qualified programmer. I not only needed to study more, but I also needed help. A contractor team arrangement, in the current vernacular, was in my thoughts—a teammate (by joint venture or subcontract) skilled in the art of software code writing. No amount of study could overcome my deficits in experience and computer programming and development in a timely manner.

As I drove back home along the New Jersey Turnpike, my mind drifted. I recalled my visit to Harry Diamond Laboratories (better known as HDL), located at Adelphi, Maryland, in 1962. Although at that time Raytheon was in initial production, it was still testing the Improved HAWK air defense missile, the I-HAWK. Each time the missile was test fired at White Sands Missile Range in New Mexico, its warhead exploded prematurely, causing the missile to miss the target. The onboard radar fuse was misfiring. This defect was baffling the Raytheon technical team, not to mention the Army project management office. It was at HDL that I met a government scientist who had dedicated his career in the government to the study and design of radar proximity fuses. In no time this elderly gentleman, who was on the verge of retirement, pinpointed the problem—to the dismay of all and to the benefit of not only Raytheon but also U.S. Army's Air Defense. The availability of such expertise in special areas of weaponization is well worth the expenditure of tax dollars to maintain our national defense laboratories.

There are a plethora of government agencies conducting internal research in a wide range of areas, from medicine, ballistic missile defense, and homeland security to pure mathematics and computer science. In many instances these same agencies have contracts for cooperative research with industry and academia. In other instances, such research is duplicative and has been drastically reduced, eliminating the in-house capabilities to respond to threats by being able to design and produce weaponry.

I side with the advocates who hold that such research should not be considered wasteful but necessary in responding to crisis and to the achievement of innovative breakthrough. More important, it provides in-house expertise to measure the quality of the services and goods delivered to the government by industry. I decided that I would find a government agent, a teammate, to help me.

The main 578-acre campus of the National Bureau of Standards (NBS) is in Gaithersburg, Maryland, on the outskirts of Washington. One could easily mistake it for the campus of Tufts or Princeton. The bureau was known for doing research in mathematics as part of its standards programs. In 1982 the Internet had not reached widespread use, but I had discovered NBS in the literature research retrieved from the Defense Technical Information Center at Fort Belvoir, Virginia, when I was preparing my proposal.

NBS, since 1988 known as the National Institute of Standards and Technology (NIST), was founded in 1901 by President McKinley as part of the Progressive era's quest for a stable, productive, and fair industrial era (see fig. 1-2). (Europe had a similar bureau in the years prior to 1900.) It is a non-regulatory agency under the Department of Commerce. During the McKinley administration the time was ripe for the establishment of a national standards library. Not only was the United States in the midst of its industrial revolution when manufacturing was king, but the age of electricity had arrived. Wall plugs for electrical devices that were mass produced in Michigan (with metal wall plates turned out in Boston) had to fit precisely and use exactly 120 volts.

The states were not even able to enforce the standards developed by the Office of Weights and Measures of the NBS because of budget constraints. No thought had yet been given to the computer and the wave of information technology products and services to come. However, by 1984, the NBS had established a series of high-level laboratories that, with some restructuring and name changes, exist to this date.

FIGURE 1-2. The Organization of the National Institute of Standards and Technology (NIST)

LABORATORIES:
Building and Fire Research
Chemical Science and Technology
Electronics and Electrical Engineering
Information Technology
- software diagnostics and conformance testing
- computer security
- statistical engineering
- mathematics & computational science
Manufacturing Engineering
Materials Science and Engineering
Nanoscale Science and Technology
Neuron Research
Physics
Technology Services

SCIENTIFIC AND TECHNICAL DATABASES:
www.nist.gov/srd/index.htm
http://srdata.nist.gov/gateway/

These laboratories respond to industry's needs for measurement methods, tools, data, and technology. The NIST mission is to promote U.S. innovation and industrial competitiveness by advancing measurement science, standards, and technology in ways that enhance economic security and improve our quality of life.

In acquiring information technology, government agencies are required to include the appropriate security policies, including the use of common security configurations. These are available through NIST's Web site at http://checklists.nist.gov.

The NIST maintains the National Vulnerability Database (NVD), a repository of standards-based vulnerability management data. The National Checklist Program (NCP) is the U.S. government's repository of publicly available security checklists (or benchmarks) that provide detailed, low-level guidance on setting the Security Content Automation Protocol (SCAP). The SCAP enables standards-based security tools to automatically perform configuration checking using NCP checklists.

NIST researchers collaborate with colleagues in industry, academic institutions, and other government agencies. Of particular interest to me in looking for a teammate was its Information Technology Laboratory, housing the mathematics and computational science and statistical engineering teams. I had hit a productivity gusher.

To my amazement I discovered that a mathematics doctorate employee had completed some basic research using nonlinear regression modeling in FORTRAN IV that had not yet been published. The software was written in the form of a series of modules for a personal computer platform that could be integrated "as is" into my effort with little software linkage. The code was owned by NBS. Commercial entities from IBM to Microsoft copyright their software code. Under U.S. copyright laws, the government cannot copyright its own literary works, including computer software code. (See chapter 9 for more details on registering computer software for copyright protection.)

NBS confirmed that my company was working on an Air Force contract and then extended its cooperation. I was allowed to share its numerous relevant "lines of code" at no cost. I estimated that the NBS prepared code saved my project some six months of intensive programming. One has to realize that code not only must be written and converted into machine language, a tedious task even with compiler machine assistance, but it also must be tested by a process called verification and validation (V&V). My efficiency had just been propelled. As I walked out of the campus to return to New Jersey, my gait was light and spirited. A ton had been lifted from my shoulders. (I should note that the campus of NBS remains under security and visits by the public should be by appointment; hence I recommend access via the Internet to www.nist.gov as a starting point.)

As in any good investigation, there was a field trip component to collect engine production information. I planned to visit two plants of the main suppliers of jet engines, Pratt & Whitney (a United Technologies Corporation company) and General Electric. The General Electric plant was in Lowell, outside Boston, and the Pratt & Whitney plant was in East Hartford. The objective of these two field trips was to gather information on the jet engine manufacturing plants and their processes and to discuss production quality issues and the basis of each plant's underlying learning curves.

Every plant has its own peculiar production learning curve, a predictive tool that relates production levels to unit costs. The theory is the more you produce a product, the lower its unit price because of efficiency in manufacturing. The collected data was to be considered in our modeling of the nonlinear regression models.

The Air Force preceded my visits with the security clearances necessary for my entry. As I reflected on these visits, I realized that security considerations today are even more heightened owing to terrorism and that my being a U.S. citizen was even then a consideration in the award of the SBIR contract to my firm.

Obtaining the requisite security clearances to perform a government contract could serve as an obstacle to bidding on a project. The contractual security requirements should be weighed in terms of time and resources before one considers going after a marketing opportunity. The visits to the plants were quite touchy. Both plants' officials knew that I was on a procurement consulting contract with the Air Force. Whatever data I collected could affect which of the two competitors would be awarded the next round of contracts for jet engine production, including the quantity of each contract.

Today we have many support firms working for a government agency. In fact the contractor's employees now sit in the very chairs that once belonged to experienced civil service employees or soldiers. The use of such support contractors for tasks from preparing solicitations for bidding to performing on-site maintenance on armored vehicles and tanks in Iraq or Afghanistan is not uncommon. The intent is to allow support tasks to be performed by contract personnel while the fighting is done by the volunteer warfighters. Such dependence has ramifications in the event of national emergencies, especially on the response to mass-scale national natural disasters such as Hurricane Katrina.

Even though I had signed confidentiality nondisclosure agreements because of the competitive and sensitive field data I collected at each plant, the GE and Pratt & Whitney managers still felt uncomfortable during my visits. I was not wearing a blue suit.

Most interesting were the discussions I had with employees on the plant floors who were assembling jet engines under contracts for low rates of production. Such contracts are intended to keep the production line "warm." Learning curves could be quite different if the plant was operating at full or surge capacity in comparison to the low rate of production I witnessed.

One machinist I met was about fifty years old. As he discussed the process of casting, grinding, and verifying the quality of the engine's turbine— probably the most critical component of a jet engine because of the intense heat environment in which turbines operate—I reflected on how precious his skills were. His ability to read the production line drawings, to test the turbine, to operate the requisite lathes in machining the turbine, and, most important, to pass those skills on to a new employee in the event the production was expanded in time of war was itself a depreciating national asset.

This meant keeping the labor talent skilled in engine manufacturing on board and qualified. As I walked each plant floor and talked to the employees, I became aware of their priceless skills. I realized that the Air Force shared production or rotated contracts to each of these plants to ensure a surge capability in the event of a national emergency. The only issue in awarding each of these contracts was what "should be" the costs of the engines under efficient production methods in each plant compared with those submitted by each of these manufacturers.

After five months of intensive work, the pilot project was completed. To my second surprise, I was invited to propose for the continuation of the project in Phase II of the SBIR program. I must have received an A+ report card in performance for Phase I. Although tempted to proceed into Phase II, I had to pass. My law practice was starting to take off.

Turning down the opportunity was difficult because Computer Sciences Corporation had invited me to team up with them to do Phase II. It is common practice for a large company to team up with a small one, especially if the smaller one has an innovative product or skilled service personnel but lacks the resources to develop its products or to render the requisite services alone. I was intrigued by the offer, but the call of practicing law was higher. After all, I had proved that I could win a federal contract on the first try and complete it successfully. The lessons learned regarding business with the government were invaluable, unbeknown to my future clients. Theory had been put into actual practice by a former warrior and a "green" attorney who was ripening fast.

When completed, most research work is published as an abstract so that other researchers can access a description of the work product. Such publication pushes the limit of the known knowledge or art by not repeating phenomena already discovered. This was also my first performance report card because I could now use this successful project as a positive reference for winning more government work. I had become a "past performer" with less risk on undertaking future related work, at least in the eyes of a government source selection evaluator.

My abstract, not including the technical report documentation submitted to the Air Force, even to this date blows my mind (see fig. 1-3).

PRACTICING BUSINESS TIPS

My experience reinforced my belief that a businessperson must be bold and flexible, and that this flexibility must include the determination to retrain oneself to meet changing conditions and the needs of the market place. The flexibility comes from a sound broad education firmly implanted in the sciences and social sciences. The SBIR program is well funded and ongoing. I recommend it if it fits. Try it as a great starter. When you let the government serve as your venture capitalist, both can benefit.

FIGURE 1-3. Abstract of the Technical Report of a
Completed Phase I DoD SBIR project, 1983

SUBMITTED BY	DEPT	AWARDED AMOUNT
Bill C. Giallourakis, A Prof Corp.	AF	$42,782
90 Monmouth Street		
Red Bank, NJ 07701		
Bill C. Giallourakis		
Title		

COST ANALYSIS SOFTWARE FOR CONTRACT ADMINISTRATION (CASCA)
TOPIC: 19b   Office: ASD/YZD

THIS PROJECT IN PHASE I, EXAMINES THE TECHNICAL FEASIBILITY OF AUTOMATING THE USE OF THE UNDERLYING LEARNING CURVE (ULC) APPROACH FOR USE BY CONTRACT ADMINISTRATION ORGANIZATIONS. THE UNDERLYING LEARNING CURVE TECHNIQUE COMBINES BOTH ENGINEERING AND PARAMETRIC ESTIMATING APPROACHES TO PROVIDE A SHOULD COST ESTIMATE OF DIRECT LABOR. ULC ALLOWS THE DISCIPLINED INTEGRATION OF THE DATA FOUND IN THE CONTRACTOR'S WORK MEASUREMENT AND COST ACCOUNTING SYSTEMS, LEADING TO THE QUANTIFICATION OF THE TIME ASSOCIATED WITH PARKINSON'S LAW. PROJECT INCLUDES REVIEW OF THE LATEST LEARNING CURVE LITERATURE, UNDERLYING LEARNING CURVE THEORIES, DEVELOPMENT OF AUTOMATED DATA SYSTEMS DOCUMENTATION AND PILOT COMPUTER SOFTWARE, AND TEST EVALUATION OF THE ULC APPROACH. FINAL REPORT INCLUDES DOCUMENTATION IN ACCORDANCE WITH DoDI 7935.1-S, AUTOMATED DATA SYSTEMS DOCUMENTATION STANDARDS.

CHAPTER 2

Market Research and Acquisition
Who's Trading What

With congressional annual appropriations at $825 billion and growing, the federal government is the largest buyer of goods and services in the United States, dwarfing General Motors, Sears, General Electric, or Wal-Mart. Expenditures by the executive departments vary from emergency rations for flood victims to rocket fuel for NASA shuttles, bullets and prosthetics for warfighters and veterans, and pistols for bear-chasing U.S. park rangers. Federal funds are not just going to Iraq or to homeland defense against terrorists.

Federal outright grants for basic science research and medical research to U.S. nonprofits, and directly or indirectly to the states and major cities for emergency and contingency planning, disaster, and reconstruction relief, call for major acquisitions. "Acquisition" is acquiring, by contract and with appropriated funds by Congress, supplies or services (including construction) by and for the use of the federal government through purchase or lease. The supplies or services may be in existence already or may need to be created, developed, demonstrated, and evaluated. The executive branch of the government has delegated procurement authority to various departments of the U.S. government.

The acquisition life cycle for products, supplies, and services purchased by the federal government is how a "need" progresses from its definition by a user to the source selection of a vendor, eventual procurement, contract administration, inventory, and final disposal. Figure 2-1 depicts the twelve steps in the acquisition cycle. This acquisition process applies whether the

United States is buying a commercial item or an adapted commercial item for military service, such as an armor-plated Hummer for service in conflicts with insurgents, a power transformer station for northern Iraq, a new carrier-based naval jet, or a new Air Force refueling tanker aircraft.

Acquisition planning should commence as soon as the agency need is identified, preferably well in advance of the fiscal year in which contract award or order placement is necessary. In developing the plan, the planner should form a team comprising all those who will be responsible for significant aspects of the acquisition (e.g., contracting, fiscal, legal, and technical aspects). If such contract performance is to be in a designated operational

FIGURE 2-1. The Twelve Steps in the Acquisition Life Cycle

#1 USER NEED

#12 INVEN-TORY DELIVERY, ACCEPT, DISPOSAL

#2 PURCHASE REQUEST

#11 CONTRACT PERFORMANCE MANAGEMENT

#3 MARKET RESEARCH

ACQUISITION LIFE CYCLE

#10 AWARD

#4 SOURCE SELECTION PLAN

#9 EVALUATION DISCUSSIONS, AUDITS

#5 WORK STATE-MENT, SPECIFICA-TION, DATA REQ.

#8 RECEIPT BID, QUOTE, PROPOSAL

#6 PUBLIC NOTICES ADVANCE, DRAFT-SOLICITATION

#7 RELEASE SOLICITATION RFQ, IFB, RFP

area overseas or supporting a diplomatic or consular mission, the planner should also consider including the combatant commander or chief of mission on the team.

The planner should review previous plans for similar acquisitions and discuss them with the key procurement staff involved in these acquisitions. On key dates specified in the plan, and no less than annually, the planner should review the plan and revise it as necessary.

Written acquisition plans are developed and coordinated consistent with the magnitude of the procurement, its complexity, and its urgency. The acquisition-cycle activities exercised follow the federal statutes and regulations, unless waived, that promote "full and open" competition before and after exclusion of any sources.

The primary competitive procedures used to fulfill the requirement for full and open competition are sealed bids, competitive quotes/proposals, the use of multiple award schedules issued by the General Services Administration, and Broad Agency Announcements (BAAs) for research work. Contracting without providing for full and open competition or full and open competition after exclusion of sources is a violation of statute, unless permitted by at least one of the seven authorized exceptions (see fig. 2-2).

FIGURE 2–2. Seven Authorized Exceptions to Full and Open Competition

1. Only one responsible source and no other supplies or services will satisfy requirements.
2. There are unusual and compelling circumstances (delay in award would cause serious injury, financial or other, to the government).
3. To maintain a facility or supplier in case of emergency or to achieve industrial mobilization; to maintain an essential engineering, developmental, or research capability; or to acquire the services of an expert or neutral person for any litigation or dispute.
4. There is an international agreement or treaty with a foreign government.
5. It is authorized or required by statute (e.g., Federal Prison Industries, 18 U.S.C. 4121-4128); Acquisition from Non-Profit Agencies Employing People Who Are Blind or Severely Disabled, Javits-Wagner-O'Day Act, 41 U.S.C. 46-48 and 41 C.F.R. 51; Robert T. Stafford Disaster Relief and Emergency Assistance Act, P.L. 93-288; 8(a) Business Development Program, Section 8(a) of the Small Business Act, 15 U.S.C. 637(a); set-asides for HUBZone Empowerment Contracting Program, 15 U.S.C. 631; and Veterans Benefits Act of 2003, 15 U.S.C. 657(f).
6. For reasons of national security.
7. It is in the public interest in the particular acquisition considered.

Before negotiating a contract or making any award without full and open competition, the contracting officer must justify the use of such an action in writing with the specific exception authority cited, certify the accuracy and completeness of the justification, and obtain the necessary approvals (known as justification and approval, or J&A) above his or her office (the competition advocate and head of the procuring activity) when the procurement is estimated to exceed $550,000 but not $57 million ($78.5 million for the DoD, NASA, and the Coast Guard). Over $57 million, the designated senior procurement executive of the agency must approve the exception. Even with the exception in hand for limiting or waiving competition, the contracting officer must solicit offers from as many potential vendors as is practical under the circumstances.

To obtain competition executive agencies must make notices of proposed contract actions available to the general public through the government point of entry on the Internet, www.fedbizopps.gov, unless the contracting officer determines that an exception exists by either regulation or statute. No further solicitation notices to the public are necessary once a contract is awarded, unless actions for additional services or supplies outside the existing scope of the awarded contract arise.

The acquisition process is flexible and can adjust to meet a contingency by the choice of the source selection procedure, contract type, and even designation of the first responsive vendor if exigency so requires. Several steps (Steps 6 and 7 of fig. 2-1) can be combined by the use of a combined synopsis/solicitation to reduce cycle time, for example.

The acquisition planners for agencies such as the DoD, GSA, U.S. Army Corps of Engineers, Department of Homeland Security, and Federal Emergency Management Agency (FEMA) can ensure that basic ordering agreements are in place with multiple vendors and that Indefinite-Delivery Contracts are negotiated and in place to be funded in order to allow for the swift award of multiple tasking and delivery orders. Because many of the requirements to prepare the nation for emergency situations are known or can be anticipated sufficiently in advance of when a contract action must be executed, many pricing actions need not be undertaken under emergency conditions.

In addition to the above, once a catastrophic event occurs the maximum use of the government credit card and simplified acquisition procedures based on expanded thresholds, among other acquisition flexibilities to be discussed in this chapter, can be used to provide emergency contracting to sustain or fill logistics gaps during early operations. Such actions are a prudent part of federal and state contingency plans, emergency disaster preparedness, and recovery plans.

MARKET RESEARCH

Federal agencies are required to conduct market research (Step 3, fig. 2-1) to meet their obligations for acquisition planning

1. before developing new requirements documents for an acquisition by an agency;
2. before soliciting acquisitions with an estimated value in excess of the simplified acquisition threshold (SAT), one hundred thousand dollars; and
3. on an ongoing basis and to take advantage to the maximum extent practical of commercially available market research methods to identify effectively the capabilities of industrial manufacturers and established service leaders, including those of small businesses and new entrants into federal contracting. The object is to be prepared to meet the surge requirements of the agency in furtherance of a contingency operation or defense against or recovery from nuclear, biological, or radiological attack.

The policy of the government is to meet its needs from commercial items (CIs) or services (so-called off-the-shelf items) leased, sold, or licensed to the general public; or items which require minor modifications that do not alter the nongovernmental function or essential physical characteristics of an item or component as far as possible before resorting to tailored procurements. Thus one should look first at the market research portion of this cycle (Step 3) through the eyes of the government buyer, who is the key member of the acquisition team.

A buyer's job, whether he or she works for the U.S. Navy or Wal-Mart, is to fill a need as soon as practical and at the least cost possible, including the cost of administration and life-cycle management (transportation, storage, distribution, maintenance, and disposal). The buyer is charged with accomplishing the acquisition by maximizing the use of quality commercial products and services and using traders who have a track record of successful performance and demonstrate an ability to perform and concurrently to promote competition. Moreover, business must be conducted with integrity, fairness, and openness while at the same time fulfilling public policy objectives.

The results of the research are used to determine if sources capable of satisfying the requirement exist. Moreover, the research is to assess if commercial items are available to meet the agency's needs or, if commercial items are not available, if nondevelopmental items that could be modified to meet agency requirements are available.

With such a balancing act, the buyer should first start with a realistic assessment/estimate as to the overall cost of the item or services to be purchased. A buyer also must keep in mind the allocated budget from the using agency involved and the urgency of fulfilling the need. With this information in hand, a source selection procedure similar to the source selection procedure matrix in figure 2-3 is helpful in choosing procurement flexibilities.

The government has more than four hundred military or other government major buildings and installations in just the United States that require a wide range of commercial supplies. Many of these supplies are purchased within the local area from local traders. Hence the popular use of the government-wide commercial purchase card for purchases not exceeding the micropurchase threshold of three thousand dollars. Purchases at or under this threshold are unrestricted as to the size of the business. However, when a need exceeds this threshold and is at least twenty-five thousand dollars and remains in the region of the simplified acquisition threshold (less than one hundred thousand dollars), purchases are limited to small businesses. During emergencies both the micropurchase threshold and simplified acquisition threshold may increase significantly to cope with the disaster, in keeping with past precedent (fig. 2-3).

PUBLIC NOTICE

Before logging onto the Internet, the market researcher should be aware that there is a mandatory requirement by the federal buyer to display a public notice, preferably by electronic posting on the GPE at www.fedbizopps.gov, of each contract action whose price is estimated to exceed twenty-five thousand dollars. Such a public notice occurs in the form of a published presolicitation "synopsis" of the proposed contract action, usually fifteen days before a solicitation is to be issued (see fig. 2-4). For contract actions under twenty-five thousand dollars, a bulletin-board posting in or near the procurement office may be adequate (see Step 6, fig. 2-1).

FIGURE 2–3. The Source Selection Procedure Matrix

Source Selection Procedure	Estimated Price Ranges—Acquisition Thresholds Supplies and Services	Who Can Be Solicited (business size)	Public Notice; Numbers of Offerors
Micro-purchase Procedure (Government-commercial purchase card)	Normal: Equal to or less than $3,000 Exceptions: Construction, Davis Bacon Act: $2,000 Services, Service Contract Act: $2,500 Contingency, Defense or Recovery Terrorism, NBC attacks: $15,000 in U.S. $25,000 overseas.	Unrestricted (small or large business)	Solicit local trade area Use oral requests for quotes
Simplified Acquisition Procedures (SAP)	Normal: Equal to or less than $100,000 Exceptions: Contingency, Defense, or Recovery Terrorism, BCC attacks: $250,000 in U.S. $1 million overseas. Commercial items $5.5 million ($11 million Contingency, Defense, or Recovery Terrorism, NBC attacks)	Only small business, including Small Business Set-Asides: "(8a)," HUBzone, Service-Disabled Veteran-Owned	Solicit: www.fedbizopps.gov if greater than $25,000; for construction, greater than $2,500 Exceptions: For less than $25,000, oral quotes, offers from three sources within local trade area. If urgent, one source will suffice for needs less than $100,000. Combined synopsis/ solicitation; or SF 1449 (commercial)
Request for Quotation (RFQ) Sealed Bidding (IFB) Competitive Proposals (RFP)	Normal: Greater than $100,000	Restricted, unrestricted, or Small Business Set-Asides	Solicit: www.fedbizopps.gov Combined synopsis/ solicitation; SF1449 (commercial);or SF 33

FIGURE 2–4. Public Notice Times between Synopsis of
a Purchase Requirement, Release of Solicitation,
and Submission of a Bid for Purchases in Excess of $25,000

Proposed Contract Action	Time (Days)
(1) Synopsis (pre-solicitation) Publication date on fedbizopps.gov	T_0
(2) Solicitation release	$T_0 + 15$
(3) Submittal, bid, quote, proposal (greater than SAT)	$(T_0 + 15) + 30$
(4) Notice of award (purchases greater than $3 million)	Day of award

Normally fifteen days are allowed from the time a synopsis of the procurement is posted on the GPE before a solicitation is to be released, except for the acquisition of commercial items, for which the contracting officer may establish a shorter period for issuing a solicitation or use the combined synopsis and solicitation procedure. Once the solicitation—Invitation for Bids (IFB), Request for Quotation (RFQ), and Request for Proposal (RFP)—is released (T0 + fifteen) (Step 7, fig. 2-1), contracting officers normally are to allow for a thirty-day response time (T0 + fifteen) plus thirty days for the preparation and submission by vendors of their quotes, bids, or proposals when the estimated procurement is over the simplified acquisition threshold; otherwise a lesser but reasonable time is to be allowed (see Step 8, fig. 2-1). Finally, all contracts awarded in excess of three million dollars are required to be posted on the day of award. This latter requirement is to provide notice to small businesses that may be interested in entering into subcontract or other teaming relationships with the winning prime contractor. Although the above is the regulatory model for notice, contract actions for the acquisition of commercial items may have shorter times or "combined" synopses and solicitations.

With the source selection procedure matrix of figure 2-3 and public notice requirements of figure 2-4, a buyer should start with the Internet, where a number of efficient market searches are possible. The Web site www.fedbizopps.gov by default has become the key instrument for conducting the market research mandated by federal law and case precedent. Before a federal buyer can start a market search of sources that may be able to fulfill a need, the North American Industry Classification System (NAICS) code or the Federal Supply Classification (FSC) code of the product or services involved must be determined.

The NAICS has replaced the Standard Industrial Classification system. The new system was developed jointly by the United States, Canada, and Mexico to provide comparability in statistics regarding business activity across North America. The 2007 series of NAICS codes replaced the 2002 series for use in the Central Contractor Registry system. NAICS codes can be determined at www.census.gov/naics. The FSC system and its index have been developed and administered by the Defense Logistics Agency under the direction of the secretary of defense for use in classifying items of supply identified under the Federal Catalog System used by the federal government. The FSC system encompasses the naming, description, classification, and numbering of all items carried under centralized inventory control by the DoD and the civilian agencies of the federal government, as well as the publication of related identification data.

The FSC is a commodity classification designed to serve the functions of supply and is sufficiently comprehensive in scope to permit the classification of all items of personal property. In order to accomplish this, groups and classes have been established for the universe of commodities, with emphasis on those items known to be in the supply systems of the federal government. The FSC code of an item can be determined at www.dlis.dla.mil/hseries.asp.

Armed with the prerequisite codes as a starting point, a federal buyer preparing to perform the market search to fill the user's need should start with the eight questions in figure 2-5. By providing answers to such queries, the buyer will be able to prepare an initial draft—mental or written—source selection plan to fulfill the need. Depending on the need (urgency, complexity, availability of commercial items, military developmental item, etc.), the plan can be as simple as one paragraph or as complex as a full-blown multipage document. The plan should define at a minimum the availability of funding, the source selection procedure to be used, and any criteria for the evaluation of the sources. Figure 2-6 depicts the initial online market search model that should be exercised by a federal buyer in attempting to answer the eight queries.

One should not forget to touch base with the small business specialists of the procuring agency itself, as well as the procurement center representative

- Are commercial or nondevelopmental items available to meet the need?
- What is the expectation of receiving several fair market price offers from responsible firms?
- Should the procurement be restricted to small businesses or unrestricted, to all vendors?
- Is there a reasonable expectation of receiving two fair market value quotes from small businesses? (If yes, restrict procurement to small businesses.)
- Should the procurement be set aside for an 8(a) Small Disadvantaged Business through the SBA, for a Historically Underutilized Business Zones–designated small business, or for a Service-Disabled Veteran-Owned Small Business?
- Is there an existing, open contract that one can piggyback the procurement onto, minimizing administrative time for delivery? (It is not uncommon for the Air Force, for example, to pay a small administrative fee to the Department of Interior or GSA to handle a procurement request.)
- Will bundling my purchases in one contract vehicle provide substantial benefits in light of the harm that may be caused to small business?
- Can we use performance-based acquisition contracting for the services needed?

FIGURE 2–6. Internet Roadmap to Market Research for Federal Contracting

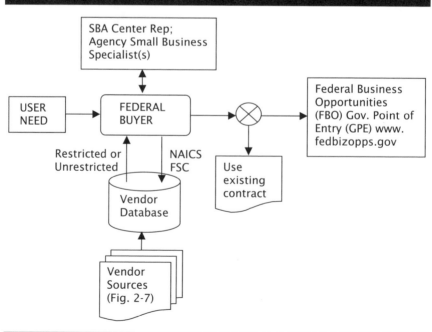

who works in concert with the agency's small business specialists, as depicted in figure 2-6. Their inputs are critical to a small business vendor since they have an understanding of the "pulse" of the procurement command they service and maintain a close liaison with the products and services offered by the vendors in the immediate locality. Figure 2-7 depicts six different databases to explore for vendor sources, including awarded contract actions.

Since 1949, the General Services Administration has been helping executive agencies better serve the public by meeting their needs for products and services and simplifying access to information. That continues to be the agency's mission. For over twelve years, GSA Advantage! has been a reliable online resource for federal employees and their buyers worldwide, offering a comprehensive selection of approved products and services from GSA contracts—from furniture, chemicals, information technology solutions, and electronics to property disposal, travel, and security services. GSA Advantage! offers an online ordering service for approved products and services from GSA/VA schedules as well as GSA Global Supply products. With over ten million commercial products and services, GSA Advantage! is a convenient shopping source to meet procurement needs.

GSA Global Supply (www.gsaglobalsupply.gsa.gov) provides easy and flexible requisition-based ordering for office supplies, tools to safety, and cleaning products. It provides global delivery of products compliant with the Federal Acquisition Regulation for DoD buyers, products guaranteed by the AbilityOne Program (formerly Javits-Wagner-O'Day) from the blind and disabled employment industries to be purchased by the federal agencies, and requisition-based ordering with no need for comparison shopping.

Moreover, the Federal Procurement Data System–Next Generation (FPDS-NG) (www.fpds.gov) takes the mystery out of procurement informa-

---

FIGURE 2-7. Databases of Vendor Sources

- Business Partner Network, the single source for vendor data (www.bpn.gov)
- General Services Administration (www.gsaadvantage.gov)
    Federal Supply Service (Consolidated Schedule)
    GSA Advantage!
- Federal Procurement Data System–Next Generation (data collection on awarded across the federal government, unclassified record of procurements) (www.fpds.gov)
- Small Business Administration (www.sba.gov)

tion. Reports are now categorized into simpler terms, based on how users typically look for information. User can now find reports based on a breakdown of who, what, where, when, and how:

- Who is winning government contracts by vendor name or type?
- What types of products and services the government has been buying?
- Where is the government spending its money, both in the United States and abroad?
- When were the procurements made?
- How did the government make the award (small business, type of competition, purchase card, etc.)? How is the government meeting its statutory goals?

The goal of FPDS-NG is to make procurement information transparent and easy to find for every user, from the experienced contracting officer to the curious member of the public. A government buyer using the database would hope to find an existing contract vehicle or instrument for the needed supplies, equipment, or services, especially if time is short (see figs. 2-6 and 2-7).

FEDERAL SUPPLY SCHEDULE PROGRAM

The buyer can search product information (i.e., national stock number, part number, common name, and review delivery options) and place orders directly with GSA schedule contractors. This would be the first step, as shown in figure 2-8. One can also place orders with GSA by using the government-wide commercial purchase card, provided the micropurchase threshold (three thousand dollars) is not exceeded.

The buyer could check with the GSA Advantage! which lists categories of supplies and services that have ongoing, open, Indefinite-Delivery Contracts with previously fixed or negotiated prices waiting to accept delivery or task orders. Such a GSA contract vehicle would have already negotiated firm-fixed prices (FFPs) and agreed-upon delivery schedules. A scheduled contractor thereafter would publish an Authorized Federal Supply Pricelist, which contains all the supplies and services offered by the scheduled contractor along with their respective price and terms and conditions.

The Federal Supply Schedule program (also known as the Multiple Award Schedules program, or MAS) provides federal agencies with a simplified

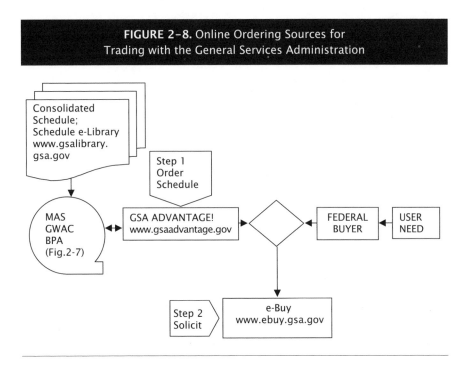

FIGURE 2-8. Online Ordering Sources for Trading with the General Services Administration

process of acquiring similar or comparable commercial supplies and services in varying quantities while obtaining volume discounts from more than one scheduled supplier. A buyer from any executive branch can request quotations from one or more scheduled vendors (the multiple awardees) who have been awarded GSA contracts, opening the gate for even lower prices than are cited in the awarded vendors' schedules. Of course, the buyer must have procurement authority. The Federal Supply Schedule program, like the U.S. Department of Veterans Affairs (VA) system, is also directed and managed by the GSA. For medical supplies, the GSA delegates to the VA the authority to purchase such supplies for the government. Because the GSA is a self-funded agency, it charges a varying schedule of industrial and contract administration fees. A buyer or vendor should coordinate with the nearest GSA office for planning purposes. Indefinite-Delivery Contracts are awarded using competitive procedures to firms by GSA. Firms provide supplies and services at stated prices associated with volume buying for given periods of time for delivery within a stated geographical area in the United States or overseas. For details on the different types of Indefinite-Delivery Contracts, refer to chapter 3. Such existing contracts allow for the purchases of products to be made at fixed prices, at fixed prices for performance of a specific task, or at fixed hourly wage rates for services. Each schedule identifies agencies that are required to use the contracts as primary sources of supply. Federal agencies not identified in the schedules as mandatory users may issue orders under the schedules, and contracting officers are encouraged to accept such orders.

Such contracts allow for a shortened cycle time for contracting because the ordering activity need not determine whether or not the price is reasonable or assess the past performance or responsibility status of the vendor. Moreover, the order being placed is considered to meet the "best value" source selection criteria without the need to go through the evaluation process.

If the user need is unable to be fulfilled in Step 1 using an order from a schedule, then one could opt in Step 2 to solicit through a new feature that uses GSA's RFQ system. To solicit the supplies or services necessary to meet the need, the statement of work would be posted on GSA's e-Buy Web site, www.ebuy.gsa.gov.

GSA's latest e-business innovation, e-Buy, is an online RFQ/RFP system designed to allow federal buyers to request information, find sources, and prepare RFQs and RFPs online for millions of services and products offered through GSA's Multiple Award Schedules and Government-wide Acquisition Contracts. Federal buyers use e-Buy to obtain quotes or proposals for services, large quantity purchases, big ticket items, and purchases with complex requirements. Firms see the statement of work and submit quotes for products or services they have in stock or that were found on a preexisting MAS. Once the lowest, responsive bid was determined and evaluated, then the purchase order could be issued electronically.

Once a firm or business has won a GSA contract, it has the extremely advantageous opportunity of placing its products and services with associated price lists on a GSA Federal Supply Service (FSS) schedule (www.gsaadvantage.gov). FSS is not only a government-to-government business with customers but also a government-to-business operation with contractors and a leading e-business enterprise and digital marketplace. It also is integrated with the GSA Advantage! Web site.

Figure 2-9 lists several Web sites that may assist a vendor in placing its products or services on a federal supply schedule. Such a placement would open the firm to a new market, the federal worldwide market. Keep in mind that to do so, the trading partner would have to have a product or service that GSA advertises as needed, then the trader would have had to compete with other traders to get its product qualified to win a GSA contract.

> **FIGURE 2-9.** Sites for Vendors Planning to Be Trading Partners with the General Services Administration

- Centralized Mailing List Service (http://apps.fss.gsa/cmls/index.cf)
  Obtain copies of schedules and publications
- GSA Schedules (www.gsa.gov/schedules)
  Getting on Schedule
  List of Eligible Ordering Activities
- Schedules e-Library (www.gsa.gov/elibrary)
  Latest contract award information on GSA/VA schedules as well as GWACs
  Information on which suppliers have contracts and what terms are available

An alternative would be to file an unsolicited proposal to GSA. In this case, the GSA conducts its own evaluation to determine whether the unsolicited proposal merits any consideration for fulfilling an unmet GSA need. The frustrating part of this marketing plan is that winning an Indefinite-Delivery/Indefinite-Quantity (IDIQ) Contract with GSA does not guarantee a steady stream of purchase orders. To the contrary, now the trader's work has really started. One has now to ferret out government users (forest rangers, infantry, helicopter pilots, field surgeons, tank commanders, etc.) and their buyers (contracting officers of material commands, training commands, supply depots, etc.) who need your services and/or products. Such buyers, once found, will be happy to avoid the time and effort negotiating prices and terms because they were previously agreed between vendors and GSA to be placed on one of its schedules. The issue here is that the trader will still have to compete with a few other traders for the sale. Nevertheless, the positive aspect is that one's chances of winning are better. The buyer now plays a big role in selecting from among several IDIQ Contract–winning vendors the one to receive the proposed product delivery or service tasking order.

Supplies offered on schedules are listed at fixed prices. Services are priced at either an hourly rate or a fixed price for performance of a specific task (installation, maintenance, or repair, for example). Ordering activities are not required to make a separate determination of fair and reasonable pricing. However, although GSA has already negotiated the pricing, ordering activities may seek additional discounts before placing an order. A buyer may undertake the conduct of a reverse auction to see if further savings can be gained for the government.

In summary, a government agency with a need can consult the GSA customer service representative or marketing specialist in its region (go to www. gsa.gov and click on "Staff Directory/Contact Us") who will assist the agency in shopping or identifying scheduled vendors. Otherwise, the regional specialist can contract for that agency under the FAR by contacting three scheduled vendors under IDIQ Contracts to compete for the business. GSA maintains eleven regional offices with staff able to handle queries in the areas of office space, office equipment, supplies, telecommunications, and information technology, among other product and service areas.

A scheduled vendor would be smart to make frequent contact with the customer service representatives who deal in their product and service areas to ensure that their federal schedules are known. What use is it to have a five-year IDIQ Contract with GSA if you receive no opportunity to compete for any tasking or delivery order requests, either from a government agency or directly through GSA?

If the government buyer did not find a GSA product listing with an existing schedule contracting vehicle, the next step could be to search in the FPDS-NG, into which the former Interagency Contract Directory has been integrated as part of the Integrated Acquisition Environment (IAE) (see fig. 2-7). On FPDS-NG one finds the Indefinite-Delivery Contracts awarded by various executive departments—the GWACs and Multiple-Agency Contracts (MACs), especially for information technology (IT). These latter contract vehicles, administered by the GSA, are part of the Multiple Award Schedule programs and similar to those found under GSA Advantage! A buyer could conceivably find a MAC covering its product need that was awarded to as many as six different firms. The buyer could elect to contact several of these firms and request quotations, selecting the lowest bidder.

A trader would find it desirable to be a winner of a GWAC or MAC. These types of contracts are called Indefinite-Quantity Contracts because the government has no obligation to order any supplies in the future after contract award except perhaps the small amount guaranteed by the contract itself. They favor the government because no significant funds are initially obligated by the government at the time of contract award. Obligation occurs at the time a specific delivery or tasking order is issued.

FEDERAL BUSINESS OPPORTUNITIES

On October 1, 2001, the Federal Business Opportunities (FBO) system became the official GPE for business opportunities for federal agencies (see fig. 2-6). The FBO system allows government buyers to post synopses, solicitations, and related documents on the Internet and interfaces with other agency applications.

The FBO is also a tool for federal buyers who are not able to find an existing contract vehicle to order the requisite supplies as commercial item(s). The Department of Homeland Security may require special airport explosive detectors. The Army may need new sand-proof wireless laptops for communications used by warfighters conducting desert operations. The U.S. Agency for International Development may have a need to build several electrical generation stations in Iraq. As a vendor, therefore, you may want to examine the FBO Web site to search out what solicitations are being posted for IFBs and RFPs to meet the tailored needs of the executive purchasing agency in which you have an interest (see fig. 2-6).

The FBO system also provides the Acquisition Notification Service, which allows vendors to register for selected notices. The service provides the capability to search for federal business opportunities and assist vendors in registering to receive notices of interest to their company (e.g., all notices for a particular solicitation number, notices from selected organizations and product or service classifications, and related procurement notices.) FBO assimilated electronically the services previously performed by a paper subscription to the *Commerce Business Daily*.

Moreover, FBO contains the database of what solicitations have closed and are thus under evaluation. This database eventually shows what contracts have been awarded and to whom. Keep in mind that in most contracts, the prime contractor will need at least one and possibly several subcontractors. Knowing a firm that just won a government contract could lead to the door that makes your firm the helping hand in its performance. A phone call could turn out to be mutually beneficial.

Once FBO is used to solicit traders' responses in the form of firm bids based upon an IFB or an initial proposal from an RFP, the government will conduct its evaluation and announce the winner through the same Web site. It is the intent of the buyer to exercise the procurement cycle at figure 2-1 on line to the extent possible to achieve economy for its taxpayers and, more important, efficiency and speed in its acquisitions. FBO also provides the Web site through which all exchanges between traders and buyers are expected to flow during the procurement cycle.

In addition, the Business Partner Network (BPN) (www.bpn.gov) serves as the single source for vendor data for the federal government. The BPN is a search mechanism that provides unprecedented views into several key databases across federal agencies (see fig. 2-10). The network (see fig. 2-10) includes a cluster of Web sites related to vendors that are key to federal contracting officers, especially those who are performing market searches or considering a vendor for an award. Such agents (contracting officers, contracting specialists, analysts, et al.) gain access into BPN through the Federal Agency Registration system using assigned BPN number, which is the same as their assigned number through the Data Universal Numbering System (DUNS).

The Business Partner Network includes the CCR database. Prospective contractors are required to be registered in the CCR database prior to award of a contract or agreement (basic ordering or blanket purchase), except for purchases that use a government-wide commercial purchase card, classified procurements to safeguard national security information, contracts awarded by deployed contracting officers in course of military operations or in the conduct of emergency operations, and responses to natural or environmental

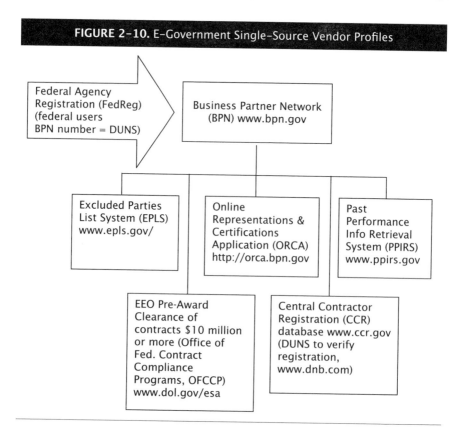

FIGURE 2-10. E-Government Single-Source Vendor Profiles

disasters or national or civil emergencies (e.g., the terrorist attacks of September 11, 2001, and Hurricane Katrina in 2005).

The CCR database allows one to search, as an example, for any firms that have registered as being in the business of designing and manufacturing explosive detectors or ruggedized laptops, including firms with construction experience in building bridges and power-grid systems (fig. 2-11). An MPIN is created at the time of a contractor's registration in the CCR profile to allow for access to that contractor's Past Performance Information Retrieval System file. The CCR also now serves as the mailing list for notices of pending and future business opportunities by federal contracting officers. The prior paper mailing lists kept by buyers have been discontinued in the government's move to a paperless system, e-Procurement. The CCR also facilitates the fast electronic payment of trader invoices.

New traders, before attempting to register on the CCR, should first apply to obtain a Commercial and Government Entity (CAGE) code and a DUNS number. DUNS is required to verify registration. These two numerical industry codes are always requested from vendors by the U.S. buyer.

A U.S. vendor can obtain the CAGE code from the Defense Logistics Information Center (www.dlis.dla.mil/cage_welcome.asp) or from the CCR

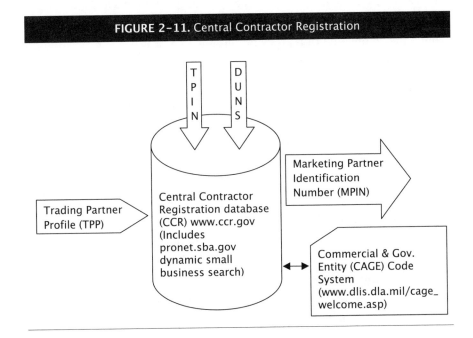

FIGURE 2-11. Central Contractor Registration

when you register. The CAGE code is used to support a variety of mechanized systems throughout the government. It provides for a standardized method of identifying a given facility at a specific location. The code may also be used for facility security clearance, a pre-award survey, automated bidder's lists, pay processes, and sources of supply. Foreign vendors must contact their country representative to receive their CAGE code (www.dlis.dla.mil/natopoc.asp).

The DUNS nine-digit number can be easily obtained by contacting the Dun and Bradstreet (D&B) information service (www.dnb.com; http://fedgov. dnb.com/webforum; 1-866-705-5711 within the United States). The number is used commercially to identify trading partners (vendors, sellers). It is also the number assigned by D&B to each office in an agency. Since each federal buyer and seller office must have a DUNS number, it is logical (saving time and effort) to use the D&B database of this associated information that D&B has collected to serve as the BPN number. In essence the BPN number equals the DUNS number.

The Online Representations and Certifications Application (ORCA), part of the BPN (shown in fig. 2-10), allows offerors to submit their Annual Representations and Certifications and to efficiently keep them current, accurate, and complete. ORCA eliminates the burden for contractors of submitting the same information to various contracting offices when responding to solicitations that, under the Uniform Contract Format (Part IV, Section K) require the completion of representations and certifications (e.g., small business self-certification, certificate of independent price determination, Taxpayer Identification Number [TIN], type of organization, certification reference to debarment, and compliance reporting involving the Equal Opportunity Act and Buy American Act). ORCA establishes a common source for this information to procurement officers throughout the government concurrent with registration by a trader in the CCR.

When a firm registers on the CCR, it has the opportunity to provide its Trading Partner Profile (TPP). Figure 2-12 depicts some of the elements of such a profile. The prospective trading partner (vendor) has the opportunity to describe its organization, business model, products, and services using the FSC system and the NAICS. The search by either a buyer or trader could reveal, for example, all possible sources for explosive detectors and protective flak vests. It behooves a new business to register on the CCR even if it has no near-term hope or interest in directly participating and winning a contract.

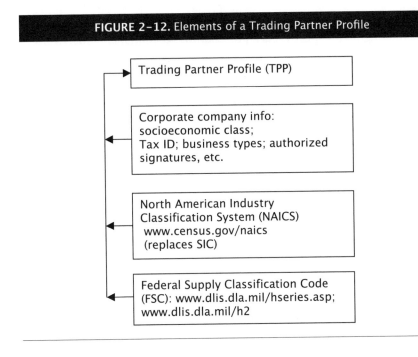

FIGURE 2-12. Elements of a Trading Partner Profile

Trading Partner Profile (TPP)

Corporate company info:
socioeconomic class;
Tax ID; business types; authorized
signatures, etc.

North American Industry
Classification System (NAICS)
www.census.gov/naics
(replaces SIC)

Federal Supply Classification Code
(FSC): www.dlis.dla.mil/hseries.asp;
www.dlis.dla.mil/h2

Once your Trading Partner Profile and other data is inputted into CCR you will be provided with your firm's Trading Partner Identification Number (TPIN) (fig. 2-11). The TPIN is the password that is used to access your CCR data. CCR data includes your banking information and other sensitive data such as your Marketing Partner Identification Number (MPIN). Therefore CCR recommends that you do not disclose your TPIN to anyone under any circumstances. If you have distributed your TPIN or MPIN, or believe that either has been compromised, you need to obtain a new one.

Always protect your TPIN with the highest level of security. No one outside of your organization should know what your secure TPIN number is. If your TPIN has been compromised, it is possible for unknown sources to obtain your financial information and even redirect any (EFT) payments to their own benefit.

Registration on the CCR is a must for a small business. It is the best road to becoming a subcontractor to a prime contractor. Before being awarded to a large business, by law each major government contract (in excess of $500 million) now requires a small business subcontracting plan to be submitted to and negotiated with the contracting office prior to award. The small business subcontracting plan's approval is a precondition to announcing the award of a contract to a large business that was evaluated as the winner.

A prime contractor preparing its proposal for submission to the government would search the CCR database for small business firms that have self-certified themselves in the locality that could be used to meet its subcontracting goals. This database is a valuable resource for locating local firms able to respond to local disaster and reconstruction procurements.

These firms would be identified, contacted, and listed as prospective subcontractors in the prime contractor's small subcontracting plan for selected portions of the overall prescribed work statement once the contract is awarded. The government monitors this plan to ensure compliance and to preclude "bait and switch" tactics. Bait and switch is when a prime contractor switches subcontractors after the contract is won. The buyer rewards the prime contractor with incentives and a positive performance evaluation rating for correctly executing its small business subcontracting plan. A high rating could be the key to winning the next competition.

The CCR also allows Uncle Sam to develop and maintain a list of possible suppliers or contractors. It opens the door to useful exchanges of information early in the procurement cycle. The buyer could check the SBA's procurement preference programs participation by self-certified small businesses. Procuring agencies and contracting officers who relied on PRO-Net as the authoritative source for vendors who are certified in SBA's 8(a) Business Development Program, HUBZone Empowerment Contracting Program, and Small Disadvantaged Business Program now access this information through CCR. To conduct market research and confirm eligibility for SBA's procurement preference programs, users may go to the CCR Web site and click on the "Dynamic Small Business Search" link. On January 1, 2004, CCR assumed all of Pro-Net's search capabilities and functions. Small business from 2004 no longer needed to register in both SBA's Pro-Net and CCR. We now have one portal for entering and searching small business sources. The CCR also gives the contracting officer access to the database to validate a trader's TIN.

If this effort proves to be inadequate, inappropriate for the services or products needed, or you turn up empty-handed, then the buyer can use the GPE, FedBizOpps. The buyer can release on the Internet an RFI or even a draft performance-based acquisition specification or solicitation asking industry to respond with an exchange of information on the proposed draft purchase (see fig. 2-6).

By using an RFI or a draft IFB or RFP the government is asking vendors, What do you think about the proposed requirement and how could it be met? The buyer can make such a request on an unrestricted basis (both large and small business) or restricted to just small businesses or even to just women-owned small businesses. Eventually, with constructive responses from prospective sources, the buyer will be able to finalize a procurement package. The buyer uses his or her integrated team of users, cost specialists, and technical staff to prepare and release an IFB or RFP (see Step 7, fig. 2-1).

The buyer will place the IFB or RFP on the Internet at www.fedbizopps. gov for traders to review and hopefully respond to in the time set for submissions (see fig. 2-6). This placement on the Internet satisfies the statutory requirement for advertising to meet the criteria for full and open competition among vendors. U.S. policy is to use competitive procurement processes to award the contract to the best-value or lowest-priced responsible offeror with an acceptable past performance record.

Through one portal, FedBizOpps, commercial vendors seeking federal markets for their products and services can search, monitor, and retrieve opportunities solicited by the entire federal community. The requirement is to allow as many firms as possible to compete on a "level" playing field, void of favoritism or discrimination. The award to a firm on a sole-source basis is anathema to the system but is allowed under seven circumstances (see fig. 2-2) related to the need for exigency, such as a natural catastrophe or national security, when approved by the procurement authority, executive order, or U.S. statute.

EMERGENCY AND CONTINGENCY ACQUISITION

The acquisition cycle (fig. 2-1) should not be viewed as a series of sequential steps. Within the established statutes and regulations, the cycle should be flexible, compressible, and able to accommodate planning for emergencies and contingencies to facilitate the national defense. More important, the acquisition process must be able to be used by trained procurement professionals to "breathe life" into existing plans to provide the supplies, services, and construction required for military operations or in the immediate aftermath of a disaster (natural or man-made), including but not limited to the resources for evacuation, security, damage minimization, medical support, damage repair, and reconstruction. Awarding of an emergency response contract refers to a contract with a private entity that supports assistance activities in a major disaster or emergency area, such as debris clearance, distribution of supplies, or reconstruction. Contracting for emergencies or contingencies requires, as a start, the following:

1. Advance planning for various contingencies or emergencies (human caused and natural), which includes logistics (supplies, services, heavy equipment, transportation, shelters, inspectors) and the related preidentified contingency contracting officers (CCOs), who are necessary once the emergency or contingency is triggered.
2. Pre-event (contingency for military operations or national disaster relief) stockpiling and warehousing of logistics for the duration or aftermath of an event to minimize loss of life and human suffering, such as provisions for temporary shelter (tents, stadiums, gymnasiums, house trailers), emergency rations, water, medical supplies, construction supplies, and spare parts for emergency repair of community infrastructure (hospitals, bridges, railroads, water supply systems, power stations). The requisite emergency contracting officer kits (preprepared credit cards, procurement forms) need to be in place before an event happens.

To accomplish emergency or contingency planning, one must take some of the following procurement actions, singly or in combination:

1. The solicitation and award of appropriate multiyear Indefinite-Delivery-type contracts (one year plus four year options, etc.) to responsible vendors that can be funded when an emergency or contingency plan is activated.
2. The award of MACs and GWACs using IDIQ Contracts negotiated for more than one year in advance and ready to be exercised but annually reviewed.
3. The issuance of tasking orders for services and delivery orders for supplies or products at the prenegotiated fixed prices, when an event is forecasted to occur, to vendors located near the geographical area of the event in quantities needed depending on the severity of the projected event.

In the planning and execution, consideration should be given to establishing substantial award fees above and beyond a normal profit rate to provide the incentive for prompt, quality performance. Liquidated damage fees should be incorporated into such contract vehicles for untimely delivery or other poor performance reflecting lack of urgency and competence. A vendor accepting a cost-type contract with a fixed funded cost ceiling of $10 million and a fixed profit fee of 10 percent of the ceiling cost to rebuild a partially washed out railroad-road bridge, for example, certainly has incentive if he also has an award fee of one hundred thousand dollars waiting for him if he completes the repairs to the bridge within fifteen days of award or faces a hundred thousand dollar penalty for each day of delay.

The planning should include using to the maximum the government-wide purchase credits cards at various levels of authority in relation to the micro-purchase threshold, which should be increased for emergencies by a standby authority that becomes effective when the event occurs. The micropurchase threshold in the immediate aftermath of Hurricane Katrina increased from $2,500 to $250,000 for selected procurement officers. Within two months, the threshold was reduced back to $2,500. Currently it remains at $3,000.

Simplified acquisition procedures should be used and the simplified acquisition threshold increased for military supplies as well as commercial items. Procurements under such procedures are not required to establish formal evaluation plans or competitive ranges, conduct discussions with vendors, or score quotations from offerors. They are exempt from the requirements of full and open competition. See figure 2-3 for current thresholds.

Planners should have developed a list of procurement laws and regulations required to be waived to further accelerate contract execution for a particular plan, including proposed legislation drafted to be submitted when the emergency/contingency plan is triggered. Competitive sourcing must still be exercised to the extent practical, including exercising sound, established federal contracting practices.

In a move toward greater emergency acquisition flexibility, the Local Community Recovery Act of 2006 amended the Robert T. Stafford Disaster Relief and Emergency Assistance Act to strengthen the government's ability to promote local economic recovery. The law allows preferences to be given to specific geographical areas within a presidential declaration of disaster or emergency for the grant of contracts to set-asides for local business to conduct debris clearance, distribution of supplies, reconstruction, and other disaster and recovery assistance activities. The act does not replace small business set-asides (see chapter 7), since both types of programs can be used concurrently.

The procurement official need not justify why unrestricted or full and open competition was not used.

The act requires the Department of Homeland Security to provide preference in debris removal contracts to firms residing or doing business in the area affected by a major disaster. No abuse was found by the judiciary in the agency's use of its discretion to implement the statute's scheme of using set-asides to provide that preference in Mississippi after Hurricane Katrina.

In emergencies one must not forget that procurement officials have been authorized or can be delegated the authority to enter into, amend, or modify contracts in order to facilitate the national defense under the extraordinary emergency authority granted by Public Law 85-804 and implemented in the FAR.

Government procurement officials can take these actions without regard to other provisions of law related to making, performing, amending, or modifying contracts without consideration, correcting or mitigating mistakes, or formalizing informal agreements whenever the president considers that such action would facilitate the national defense. Such actions authorized by the Local Community Recovery Act must be accomplished expeditiously as possible, consistent with the care, restraint, and exercise of sound judgment appropriate to the use of such extraordinary authority. Under the act advance payments to contractors are allowed to facilitate the purchase of supplies and meet emergency payrolls among other needs.

The legislative history of PL 85-804 indicates that it may also be used as the basis for making indemnity payments under certain government contracts, the so-called residual power. This need for an indemnity provision has in the past arisen from the advent of nuclear power and the use of highly volatile fuels in the missile program. The magnitude of risks involved under procurement contracts in these areas have rendered commercial insurance either unavailable or limited in coverage. The emergency indemnification flexibility provided by PL 85-804 has been applied to procurements involving ammunition plants.

Finally, to better support emergency and contingency procurement, the Support Anti-Terrorism by Fostering Effective Technologies Act, known as the SAFETY Act, was formulated to provide broad protections from liability for products designated by the Department of Homeland Security as "qualified anti-terror technology" (QATT) if they failed to prevent injuries or damage caused by a terrorist attack.

Department of Homeland Security certification of the product in advance, though, is required. The aim of the SAFETY Act, in which Congress created the DHS, is to encourage innovation by entrepreneurs who might not be so eager to create better explosives- and weapons-detection systems, protective gas masks, and chemical, biological, or radiological release detectors or might not wish to provide passenger baggage screening services if they risked being sued for hundreds of millions of dollars should their products or services flop in their hour of greatest need.

The SAFETY Act shields not only sellers of the technology but also subcontractors, suppliers, and purchasers. Most important is the fact that the law codified the "government-contracts defense," hitherto a common-law immunity from litigation for companies doing business with the federal government. The manufacturer obtains the "government-contractor defense" whether it sells the product to the federal government or to the commercial market.

AVAILABLE ACQUISITION FLEXIBILITIES

Available acquisition flexibilities are used in support of contingency operations; to facilitate the defense against or recovery from nuclear, biological, chemical, or radiological attacks against the United States; and when the president declares an incident of national significance, an emergency, or a major disaster. The acquisition flexibilities do not require an emergency declaration or designation of a contingency operation. A number of procurement-related actions, although not inclusive, can be taken by contracting officers depending on the conditions fitting a particular situation:

- Exempt contracts awarded to support unusual and compelling needs or emergency conditions from the requirements pertaining to registration on the CCR
- Do not require the synopsis of proposed contract actions
- Restrict the number of sources to be solicited for full and open competition
- Emphasize the use of existing federal supply schedule contracts, multiagency basic ordering agreements, or multiagency IDIQ Contracts
- Do not enforce qualification requirements
- Use the Defense Priorities and Allocation System (DPAS) to set manufacturing and delivery priorities to maximize use of scarce raw materials, skilled labor, and plant facilities

- Disregard the mandate to purchase supplies from the Federal Prison Industries, Inc.
- Disregard trade agreements to acquisitions not awarded under full and open competition
- Waive the need to obtain prior authorization for the use of patented technology
- Allow overtime approvals to be retroactive
- Award contracts to Service-Disabled Veteran-Owned Small Business Program, HUBZone Empowerment, and 8(a) Business Development Program businesses on a sole-source basis
- Waive the requirement for the electronic transfer of funds
- Grant the procuring agencies protest override procedures so that essential contract awards can proceed, allowing the head of the contracting activity to determine that the contracting process may continue after the Government Accountability Office (GAO) has received a protest
- Allow contractors rent-free use of government property with FEMA concurrence
- Treat the product or service as a commercial item (see chapter 5)

INNOVATIVE CONTRACTING

The FAR outlines procurement policies and procedures to be used by members of the acquisition team. The team comprises not only representatives of the technical, supply, and procurement communities but also the customers they serve and the contractors who provide the products and services.

If a policy or procedure, or a particular strategy or practice, is in the best interest of the government and is not specifically addressed in the FAR or prohibited by law (statute or case law), executive order, or other regulation, government members of the team should not assume that it is prohibited. Rather, absence of direction should be interpreted as permitting the team to innovate and use sound business judgment that is otherwise consistent with law and within limits of their authority.

An innovative contracting procedure pioneered by the U.S. Navy is "alpha contracting." This form of contracting is intended to streamline the acquisition process (fig. 2-1) to reduce "cycle time" for contracts. It emphasizes conducting actions concurrently with a close relationship between an integrated government team and contractors, the acquisition team. Such contracting fits procurements designated as sole-source acquisitions. Under alpha contracting the government and contractors may work together to develop a solicitation package that meets the government's needs while also addressing contractor questions and concerns with it.

As the contractors complete the development of portions of their technical and cost proposals, an integrated government team may review the proposal and attempt to resolve issues the team identifies. The integrated government team may include representatives from the program office, the contracting office, the contract administration office, and the Defense Contract Audit Agency (DCAA). When the completed proposals are then formally submitted to the contracting officer, much of it may already be negotiated.

This approach is much more likely to result in an optimized program with achievable scope, improved performance or quality, and the avoidance of non-value-added requirements at a lower overall cost than was originally contemplated. Alpha contracting, aside from its use in sole-source acquisitions, is also a good process to perform contract planning before an emergency occurs. More important, the team, having worked together in the past, will perform even better when the crisis erupts.

In summary, alpha contracting involves many activities performed jointly by the government and contractor teams. This process offers a number of performance enhancements, such as improving communications; decreasing the number of formal RFP iterations, revisions, and rework required to correct misunderstandings, errors, and mistakes; and reducing the procurement administrative lead time required for contracting. The benefits of alpha contracting are not limited to reducing procurement acquisition lead times. One benefit includes the early involvement of audit personnel (the DCAA) in the immediate utilization of overhead rate and other pricing recommendations, rather than at some later date when significant updates would have occurred. The contractor benefits by significantly reducing proposal preparation costs. Alpha acquisition is a framework to eliminate any unnecessary processes and reviews and to streamline and conduct in parallel the required ones. Nevertheless, the same issues addressed in standard procurements are addressed in alpha acquisition, the same questions asked, and the same support provided. It is simply done more quickly and started earlier in the process in alpha contracting. Go to www.dau.mil (use the "Enterprise Search Engine" near the top of the page and enter "alpha contracting") for more information.

PRACTICING BUSINESS TIPS

The conduct of market research for products and their sources in support of designing, planning, and executing an acquisition plan for products or services is an obligation of procurement professionals for normal peacetime acquisitions, natural disasters, and contingencies involving military operations. Central to such mandatory efforts is the Business Partner Network, which includes the pivotal CCR database.

The use of the government-wide point of entry, FedBizOpps, and the e-government databases now established provide the vendor and contracting officer a flexible tool to promote trading with Uncle Sam. These Web-based tools are not intended to replace the "personal contact" between the integrated team and the exchange of information and communications regarding how to best fulfill the government's needs. Whether one is in government or industry, there is always the need to exchange views. An effective practical product that stops bullets, identifies the enemy, locates improvised explosive devices, or can produce vaccines on a mass scale as a function of a variable human health threat are just a few of the challenges that can be tackled by an integrated procurement team (IPT) of government and industry.

Recent experiences from the Global War on Terror, fighting in Iraq and Afghanistan, and natural disasters such as Hurricane Katrina have placed greater emphasis on defining acquisition flexibilities and emergency planning. Government procurement specialists and industry need to understand the new laws, revisit laws already on the books, and be prepared to exercise both.

CHAPTER 3

The Federal Contract

A contract is a promise or set of promises for the breach of which the law gives a remedy, or the performance of which the law in some way recognizes as a duty.

BLACK'S LAW DICTIONARY

A federal contract as a matter of public policy is a writing that contains the agreement of parties, with terms and conditions, and serves as a proof of obligation. In key aspects, regardless of the nature of the contract, a federal or a commercial contract has the same essential elements (see fig. 3-1).

A contract involves the tendering of an offer by the trader. In contracts, the offeror is the party who makes the offer and looks for acceptance from the offeree. An offer generally describes the need for a product or services requiring a combination or mix of research, design, production, performance, or delivery, including any quality assurance features and technical data. The offer is transmitted, via the Internet unless otherwise instructed, then accepted by the buyer or met with a counteroffer, and the cycle repeats until the revised offer is accepted by the buyer. This act is known as "acceptance."

Coincident with acceptance by the buyer is the agreement on what the buyer is willing to pay, the "consideration." The consideration can be in the form of dollars, goods, or some form of forbearance in return for the performance of the described services or delivery of a product.

FIGURE 3–1. Elements of an Enforceable Agreement

- Offer
- Acceptance
- Consideration
- Mutuality of Agreement and Obligation
- Competent Parties
- Legal Subject Matter

The common elements of an enforceable agreement (see fig. 3-1) are found generally in a written document that states the intent of the two parties to be bound, which then leads to what is called the "mutuality of agreement and obligation" by the two parties. This final executed document is the "contract." Oral contracts must comprise the same elements, but since they are not memorialized in written form, they are not recognized for the purposes of federal contracting except in exceptional circumstances. For the contract to be enforceable, however, the two parties must be competent and the subject matter involved must not violate any criminal or civil laws.

Government contracts are solicited and awarded on behalf of the United States, the principal, by agents who are specifically trained and chartered by the procurement authority. Such agents are known as "contracting officers" (see fig. 3-2). Only the contracting officer has the express, implied, and customary authority by title and authorization to commit and obligate the United States to a third party. Privity of contract flows only from the contracting officer to the third party, the contractor or a vendor entity, such as a recognized partnership or joint venture.

Such privity of contract does not flow from the government to any subcontractors of the contractor. This of course does not preclude a prime contractor from flowing down to its subcontractors and suppliers in its own subcontracts or commercial purchase orders pertinent federal procurement regulations such as clauses or other requirements found in the contract between the government and the contractor.

The contracting officer is the agent of the government with the authority to enter into, administer, and terminate contracts and make determinations of findings. A single contracting officer may be responsible for duties in any or all of these areas. Any changes to the statement of work, delivery dates, or

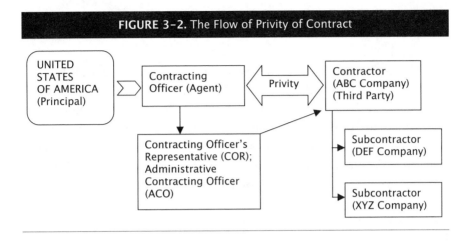

FIGURE 3-2. The Flow of Privity of Contract

adjustments to the statement of work and contract price can only be negotiated and agreed to in writing under the signature of the contractor and the contracting officer.

Contracting officers have the inherent authority based on their charter to delegate selected procurement functions, but not responsibility, to other government officials for proposal evaluation and source selection, contract administration, quality overwatch, and technical review and assessment. That authority goes to such officials as contract specialists working in the contracting office, contracting officer's representatives (COR), the contracting officer's technical representatives (COTR), the administrative contracting officers (ACO), and others.

Delegation of such authority should be transcribed to written instructions, and a contractor should be informed of said delegation and provided a copy of the instructions. Contractors invariably get in trouble by making changes in the scope of ongoing work or work processes, quality control, testing, delivery dates, and other contractual matters that increase the scope of work and contract price without authority. For the contractor to be paid for its work, there must be a direct connecting link between the contracting officer and the government official in a particular area or specialty who may be interfacing with the contractor regarding the product or services being supplied (see fig. 3-2).

If a contractor takes actions that have not been authorized by the agent of the government or that exceed the express, implied, and customary authority of the agent, then the contractor as the third party risks being paid its costs and efforts. In fact, the contractor may be unable to show that a constructive change to the contract had occurred. (See chapter 11 for further discussion of this issue.)

What is also different in government contracts is the IFB or RFP. For federal procurements, in both processes the buyer prepares a statement of work that includes a design or performance-based acquisition specification and is released as part of the solicitation on the Internet for all possible traders for a response. Military standards, specifications, and technical drawings not attached to the released solicitation can often be viewed or downloaded from Web sites identified in the solicitation itself. The trader responds to the IFB, RFQ, or RFP with an offer in the form of a sealed bid, quote, or proposal at the designated place, date, and time using the designated media, which generally is the Internet. The government has the obligation not to withdraw its solicitation without good cause (such as major change or deletion of requirement, no funds).

For a sealed bid, the bid cannot be withdrawn at anytime after its submission for a stated period of time, the bid acceptance period, normally sixty or ninety days. This is known as the "firm bid" rule. On the other hand, a timely proposal submitted in response to an RFQ/RFP to the government may be withdrawn at any time up to the date of contract award. It may also be revised because of discussions with the buyer, as mutually agreed. Unilateral revisions by the trader to its initial proposal are not allowed.

A government contract can be unilaterally terminated for the "convenience of the government" at any time without the payment of profit for the uncompleted work. Of course the completed work and that in progress is paid along with any pro-rata associated profit to the date of termination. Even if a firm has a multimillion-dollar government contract, the government for a variety of recognized reasons (change in requirements, threat change, reprogramming of funds, lack of congressional appropriation) can terminate the contract at will.

Lastly, the buyer can order more work to be undertaken or change how the work is being performed within the original scope of the contract. The trader is required under the "changes" clause of the Federal Acquisition Regulation to perform the work under protest before a price adjustment in the form of a written contract modification is negotiated. Such a protesting trader may, however, submit a claim for reimbursement on the disputed work and any impact it may have sustained on the completed and remaining undisputed work to be completed.

Remember that when the government is the paying party to the agreement, one has full faith in the power of the federal government. One need not worry about bankruptcy, a party disappearing, or a bounced check. It is extremely frustrating to perform a service only to find out the party that received the benefit does not have the money to pay, but having the government as your client ensures that eventually you will be paid.

The government may be slow in paying, but one will eventually be paid—plus interest—under the prompt payment provisions of most contracts. Moreover, your banker will be more than amenable to extend to your firm a line of credit against the contract's receivables, especially if you have a Fixed-Price Contract. Most government contracts include the "assignment of claims" clause (see chapter 11), which allows your bank to directly receive the earned proceeds of the government contract as collateral to a loan. Banks really like this collateral. Boeing, Lockheed Martin, and General Electric are not the only firms that enjoy such lines of credit. Even a small business can.

The government provides you an assured support base as you build up your commercial customers. One can use the assured payments from the government contract to refine the skills of one's work force and develop your government product line into commercially adapted goods and services. In many instances the services or products you sell to the government can be repackaged for commercial markets. With the sunk costs having been already borne by the government, commercial sales represent substantial clear profit.

THE UNIFORM CONTRACT FORMAT

The Department of Defense, NASA, and the GSA use the Uniform Contract Format (see fig. 3-3) for their RFQ, IFB, or RFP above the simplified acquisition threshold of one hundred thousand dollars. The format can be found in Standard Form (SF) 33, Solicitation, Offer and Award. (SF forms such as SF 33 and others discussed below may be obtained from the GSA Forms Library at www.gsa.gov/formslibrary/.)

The same general format applies to all other executive agencies (the departments of Treasury, Commerce, Transportation, Interior, and Homeland Security) and independent federal entities such as the U.S. Postal Service and the federal judiciary. Oral contracts and simple letter contracts, except for emergencies and in response to terrorism avoidance or recovery from a terrorist act, are to be avoided and are against public policy.

FIGURE 3–3. The Uniform Contract Format (Standard Form 33)

SECTION   Description

PART I. THE SCHEDULE
A   Solicitation/contract format
B   Supplies or services and prices/costs
C   Description/specifications/work statement
D   Packaging and marking
E   Inspection and acceptance
F   Deliveries and performance
G   Contract administration matters/data
H   Special contract requirements

PART II. CONTRACT CLAUSES
I   Contract clauses

PART III. LIST OF DOCUMENTS, EXHIBITS, AND OTHER ATTACHMENTS
J   List of attachments

PART IV. REPRESENTATIONS AND INSTRUCTIONS
K   Representations and certifications, and other statements of offerors
L   Instructions, conditions, and notices to offerors
M   Evaluation factors for award

Use of the format facilitates the preparation of the solicitation and the contract itself. The format may be adjusted or modified when a commercial item is purchased using SF 1449, Solicitation/Contract/Order for Commercial Items, or even a commercial format may be used.

The four parts of the Uniform Contract Format are shown in figure 3-3. This format is similar for solicitations for both IFBs and RFPs. As time goes on more portions of this format will be able to be completed electronically in advance and updated annually. One such example is Section K, Representations and Certifications, which can be submitted online and periodically updated at http://orca.bpn.gov.

The uniform format also allows traders to readily find portions of a solicitation that are of particular interest, regardless of which federal agency has posted the solicitation. The format serves as a handy checklist.

CONTRACT TYPES

The type of contract vehicle to be used is a function of variable factors being considered for trade-offs. The selection of the type of contract to be awarded by the contracting officer is different from the decision as to what procurement procedure to use for the selection of a vendor. Some of these trade-off factors are shown in figure 3-4.

Figure 3-5 classifies the types of contracts by risk associated with the type of work. They are placed into various risk clusters as seen from the trader's or buyer's point of view. As a trader you should make sure that you understand the type of contract proposed by the government for a particular service or product. The issue involved is directly related to which party assumes the risk of the costs of performance. The objective is to arrive at a contract type and price or estimated cost and fee that will result in reasonable trader risk and provide the trader with the greatest incentive for efficient and economical performance.

In the next few pages each type of contract will be discussed in more detail and portrayed graphically to gain a better understanding of the variables of a particular type of contract as they affect price, cost, and profit or fee.

Firm-Fixed-Price Contracts

If the product or service to be delivered can be specified in a design or a performance specification for bidding or a request for proposal, then the risk of

---

FIGURE 3-4. Factors for Selecting the Contract Type

- Availability of appropriated funds
- Contractor's technical capability and financial responsibility
- Adequacy of the contractor's accounting system
- Extent of projected price competition
- Whether price analysis can provide realistic pricing
- Availability of cost estimates for cost analysis to support negotiations
- Product maturity
- Types and complexity of requirements
- Period of performance or length of product run
- Urgency of the need
- Concurrent contract
- Extent and nature of proposed subcontracting
- Acquisition history

FIGURE 3–5. Types of Contracts	
CONTRACT TYPE	APPLICABLE TYPE OF WORK/SERVICES
Fixed-Price: Firm-Fixed-Price; Fixed-Price w/ Economic Price Adjustment; Fixed-Price Incentive; Fixed-Price with Award Fees	Commercial item(s); construction; build to drawings; full production; low initial rate production.
Cost-Reimbursement: Cost; Cost-Sharing; Cost-Plus-Fixed-Fee; Cost-Plus-Award-Fee; Award-Term Incentive; Cost-Plus-Incentive-Fee	Research, development; prototyping; initial production line; risky technology; no firm specifications; new software code; wartime or antiterrorist national response; national emergency surge requirements for supplies, products, or services.
Indefinite-Delivery: Definite-Quantity; Indefinite-Requirements; Indefinite-Quantity	Services or products ordered by use of delivery orders or tasking orders issued as fixed price, cost reimbursement, time and material when needs occur and funds are authorized.
Time-and-Materials; Labor-Hour; Letter Contracts	Level of effort work; needed to supplement government resources; wartime or antiterrorist national response; emergency surge requirements for supplies, products, or services.

the cost of performance shifts to the contractor. In such cases, a Firm-Fixed-Price Contract is the proper vehicle. The analytical representation of such a contract is shown in figure 3-6. One hundred percent of the risk falls on the trader. None falls to the government, as shown in the slope of the straight line in the diagram. It behooves the trader, therefore, to perform the contact work as efficiently as possible and to accomplish the work satisfactorily. The less the cost of satisfactory performance, the greater the profit. Conversely, the more the cost, the smaller the profit. If the cost is excessive, negative profit will occur, or in the actual world the trader will be paying out of its pocket for cost of work and receive no profit. If the project costs less than the contract price, the contractor reaps that benefit along with whatever profit was included in the fixed price at the time of award.

Regulations mandate that commercial items be purchased on a fixed-price basis. Recurring acquisitions of a product such as spare parts for an

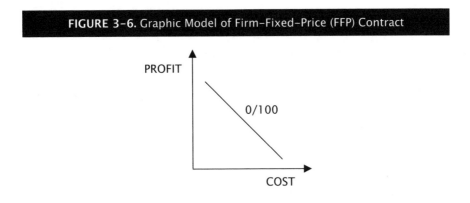

FIGURE 3-6. Graphic Model of Firm-Fixed-Price (FFP) Contract

armored vehicle or aircraft (build to government provided drawings) lend themselves to a Firm-Fixed-Price Contract. The supplier assumes the entire risk of performance. This type of contract is not subject to any adjustment on the basis of the contractor's cost incurred in performing the contract.

Such a supplier keeps all of the profit with no recourse by the government, unless fraud or a defective product is involved. The government has no cost analysis oversight of contract performance to assess compliance with the cost-accounting standards. The contract price was established by the bidding of several offerors, after which the lowest responsible offer was selected. Vendors seek such contracts because they find the government causes little interference in their contract administration, which allows them to focus on performance.

Fixed-Price with Economic Price Adjustment Contracts

Where serious doubts exist as to the stability of market or labor conditions (such as in Iraq or Afghanistan) that will exist during an extended period of contract performance, one may propose a variant of the Firm-Fixed-Price Contract. This variant is a Fixed-Price with Economic Price Adjustment Contract. In such a contract, revisions to the contract price can be made upon the occurrence of contingencies specifically defined in the contract. Some contingencies for adjustments are based on (1) established prices, (2) the actual cost of labor or material, and (3) cost indexes of labor or material.

Fixed-Price Contracts with Award-Fees

Award-fee provisions may be used in Fixed-Price Contracts when the government wishes to motivate a contractor and other incentives cannot be used because contractor performance cannot be measured objectively. Such contracts establish a fixed price, which includes normal profit for the effort. This price will be paid upon satisfactory performance. (See fig. 3-7.)

The award fee earned out of the award-fee pool, if any, will be paid in addition to that fixed contract price (Equation 1), thus establishing the final contract price (Equation 2):

Equation 1: fixed contract price = normal profit + contract cost
Equation 2: final contract price = fixed contract price + award fee

Such contracts provide for periodic evaluation of the trader's performance (e.g., cost control, quality, timely completion, cooperation, etc.) against an award-fee plan administered by a preestablished award-fee board. The amount of the award fee is not appealable under the disputes provisions of the contract once it has been approved by the contracting officer's superior.

Fixed–Price Incentive (Firm Target) Contracts

The Fixed-Price-Incentive (FPI) Contract provides for adjusting profit according to a formula based on the relationship of the final negotiated total cost to the total target cost. In an FPI (firm target) Contract, the following items are negotiated: target cost, target profit, ceiling price (but not a profit ceiling or floor), and the percentage sharing formula for establishing final profit and price. (See fig. 3-8.)

The share formula is expressed as a share ratio, 60/40. The figure to the right (40) represents the contractor's share, and the figure to the left, the gov-

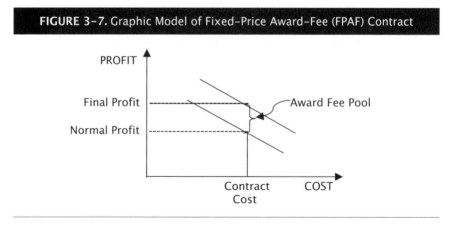

FIGURE 3–7. Graphic Model of Fixed–Price Award–Fee (FPAF) Contract

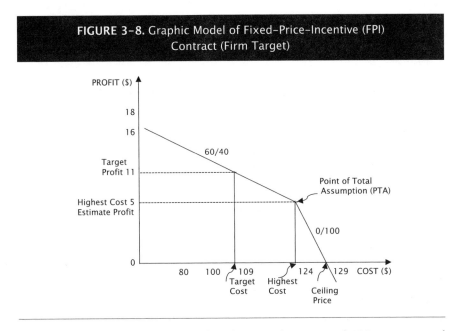

FIGURE 3–8. Graphic Model of Fixed–Price–Incentive (FPI) Contract (Firm Target)

ernment's share (60). The total of both must always equal 100 percent, and the government share should not normally be less than 50 percent.

The ceiling price is the maximum that may be paid to the contractor. The sum of the actual cost and the earned profit at that actual cost may not exceed the ceiling price. If it does the government will pay only the amount of the ceiling price. At the Point of Total Assumption (PTA), the sum of the actual cost plus earned profit at that cost equals the ceiling price. From this point on, as costs increase, the contractor's earned profit decreases by one dollar for each dollar of cost. Since the ceiling price may not be exceeded, as costs increase the earned profit must decrease. A Fixed-Price Incentive Contract changes its character to a Firm-Fixed-Price Contract at the PTA.

When performance of the contract is completed, the final cost is negotiated and the contract price is established by using the formula. When the final cost is less than the target cost, the application of the percentage sharing formula will yield a final profit greater than the target profit. Conversely, when the final cost is more than the target cost, application of the formula results in a final profit less than the target profit, or even a net loss. If the final negotiated cost exceeds the price ceiling, the contractor absorbs the difference as a loss.

Such a contract is appropriate if its intent is to have the contractor assume some cost responsibility. At the onset a firm target cost, target profit, and profit adjustment formula can be negotiated that will provide a fair and reasonable incentive. A ceiling price that provides for the contractor to assume an appropriate share of the risk must be established.

Fixed-Price Incentive (Successive Targets) Contract

The other variant to the Fixed-Price-Incentive Contract is the Successive Targets Contract. Such a contract specifies all of the following elements, which are negotiated at the outset: an initial cost and initial profit; an initial profit adjustment formula to be used for establishing the firm target profit, including a ceiling and floor for the firm target profit; the production point at which the firm target cost and firm target profit will be negotiated (usually before delivery or shop completion of the first article); and a maximum ceiling price that may be paid to the contractor, except for any adjustment under other contract clauses providing for equitable adjustment or other revision of the contract price under stated circumstances.

When the production point specified in the contract is reached, the parties negotiate the firm target cost, giving consideration to cost experience under the contract and other pertinent factors. The firm target profit is established by the formula. At this point, the parties have two alternatives. They may (1) negotiate a firm-fixed price, using the firm target cost and the firm target profit as a guide, or (2) if negotiation of a firm-fixed price is inappropriate, negotiate a formula for establishing the final price using the firm target cost and firm target profit. The final cost is then negotiated at completion, and the final profit is established by formula, as under the Fixed-Price-Incentive Contract discussed above.

Such a contract is appropriate when available cost or pricing information is not sufficient to permit the negotiation of a realistic firm target cost and profit before award. However, sufficient information must available to permit negotiation of initial targets, and there should be reasonable assurance that additional reliable information (under the contract itself but also other contracts for the same or similar items) will be available at an early point in contract performance. Such data should allow negotiation of a firm-fixed price or firm targets and a formula for establishing a final profit and price that will provide a fair and reasonable incentive.

Cost-Reimbursement Contracts

A Cost-Reimbursement Contract fits a project involving research and development services. The type of project whose uncertainties involved in contract performance do not permit cost to be estimated with sufficient accuracy to use a Fixed-Price Contract. In a pure cost contract, the trader is reimbursed for cost only and receives no fee. This type of contract is used for facilities contracts and research and development contracts with nonprofit organizations.

In a cost-sharing contract, the contractor receives no fee and is reimbursed for only a portion of its costs. This type of contract is used where the benefits of a research and development contract accrue to both parties. If the product is projected to have wide commercial application, the trader may convince the government that cost sharing would be in the best interests of both parties.

Cost–Plus–Fixed–Fee Contracts

The Cost-Plus-Fixed-Fee Contract is a Cost-Reimbursement Contract that provides for payment to the contractor of a negotiated fee that is fixed at the inception of the contract. The fixed fee does not vary with actual costs but may be adjusted as a result of changes in the work to be performed under the contract (see fig. 3-9). This type of contract permits contracting for efforts that might otherwise present too great a risk to contractors. It provides the contractor only a minimum incentive to control costs. It should not to be used in major weapon systems. This type of contract should be used when a Cost-Plus-Incentive-Fee Contract, discussed below, is not practical.

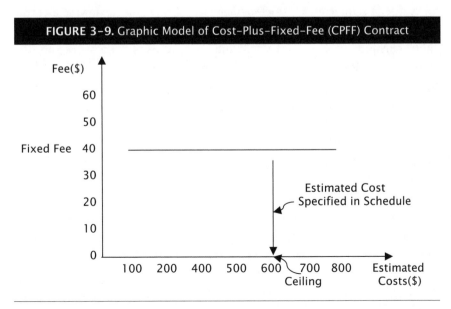

FIGURE 3-9. Graphic Model of Cost-Plus-Fixed-Fee (CPFF) Contract

Perhaps a small prototype needs to be built, a vaccine developed as a defense to a projected biochemical terrorist threat or flu epidemic, or software created to interpret encrypted data received from a surveillance satellite. Cost-Plus-Fixed-Fee Contracts are particularly applicable to initial responsive contracting in the aftermath of a natural disaster or terrorist attack where the scope of work cannot be defined (e.g., the unknown extent of the physical damage to levees in New Orleans after Hurricane Katrina).

Under such a contract, the government assumes the cost risk. The trader will be paid the incurred costs up to the agreed estimated cost specified in the contract's schedule. This estimated cost to be paid for the specified work, whether it be from incremental or complete funding, is the ceiling cost depicted in figure 3-9, unless increased by the contracting officer under proper authority. (For a discussion of limitation of funds or cost clauses, see chapter 11.) In addition, a fixed fee will be negotiated and set in the contract and paid incrementally as the work is performed, not to exceed 10 percent of the estimated cost objective for supplies or services. For research and development projects, a maximum fee of 15 percent is allowed.

Both the trader and buyer in such a contract have an obligation to "track" and "report" costs to ensure the ceiling or the estimated cost specified in the schedule set at the beginning of the contract has not been exceeded causing an "overrun." Overruns are anathema to the government.

Since the government accepts the risk of performance on such contracts, it exercises a significant contract management function by reviewing incurred versus projected cost-schedule reports, mandating the use of certified earned value management systems (EVMS) and periodic visits at the work site. The agreed estimated cost specified in the schedule may not be exceeded by a trader, except at its own risk, without approval of the government contracting officer. Periodic payments are scrutinized to ensure each cost category is allowable.

For a cost item to be allowable, it must be reasonable and allocable to the particular contract work itself. Moreover, the cost must be one whose expense meets preestablished cost-accounting standards. Each cost, including general and administrative expenses, reflected in overall overhead rates are reviewed or audited before payment. (See chapter 8 for more on this.)

Such a contract may take one of two basic forms: completion or term. The completion form describes the scope of work by stating a definite goal or target and specifying an end product. This form of contract normally requires the contractor to complete and deliver the specified end product (a report, prototype sample, or software code) within estimated cost, if possible, as a condition for the payment of the entire fixed fee. In the event the work cannot be completed within the estimated cost, the government may require more effort without an increase in fee, provided the government increases the estimated cost.

The term form describes the scope of work in general terms and obligates the contractor to devote a specified level of effort for a stated period of time. Under this form, if the performance is considered satisfactory by the government, the fixed fee is payable at the expiration of the agreed-upon period upon contractor statement that the level of effort specified in the contract has been expended in performing the contracted work. Renewal for further periods of performance is a new acquisition that involves a new cost and fee arrangement.

The completion form of Cost-Plus-Fee Contract is preferred by the federal buyer because of the differences in obligation assumed by a contractor, provided the work or specific milestones for the work can be defined sufficiently to permit the development of cost estimates within which the contractor can be expected to complete the work.

Cost–Plus–Award–Fee Contracts

The Cost-Plus-Award-Fee Contract involves a target cost, a fixed-base fee, and an award fee based on evaluation criteria that assess the contractor's performance in areas such as timeliness, quality, ingenuity, and cost effectiveness (see fig. 3-10). If the contractor's performance meets the stipulated criteria, an adjustment is added to the base fee up to a specified maximum limit. The amount of the government's award fee is not appealable under the Disputes clause of the contract.

Award–Term Incentive Contracts

Instead of a profit award-fee incentive, Award-Term Incentive Contracts include a provision allowing an agency to extend performance by the contractor. A true Award-Term Incentive Contract rewards the contractor with legal entitlement to a contract extension, not an additional option. An option is a unilateral right of the government; a contractor is not entitled to the exercise of an option. A contractor is entitled to nothing. But under such a contract, if the contractor's performance meets the award-term criteria stipulated in the contract and if any stipulated conditions—such as continuing need and

FIGURE 3–10. Graphic Model of Cost–Plus–Award–Fee (CPAF) Contract

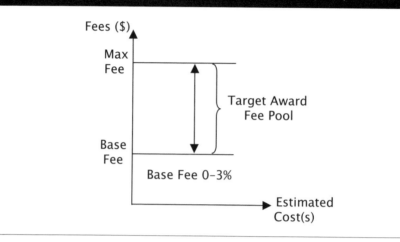

availability of funds—are met, then the government must either extend the contract or terminate it for convenience or default.

A contract providing for such extension would be required to include performance standards and be performance-based to the maximum extent practicable. There is intuitive appeal to such a contract since contractors are offered the opportunity to obtain more business without having to compete as a mechanism for motivating exceptional performance. The opportunity for extension is in lieu of or in addition to just being granted a profit incentive. This commercial-style practice creates a win-win situation for the government and contractors alike if agencies are vigilant about (1) conducting new competitions when cost savings are no longer accruing through the existing contract, and (2) limiting the overall term of the contract to a reasonable time frame so that the full benefit of marketplace competition can be applied to secure favorable pricing and refresh terms and conditions.

In summary, the Award-Term Incentive Contract is a relatively new development in government contracting, which instead of rewarding a contractor for excellent performance with additional fee or profit incentive, rewards the contractor by extending the contract period of performance without a new competition. The extension could be awarded in addition to the earned profit incentive. Under such a contract the government monitors and evaluates the contractor's performance, and if the designated government incentive award official (normally the contracting officer) decides that the contractor's performance was excellent, then the contractor earns an extension.

Cost–Plus–Incentive–Fee Contract

The government may also want to add an incentive feature to the Cost-Reimbursement Contract, renaming the contract a Cost-Plus-Incentive-Fee (CPIF) Contract. There is a target cost, target fee, a minimum and maximum fee, and a fee-adjustment formula, or sharing ratio. In such a contract, the initially negotiated target fee is adjusted after contract performance by a formula based upon the relationship of total allowable costs to total target costs. There is no ceiling price as found in a Fixed-Price-Incentive or Cost-Plus-Fixed-Fee Contract (see fig. 3-11).

The "target cost" is initially the cost figure developed from cost analysis as the government's prenegotiation goal for costs. After negotiations, it represents the cost figure agreed on by both parties as the most likely cost outcome of the contract's performance.

The "target fee" is initially the profit figure developed through the application of weighted guidelines or an unstructured profit methodology as the government's prenegotiation objective (see chapter 8). After negotiation, it

FIGURE 3-11. Graphic Model of Cost–Plus–Incentive–Fee (CPIF) Contract

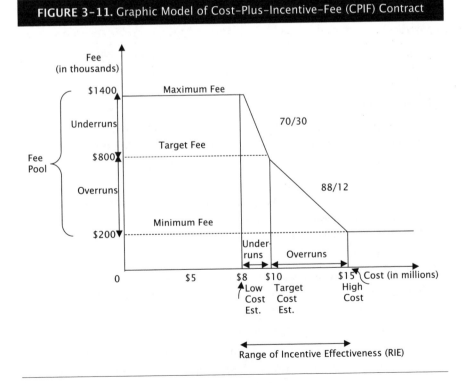

represents the profit figure agreed on by both parties as a reasonable fee for performance at the target cost.

The "fee adjustment formula" or "share ratio" provides, within limits, for increases in fee above the target fee when the total allowable costs are less than the target costs and decreases in fee below the target fee when the total allowable costs exceed the target cost. This increase or decrease is intended to provide an incentive for the contractor to manage the contract effectively.

A share ratio may be expressed as 70/30. The figure to the right (30) represents the contractor's share, and the figure to the left (70), the government's share. The total of both must equal 100 percent, and the government's share should not normally be less than 50 percent. These figures describe how the risk will be shared in contract performance. Essentially, a 70/30 share ratio states that the contractor's earned profit will be increased from the target fee by thirty cents for every dollar its actual cost is less than (underrun) target cost, and that for every dollar by which its actual cost exceed (overrun) the target cost, seventy cents will be deducted from its target fee. This increase or decrease is calculated as a plus or minus from target fee. The intent is to extract better performance from the trader.

The high cost estimate and low cost estimate are initially developed as a part of the cost analysis as the highest and lowest probable costs of contract performance by the government. After negotiations, they represent the agreement by both parties as to the highest probable cost and lowest probable cost.

The "minimum fee" is that which is determined to be reasonable for work performed at the high cost estimate. The minimum fee will be paid regardless of the final cost outcome. Should the contractor's final cost exceed the high cost estimate, it would still earn the minimum fee, assuming it completes the contract. This is guaranteed. Thus the CPIF arrangement changes its character to a Cost-Plus-Fixed-Fee Contract at the point where the contractor's costs earn it only the minimum fee.

The "maximum fee" is the fee determined to be reasonable for work performed at the low cost estimate. It may not exceed the statutory limitation of 15 percent of the estimated costs for research and development work and 10 percent for supply/service contracts. The maximum fee is the ceiling on the fee.

The "range of incentive effectiveness" (RIE) is a cost-related term referring to the range of possible costs over which the incentive arrangement works. Thus the total RIE would extend from the cost figure where the maximum fee is earned (low cost estimate) to that cost figure where the minimum fee is earned (high cost estimate). The term may also be applied to that range of costs between target cost and the cost for either the minimum fee or maximum fee. In graphics the RIE can be considered as a change in cost. The term is more often used in relation to a CPIF-type contract than an FPI type. The RIE is usually expressed as a range ($8 million to $15 million) but can also be expressed as the value of the change ($7 million).

The "fee pool" or "fee swing" refers to a change in fee, such as a change from target fee to maximum fee or from target fee to minimum fee. It can be expressed as a range ($800,000 to $1.4 million) or as the value of the change ($600,000). This term is more often used in relation to a CPIF arrangement than an FPI arrangement. If used in relation to FPI, the word "profit" would be substituted for "fee." We urge that one graph on a laptop the incentive arrangement displayed in figure 3-11 to efficiently show the consequences in variations of the parameters when negotiating an incentive contract when the parties meet face to face.

The Cost-Plus-Incentive-Fee Contract is ideal for services or development and test programs for a new helicopter anti-heat-seeking missile defense system, a new roadside improvised explosive device detector and neutralizer, new light materials research for body vests, the next generation of "laser guided" or "smart" munitions, a new orbiting platform for NASA or the Air Force, or for providing advisory services to a new Iraqi military police academy. The intent of the Cost-Plus-Incentive-Fee Contract is to extract a better performance from the trader when performing such critical projects.

Indefinite-Delivery Contracts

Indefinite-Delivery Contracts are now commonly used throughout the federal government, especially for commercial supplies and services. They are excellent instruments, allowing the government in many instances to award contracts to multiple sources, geographically disbursed, who are found qualified to deliver the requisite products or services. They allow the government in a tight budget environment to lock in prices for multiple years using fixed prices or rates. Such contracts assist logisticians and their procurement staffs to support "planning" for contingency operations (natural disasters, pandemics, terrorist attacks, recovery, reconstruction, and military operations). Figure 3-12 describes the characteristics of the three types of Indefinite-Delivery Contracts.

FIGURE 3–12. Indefinite–Delivery Contracts			
Indefinite-Delivery Contracts	**Exclusive Right to Fill Government's Needs**	**Legal Obligation**	**Funds Are Obligated**
Definite-Quantity	Total quantity specified	Yes	Contract itself
Indefinite-Requirements	Realistic estimated total quantity for planning; minimum and maximum order limitations	None, except to order from contractor only	Issue of Task or Delivery Order based on needs
Indefinite-Quantity (Note: For advisory and assistance services, multiple awards are mandated if longer than three years and more than $10 million, including options.)	"Guaranteed" minimum goods and services are speci-fied; "Guaranteed" minimum must be more than just "nomi-nal" amount. Mini-mum and maximum quantities covered by contract must be realistic and based on most current available information.	Order guaranteed minimum amount	Contract itself for guaranteed minimum; other by issuing Delivery or Tasking Order on needs

The Federal Acquisition Regulation related to Indefinite-Delivery Contracts does not in any manner restrict the authority of the General Services Administration to enter into federal schedule, multiple-award, or task or delivery order contracts. GSA regulations take precedence.

An Indefinite-Delivery/Definite-Quantity (IDDQ) Contract requires the trader to manufacture a fixed number of items or products for a fixed price. Put another way, the government is obligated to order the set quantity. Funds are obligated at the time the contract is awarded. The only variable is the date of delivery of each completed lot and the designated receiving location. Under such a contract, the trader knows it will be paid a fixed sum. It can initiate contract performance at its own schedule provided the trader can meet the delivery date(s) at designated locations upon order.

An Indefinite-Delivery/Indefinite-Requirements (IDIR) Contract is one in which the government does not guarantee any performance. Under such a contract, the government issues delivery orders for products or tasking orders for services. The buyer has no contractual obligation to issue any orders—not even a minimum quantity. The effort to win such a contract may have been indeed substantial, consuming nonrecoverable company overhead costs. One may wonder then, what is the value of such a contract? The answer is that the government is required to come to the trader that was awarded the contract and none other. The traders really need to scrutinize a solicitation, especially the estimated amount of business that the government could order provided funds were authorized. Since such a contract vehicle may extend over five or more years, the pricing schedule negotiated for various tasks or products is crucial to not only profitability but also the budgeted cost for performance.

Minimum and maximum order limitations are placed in such type contracts. The minimum order limitation is to assure the vendor that orders will not be placed in such a manner as to be administratively burdensome. These minimum order limitations must not be confused with guaranteed minimums, which are used in Indefinite-Quantity Contracts (discussed below). Maximum order limitations are apparently intended to permit the contractor to determine the maximum resources that must be committed to the contract at any time during the performance. These limitations are important if performance is required within a short period of time after placement of orders.

In this type of Indefinite-Delivery Contract, the vendor may be able to be reimbursed if the government does not order the estimated order quantity found in the contract itself. Case example involves a requirements contract to repair military family housing units. The government ordered only 31 percent of the contract's estimated work, and that order shortfall entitled the contractor to recover its unabsorbed overhead costs.

Moreover, a contractor may be able to use the FAR variation in estimated quantities (VIQ) clause found in such contracts. Under the standard VIQ clause, if the quantity of a unit-priced item in the contract is an estimated quantity and the actual quantity of the unit-priced item varies more than 15 percent above or below the contract's estimated quantity, either party is entitled to an equitable adjustment based on the increased or decreased cost resulting from the variation above 115 percent or below 85 percent of the estimated quantity. Recent administrative board of contracts appeals have confirmed that fixed overhead costs that are not absorbed because the government orders less than the estimated quantity come within the type of costs contemplated by the VIQ clause found in the awarded contract. Hence such a finding will allow the contractor to receive an equitable adjustment to its contract.

An important limitation is that no such contract type should be used for advisory and assistance services in excess of three years and ten million dollars unless the contracting officer or other designated procurement agency head determines in writing that the services required are so unique or highly specialized that it is not practical to make multiple awards under the regulations.

Of the three types of Indefinite-Quantity Contracts, this one appears to carry the highest risk for the trader. Yet the trader can decrease the risk. It can build a conservative inventory of the listed item based upon a plot of the buyer's historic usage and current intelligence dealing with the buyer's planned usage. Just remember that the government uses such a contract vehicle because it anticipates recurring requirements but cannot predetermine the precise quantities of supplies or services that designated government activities will need during a definite time period. This type of contract is suited for responsive contracting in support of logistics plans in the event of an emergency or contingency. Generally, an Indefinite-Requirements Contract is appropriate for items or services that are commercial products or commercial-type products. Funds are obligated by each task or delivery order, not by the contract itself.

Finally, the Indefinite-Delivery/Indefinite-Quantity Contract is similar to the IDIR discussed above. It differs, however, in that the government guarantees that it will purchase a minimum fixed sum of services or goods from the trader. To be binding, an Indefinite-Quantity Contract must contain a guaranteed minimum quantity that is more than "nominal" in relation to the services or products estimated to be purchased. The government's failure to order the minimum guaranteed quantity will constitute a breach of contract in favor of the contractor. In this regard, a trader can better plan his current and projected workloads.

Such contract vehicles are valuable when a recurring need is anticipated but it is inadvisable for the government to commit itself for more than a minimum quantity and funding levels may not have been as yet established. This Indefinite-Delivery-type contract fits the acquisition plan, providing contingent flexibility, especially when the precise quantities of supplies or services cannot be predetermined.

In such a contract vehicle, the maximum possible order will be stated so that planning can take place to handle such requirements. Likewise, the minimum order that may be placed is provided. Once again the buyer issues delivery (for products, commercial items, construction) or tasking orders (for services) against a fixed-price schedule previously negotiated for both services and products, including labor, time, and materials. A tasking order may include a combination of services to be delivered, as well as hardware, but the predominate work statement should be for the delivery of services.

The type and size of the tasks may vary and negotiations may take place, however, the labor rates as a minimum are set when the contract is initially awarded. The difficulty with such a contract vehicle is that the government (DoD, GSA, FEMA) prefers awards of such contracts for the same services or products to multiple sources. Whether or not multiple awards will be made depends upon the determination of the contracting officer as part of acquisition planning. Some traders have called such IDIQ agreements nothing more than the opportunity to further compete among a smaller group of selected bidders.

The use of multiple awards under a single solicitation for the same or supplies or services to two or more sources, however, is mandated in the event of advisory and assistance services that are not incidental and are a significant component of the contract(s) and exceed three years and $10 million, including options, unless

1. multiple awards are not practical as attested to by the head of the procurement agency or contracting officer inasmuch as only one contractor can reasonably perform the work because either the scope of work is unique or highly specialized or the tasks are integrally related;
2. the contracting officer or other designated official by the head of the agency determines in writing after evaluation of offers that only one offeror is capable of providing the services required at the level of quality required; or
3. only one offer is received.

Buyers and sellers in their planning should note that advisory and assistance services have been defined by regulation and precedence as management and professional support services encompassing accounting, budgeting, data collection, and performance auditing; studies, analyses, and evaluations;

and engineering and technical services, including support for conference and training programs.

The advantage on the part of the government using an IDIQ contract is that its buyers no longer need to synopsize or advertise purchase orders under Indefinite-Delivery Contracts once awarded. However, the buyer must develop order placement procedures that are preestablished and found in each solicitation and that provide each awardee a "fair opportunity" to be considered for each order exceeding three thousand dollars by providing for the multiple award of separate task or delivery order contracts for the same or similar services to two or more sources.

Figure 3-13 depicts the seven steps of the model for the processing of a requirement based on a Request for Task Execution Plan (RTEP) or Task Request for Proposal (TRFP) to fulfill a product or service need from an existing awarded IDIQ Contract or from multiple vendors awarded identical IDIQ umbrella contracts.

FIGURE 3–13. Indefinite–Delivery/Indefinite–Quantity (IDIQ) Contract Task or Delivery Order Processing Model

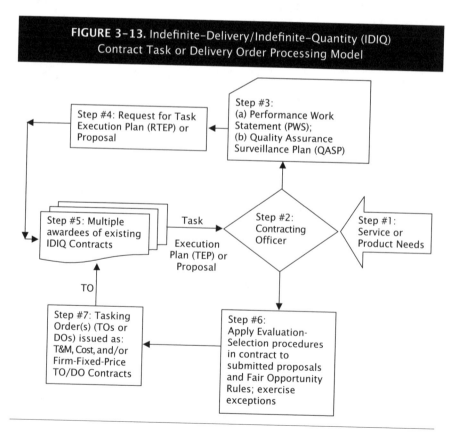

Using figure 3-13, based on a need (Step 1), the contracting officer or administrative contracting officer (Step 2), using his procurement team, develops the work statement along with the necessary quality assurance plan (Step 3). These documents are incorporated into the issued RTEP or TRFP (Step 4) to all the contractors awarded one of the multiple-agency contracts (Step 5). The government's request, needless to say, should describe the services to be performed or supplies to be delivered so that the full cost or price for the performance of the work can be established when the order is placed.

If the contract or order is for services, the RTEP prepared by the government must include a performance-based work statement(s) (see chapter 4). Orders are required to be within the scope of work of the awarded contract, issued within the period of performance, and within the maximum value of the awarded main contract. If the contract did not establish the price for the supply or service, the contracting officer must establish prices for each order using the policies and methods related for the conduct of price analysis or cost analysis, as appropriate. The contracting officer should keep submission requirements to a minimum. Streamlined procedures may be used including oral presentations. Each contractor then prepares and submits its Task Execution Plan (TEP) (Step 5) to meet the needs of the government for a particular task. Those contract holders that are not able or interested in submitting a TEP in response to the RTEP should notify the government contracting officer.

Of course, price or cost will be considered with each order in addition to technical approach, staffing levels, expertise, small business participation, and past performance. There are only four exceptions (Step 6) to providing each awardee a "fair opportunity" to compete for a delivery or tasking order:

1. Providing a fair opportunity would result in unacceptable delays.
2. Only one contractor is capable of providing the supplies or services ordered at the requisite level of quality owing to their uniqueness or high specialization.
3. The order must be issued on a sole-source basis in the interest of economy or efficiency as a logical follow-on to a delivery order already issued on a competitive basis.
4. The minimum guarantee agreed to in the main IDIQ Contract must be satisfied.

Once the TEPs have been evaluated, tasking orders (TOs) will be issued with or without negotiations at the discretion of the contracting officer, using generally a Time-and-Materials (T&M), Cost, and/or Firm-Fixed-Price TO (Step 7). (Each TO is a contract within itself under the terms and umbrella of the previously awarded IDIQ.)

To reduce the misuse and favoritism in the issuance of tasking or delivery orders, enhanced competition requirements for task and delivery order contracts are imposed. In essence, no task or delivery order contract in an amount estimated to exceed $100 million (including all options) may be awarded to a single contractor unless the head of the agency determines in writing that

1. because of the size, scope, or method of performance of the requirement, it would not be practical to award multiple task or delivery order contracts;
2. the task or delivery orders expected under the contract are so integrally related that only a single contractor can reasonably perform the work;
3. the contract provides only for firm-fixed-price task orders or delivery orders for the products for which unit prices are established in the contract or the services for which prices are established in the contract; or
4. only one contractor is qualified and capable of performing the work at a reasonable price to the government.

In the case of a task or delivery order in excess of five million dollars, the requirement to provide all contractors a fair opportunity to be considered is not met unless all such contractors are provided at a minimum with the following:

1. A notice of the task or delivery order that includes a clear statement of the agency's requirements
2. A reasonable period of time to provide a proposal in response to the notice
3. Disclosure of the significant factors and subfactors, including cost or price, that the agency expects to consider in evaluating such proposals, and their relative importance
4. In the case of an award that is to be made on a best value basis, a

written statement documenting the basis of award and the relative importance of the quality and price or cost factors
5. An opportunity for post-award debriefing

One must also keep in mind that the ordering period of a task-order contract for advisory and assistance services, including all options and modifications, normally may not exceed five years.

Lastly, orders placed by another agency under a GWAC or multiple-agency contract or an existing task-order or delivery-order contract are not exempt from the development of acquisition plans, rules on the use of funds, or the requirements for a bundled contract. A MAC is a tasking or delivery order contract established by one agency for use by other government agencies to obtain supplies, information technology, and services consistent with the Economy Act.

Agencies must designate a task and delivery order ombudsman who shall be responsible for reviewing complaints from contractors and ensuring that all contractors are afforded a fair opportunity to be considered under multiple-award contracts. If an agency designated an ombudsman prior to the Federal Acquisition Streamlining Act (FASA), the duties of that designated individual could also include these responsibilities.

After an award, contractors can protest the issuance of orders on the grounds that the order increases the scope, period, or maximum value of the contract. The ombudsman thus plays an important role. He or she must be a senior official who is independent of the contracting office awarding the multiple-award contract. The ombudsman does not have the authority to overturn award decisions or adjudicate formal contract disputes.

Moreover, no protest to the issuance or proposed issuance of an order under a task-order contract or delivery order contract is authorized, except for a protest on the grounds that the order increases the scope, period, or maximum value of the contract under which the order is issued or a protest of an order valued in excess of ten million dollars, in which case the comptroller general of the United States will have exclusive jurisdiction. See chapter 6 for more information on protests to the Government Accountability Office. One is not precluded, however, from discussing a complaint with the procuring agency's ombudsman.

Most agencies that appoint an ombudsman do so at a relatively high level. For example, the Department of Veterans Affairs has established the ombudsman at the Office of the Associate Deputy Assistant Secretary for

Acquisition. The Defense Information Systems Agency (DISA) has assigned the deputy director for procurement and logistics as the ombudsman. The Internal Revenue Service's ombudsman is the chief of the Policy and Procedures Branch, Office of Procurement Policy. In other agencies this role has been assigned to the competition advocate. In the Department of Energy (DOE) all heads of contracting activities designate a senior manager who is totally independent of the contracting officer and has no connection to the award of the order to perform ombudsman duties. The DOE also has a headquarters ombudsman.

Time–and–Materials Contracts

A Time-and-Materials Contract allows the buyer to provide supplies or services on the basis of loaded direct hours for the labor. Loaded labor rates are hourly rates that include basic wages, overhead, general and administrative expenses, and profit. The provided materials are billed at cost plus their associated material-handling costs. Such contracts should be awarded only when it is not possible at the time of placing the contract to estimate accurately the extent or duration of the work or to anticipate costs with any degree of confidence.

Use of such a contract would be appropriate in the event of fast-moving combat operations, such as during Operation Iraqi Freedom, where contractor support is required for fuel and fresh subsistence supplies. It could also be used in a national emergency. The buyer must justify such a contract (determination and findings) and place a ceiling price or any subsequent changes to such ceiling that the contractor exceeds at its own risk of nonpayment. However, in most cases such contracts are to be avoided for the purchase of commercial items or the issuance of delivery or tasking orders for commercial products or services.

Under this type of contract there is no requirement to withhold 5 percent of the payments due, unless it is necessary to withhold payment to protect the government's interest or if it is otherwise prescribed in the contract schedule. It requires a contract modification to make payment withholding and, in the event withholding is required, the contractor is responsible to withhold the amounts from its billing up to fifty thousand dollars for the contract.

Labor–Hour Contracts

Of course we can use Labor-Hour Contracts without supplies under the same rules. A Labor-Hour Contract is only a variation of the Time-and-Materials

Contract without materials. When an IDIQ Contract is awarded with services priced on a time-and-materials or labor-hour basis, contracting officers are required to the maximum extent practical to structure the contract to allow for the issuance of tasking orders on a firm-fixed-price or fixed-price with economic price adjustment basis. Varying from this requirement necessitates that the contracting officer provide a determination and findings to support the basic contract and also to explain why providing for an alternative from the fixed-price or fixed-price with price adjustment pricing structure is not practical.

Letter Contracts

A Letter Contract is an emergency measure that authorizes the trader to begin performance, manufacturing supplies, or rendering services immediately. Such contracts are necessary in regional natural disasters, such as hurricanes and flooding; a shooting war, as in the preparations for the invasion of Normandy in World War II; or the buildup for the liberation of Kuwait or invasion of Iraq. There just is no time to negotiate or make definitive a contract. If the opportunity exists for price competition, then the contracting officer includes the overall price in the letter contract.

Within the Letter Contract, there is a requirement to include a schedule for converting the letter contract to a definitive one. Dates are included for a trader to submit its price proposal, subcontracting plans, and a target date for completing the definition of the contract. The objective is to have defined the contract within 180 days or before 40 percent of the work to be performed has been completed, whichever occurs first.

The contracting officer may in selected cases authorize an additional period for defining the contract. If, after exhausting all reasonable efforts, the contracting officer and contractor cannot negotiate a definitive contract because of failure to reach agreement as to price or fee, the contractor can be required to proceed with the work and the contracting officer may, with the approval of his or her superior, determine a reasonable price unilaterally subject to appeal as provided in the disputes clause of the contract.

Under this type of contract, the government limits its liability based upon the estimated amount necessary to cover the contractor's requirements for funds before the development of the defined contract. This limit may not exceed 50 percent of the estimated cost of the definitive contract unless approved in advance by the official who authorized the letter contract.

BLANKET PURCHASE AGREEMENTS

A Blanket Purchase Agreement (BPA) is a simplified method of filling anticipated repetitive needs for supplies or services by establishing "charge accounts" with qualified sources of supply. BPAs should be established for use by an organization responsible for providing supplies for its own operations or for other offices, installations, projects, or functions. Such organizations, for example, may be organized supply points, separate independent or detached field parties, or one-person posts or activities. The use of BPAs does not exempt an agency from the responsibility of keeping obligations and expenditures within available funds. BPAs fit under the following circumstances:

1. A wide variety of commercial items in a broad class of supplies or services are to be purchased, but the exact items, quantities, and delivery requirements are not known in advance and may vary considerably.
2. There is a need to provide commercial sources of supply for one or more offices or projects in a given area that do not have or need authority to purchase otherwise.
3. The use of this procedure would avoid the writing of numerous purchase orders.
4. There is no existing requirements contract for the same supply or service that the contracting activity is required to use.

Individual purchases should not exceed the simplified acquisition threshold. Agency regulations may establish a higher threshold. An individual BPA is considered complete when the purchases under it equal its total dollar limitation, if any, or when its stated time period expires.

PRACTICING BUSINESS TIPS

Read the solicitation carefully to understand the source selection procedure to be used to acquire a product or service. Then assess the classification of the contract instrument the government is planning to award to the winner. The federal solicitation will tell you the type of contract being proposed. The contract may or may not be correct for you depending on your risk level.

If the fixed-price type of contract proposed in a solicitation does not fit your business model—it is too risky for the product sought in acquisition, for example—but your firm is interested in performing the work, then by all means notify the buyer that you believe that the contract type is not suitable. Attempt to convince the buyer to change the type contract to a classification that fits the acquisition. This effort must be undertaken before the closing time of the solicitation, regardless of whether it is an IFB or RFP. Any formal or informal protests subsequently will fall on deaf ears. The GAO has repeatedly denied such bid protests.

No responsible firm would undertake the development, initial engineering prototyping, or even low initial production of a new aircraft missile avoidance radar on a firm-fixed-price basis. A hybrid-type contract would be easier to swallow (for example, a Cost-Reimbursement Contract to a maturity level of the system and then a Fixed-Price Contract in initial low-rate production with the appropriate labor and material price escalation clauses, including overhead escalation clauses for pension and medical costs).

Lastly, contractors, the third parties to a federal contract, are cautioned to be careful when dealing with government agents to ensure they are not undertaking work for which no compensation may be paid because the work is unauthorized.

CHAPTER 4

Writing a Winning Proposal

Section L

Proposal Submission

1. Proposal shall be submitted via electronic media using Microsoft Office 2000 products . . . in separate files as set forth below. The Offeror's Proposal shall be divided into three (3) sections. Technical; Price; and Solicitation, Offer and Award Documents and Certifications/Representations.

SOLICITATION WI5P7T-08-R-N210

There is no guarantee of success. Business development, aside from the important aspect of being out there "beating the bush" and making contacts even on military bases, eventually comes down to writing proposals. The concepts presented in this chapter apply not only to federal solicitations and grants but also to those of state agencies.

Whether it is for a response to a combined synopsis/solicitation for commercial items or services, a quote for an RFQ, an initial proposal for an RFP, or a grant proposal for the Defense Advanced Project Research Agency or the National Institutes of Health, the Web sites www.fedbizopps.gov and www.fedgrants.gov both require the submission of an offer in some specified form.

The federal buyer has good money and cannot file for bankruptcy, but it needs technical and cost proposals to review even if the trader is the incumbent "sole source" for the delivery of the service or product. Moreover, when it comes to responding to RFPs, it is wise to know all aspects of this process of government contracting, including the rules, the decision making, and the submission.

There are two steps to writing a winning proposal. The first step involves preliminary analysis of the RFP to assess your firm's capabilities and the team (joint venturers, subcontractors, suppliers, technology licensors) you need for the project. It is during this step that you determine the profitability potential of the project in comparison to other business opportunities and the risks to successful performance. It is at this step, too, that one makes the decision as to whether or not to respond to the RFPs. Assuming the decision is made to proceed, the second phase includes the actual preparation, production, and timely delivery of the proposal or offer in response to the solicitation.

The preparation of the cost volume of an overall proposal is discussed in chapter 8. Figure 4.1 shows a list of the key e-government reference Web sites, many of which are part of the Integrated Acquisition Environment (IAE), that one may consult as resources for responding to a solicitation.

At a minimum, the Web site resources in figure 4-1 will assist you in studying the numerous regulations incorporated by reference, especially at Section I of the Uniform Contract Format (fig. 3-3), in most federal solicitations under review.

THE SOLICITED PROPOSAL, ADVERTISED BUSINESS OPPORTUNITY, AND RESPONSE TO AN RFP

If the government buyer has placed a "draft" solicitation "on the street" (at the GPE), then your team should be following its progress to final release. You should be planning a tentative team to develop your response during this waiting time. Even before this time a series of RFIs may have been posted by the buyer, giving you the opportunity to reply with information about your firm's capabilities, products, and services.

Once the trader has identified a formal advertised business opportunity and has the final released version of the solicitation (RFP) in hand or knows how to access the RFP from the FBO Web site, www.fedbizopps.gov, the process to be followed should be to first assign one person as the manager of your proposal writing team. Then start the analysis of the request for proposal with all of its references and attachments, its work statement, data item requirements, and security restrictions, following a strict, disciplined methodology to first and foremost determine whether or not to submit an offer. At any time along the path described below, one may make the decision to "pass up" this one. There will always be others.

FIGURE 4–1. Key E-Government Reference Web Sites of the Integrated Acquisition Environment (IAE) to Be Used in Preparing Bids and Proposals

Federal Acquisition Regulation (FAR)	www.arnet.gov/far/; www.acquisition.gov/far/ or http://acqnet.gov/far/index.html
Defense Federal Acquisition Regulation Supplement (DFARS); DFARS Procedures, Guidelines, and Information (PGI) serves as companion resource to DFARS	www.acq.osd.mil/dpap/dars/dfars/index.htm
Defense Procurement Acquisition Policy	www.acq.osd.mil/dpap
Acquisition, Technology, and Logistics Knowledge Sharing System; Ask a Professor; Glossary & Acronyms	http://akss.dau.mil/
Information for Contractors, Defense Contract Audit Agency (DCAA): Cost, pricing, payments, sample cost proposal	www.dcaa.mil (Go to Publications, click on "Info to Contractors")
Federal Technical Data Solutions for dissemination of Sensitive But Unclassified (SBU) acquisition material (e.g., TDPs, engineering drawings) related to solicitations found on FedBizOpps	www.fedteds.gov
Wage Determinations Online: applicable to service contracts subject to Service Contract Act and construction contracts subject to Davis-Bacon Act	www.wdol.gov

The following approach is presented not as a "how-to list" but as a logical series of questions that guide the triggers for smart decision making by a business development professional seeking opportunities to contract with the United States.

Does the Proposal Fit or Involve Your Product and Service?

If you are in the business of designing, manufacturing, and operating unmanned aerial vehicles, you would be marketing to the armed services and Department of Homeland Security for border patrolling and even perhaps to the Forest Service of the Department of Interior. Hence, your marketing or business development staffs would follow all agency proposal solicitations identified with North American Industry Classification System codes 511130, 541330, and 339999. Such codes will be noted in the synopsized solicitations on the business opportunity pages of the various executive agencies. These codes identify products related to unmanned aerial vehicles, your product line.

What Is Your Competition?

Examine the cover page of the Uniform Contract Format's Part I, Section A (the Solicitation/Contract Form), which includes SF 33 of the RFP, SF 18 of the RFQ, and SF 1449 for CIs, to determine from the start whether or not the proposed acquisition is "restricted" in any manner.

The solicitation may be restricted to only small business. This occurs when the contracting officer has completed the market research and has the expectation of being able to receive from small business at least two fair market value quotes. On the other hand the procurement may be "unrestricted," allowing any size offeror to participate. In the latter event you may decide that the competitive field is too large, thus creating a low chance of winning, or that even if you did win, because of the projected competition only a very narrow margin of profit would be possible.

Perhaps you would elect to pass up responding to the solicitation or explore whether you could be a subcontractor to one of the large bidding firms, especially if the solicitation is being awarded on a sole-source basis to an incumbent firm.

Does the Buyer Require a Qualified Product?

If the buyer requires a qualified product in its solicitation, the offeror should already have its name and prequalified product on a Qualified Bidder's List (QBL), Qualified Manufacturer's List (QML), or Qualified Products List (QPL). Otherwise, the buyer needs to give you the opportunity in advance to demonstrate your abilities to meet the standards specified for qualification. Once your firm or product is on such listings, if the agency determines an acquisition is subject to qualifying standards, it may limit competition to the bidders, manufacturers, or products listed, giving you an advantage over firms that have not been prequalified.

For example, if the product (e.g., a fuselage mounted antenna) needs to be flight certified or environmentally tested (e.g., a tank computer subjected to shock and vibration tests) in advance, independent of any specific procurement action, there may not be time to do so by the date of award, much less by the solicitation's closing date for the submittal of proposals. Likewise, you may not want to undertake privately the expense to do so in hopes that there may be another, similar procurement. If you want to be ready, then by all means make the private investment to qualify your product. But also consider that there may be already sufficient firms with qualified products that listed.

Is This Acquisition Rated?

Block 1 of the solicitation form (SF 33) will indicate if the contract is a "rated order." A rated order is a prime contract for any product, service, or material that requires preferential treatment and includes subcontracts and purchase orders resulting under such contracts. The Defense Production Act of 1950, as amended, authorizes the president to require the priority performance of contracts and orders necessary to promote the national defense, including emergency preparedness activities conducted pursuant to the Stafford Disaster Relief and Emergency Assistance Act, and to allocate materials, services, and facilities to promote the national defense. The Defense Priorities and Allocations System (Department of Commerce) implements the act with respect to industrial resources. The ratings are enforced in peacetime and war or during emergencies.

Check to determine if the RFP involves a rated order certified for national defense use. If it is a rated order, then the offeror when awarded a contract must follow the requirements of the DPAS regulation. The supplier must give precedence over unrated orders so as to deliver the articles or materials in a required time period. The contractor is obligated to accept the rated order, to schedule production operations to satisfy delivery requirements of each rated order, and to extend the priority rating to suppliers to ensure that the item is delivered in the time frame requested.

There are two levels of rated orders established by the DPAS. These orders are identified by a priority rating—either DX or DO—and a program identification symbol within a plant. Rated orders take precedence over all unrated orders as necessary to meet required delivery dates. DX ratings are used for special defense programs designated by the president to be of the highest national security. All DO-rated orders have equal priority and take preference over unrated orders, including commercial orders. All DX-rated orders have equal priority and take preference over DO-rated and unrated orders.

Program identification symbols indicate which approved program is involved with the rated order. For example, "A1" identifies defense aircraft programs, and "A7" signifies defense electronics programs. If there is a work backlog in your plant or you are unable to give preferential treatment (owing to a lack of skilled manpower or shortage of parts) to such a new order, then you should not submit an offer on the solicitation.

What Are the Employee Security Clearance Levels, Site Physical Security, and Geographical Work-Site Requirements for the Project?

Closely examine the security requirements included in the solicitation (usually by an attachment, DD Form 254) regarding clearance levels, personnel, and site and operations security. Just this aspect of a project could cause you to reach a no-bid decision and spare you wasted effort. Remember that employees with dual citizenship and even permanent green cards may not be able to receive timely security clearances—or any security clearances at all.

In addition to the costs of compliance caused by the numerous clauses incorporated into the solicitation at Section I of the Uniform Contract Format, the need for physical security of the work site and for your employees and subcontractors must be estimated. These latter security costs may be significant if contract performance extends your firm's operations in a combat-supporting role overseas. In such an event, the profit margin, recruitment costs, and risks to your team could become unacceptable in comparison to other markets.

Be alert to determine from the solicitation whether your firm's team or subcontractor personnel will be required by the combatant commander to deploy to a designated operational area outside the United States for the conduct or support of specified military operations, including contingency operations, humanitarian or peacekeeping operations, and military exercises. This also includes solicitations that require a contractor to provide personnel to support diplomatic or consular missions. Such solicitations involve special costs (weapons training, security, logistics, medical, hazard pay, etc.) not normally included in a bid for performance of work in the United States.

Keep in mind that it is possible you may not be able to provide skilled employees because your personnel may be unwilling to work overseas in high threat areas owing to terrorists or civil strife.

How Is the Winner Determined?

If you do not feel the methodology including the order of importance of the evaluation factors and subfactors to be used is fair, you should consider passing. First, closely study the evaluation criteria for selecting the winner under Section M, Evaluation Factors for Award, of the Uniform Contract Format to determine whether the solicitation favors a trade-off process or the lowest price that is technically acceptable. The former is based on trade-offs among the preannounced factors that will be evaluated (price or cost, technical, small business participation plan, performance risk assessment) to find the "best value" and possibly to award the contract to other than the lowest-priced offeror; the latter process awards the contract to a technically acceptable proposal with the lowest evaluated price. This best value methodology is also known as "pass/fail." The pool of offerors who pass technically are then evaluated by which one offers the lowest cost.

What Effort Will It Take to Submit a Proposal?

The solicitation's instructions to bidders found in Section L, Instructions, Conditions, and Notices to Bidders, of the Uniform Contract Format specifies what e-paperwork has to be submitted, when, and in what format. This step is no different from what a college student must do when a professor issues a research assignment. A cursory examination will allow management to decide approximately what resources and time will be required, based upon past historical bid and proposal (B&P) costs as a function of the current budget for such overall activities across the firm.

More than the proposal's preparation costs should be considered; you must also factor in production (printing) and required delivery costs. Teaming in a joint venture or partnership business arrangement allows cost sharing for the competition phase. Moreover, a joint venture brings strength to the submitted proposal owing to the special capabilities and complementary technology each venturer contributes to the team's overall proposal. Such contractor team arrangements are looked on favorably by contracting officers because both joint venturers are required to sign the contract and are thus responsible collectively and individually for performance.

What Did the Government Pay for the Product or Service Last Time?

Visit the buyer's Web site e-library, which is identified in the RFP, to review prior and any pending acquisitions and to obtain the built-to drawings and/

or work statements for the product or services needed, other technical data package information, any past historical cost data or pricing data on project services or products, and all other available past data on the project's products or services (e.g., copies of issued delivery or tasking order contracts). Convert and download the information you need into your word-processing program so that you can manipulate relevant information into your response to the RFP.

Otherwise, you may have to use the Freedom of Information Act (FOIA) to require the government to provide the information from its files, which means you may not receive it in time to influence your assumptions and decisions prior to the date your initial proposal must be submitted.

How to Get the Solicitation's Specifications, Standards, References, and Related Requirements

There are three basic types of specifications. In practice, it is rare to find specifications that fit completely into one of these categories, however; most specifications are a combination of the following:

1. Performance specifications. These contain performance characteristics desired for the item. Examples: The radio must operate over a forty-mile radius. The floor must be free of stains, spots, and streaks.
2. Design specifications. These contain precise measurements, tolerances, materials, in-process and finished-product tests, quality control and inspection requirements, and other detailed information for manufactured items. The information furnished is sufficiently detailed to ensure that all items manufactured to the specifications are the same. Example: Detailed manufacturing drawings.
3. Purchase order descriptions. These specifications identify the item by a brand name with the optional use of an "or equal" statement to allow competition.

Specifications are comprehensive descriptions of the technical requirements for material, equipment, and services. In addition to its specifications, the DoD uses standards that establish the engineering and technical limitations and applications of items, materials, processes, methods, and engineering practices.

Standards are used to ensure maximum uniformity in materials and equipment and to foster interchangeability of parts used in these products. Standards may be separately stated in a description of a need, but frequently they are also included in military specifications. Though use of military specifications and standards continues within the DoD, there is an emphasis on maximizing the utilization of commercial specifications and standards whenever practicable.

Military and Federal Specifications and Standards

Agencies prefer to provide complete technical data packages with their solicitations. However, many acquisitions are accomplished using only the manufacturer's name and part number, namely when an agency does not have or own the technical data. The most common reason agencies do not have the technical data is the proprietary designation. Most of the parts we buy today are financed and developed by private industry. Therefore, we have no control or right to use such data for procurement purposes and, in most cases, the cost of purchasing this data far exceeds any savings that may be realized through competition.

For access to specifications the Department of Defense is able to provide, go to ASSIST-Online (Acquisition Streamlining and Standardization Information System), a comprehensive Web site providing access to current information associated with military and federal specifications and standards in the management of the Defense Standardization Program. It provides public access to standardization documents over the Internet and is the official source for DoD specifications and standards. For more information about ASSIST-Online and to register, go to http://assist.daps.dla.mil/online/faqs/overview.cfm.

Some agencies provide drawings or "bidsets" for contractors' use in bidding on currently open solicitations. A bidset is a collection of engineering technical data that has been determined to be technically adequate for the manufacturing of an item of supply in a fully competitive procurement environment. A bidset is defined by an associated National Stock Number (NSN). Not all NSNs or items managed by an agency have bidsets. For information on obtaining a bidset on an open solicitation, the solicitation itself should be examined to ascertain the recommended Web site.

The next step is to obtain the necessary standards and specifications to include data item descriptions, not provided but incorporated by reference in the solicitation so that you can price the work, unless they are available in your company's proposal library. (Refer to chapter 8 for preparation of cost estimates.) As you study the RFP particular attention should be paid to those requirements that carry a large price tag in delivering either the specified product or the required services (e.g., warranties, delivery schedule, labor rates such as wage determinations under the Service Contract Act or Davis Bacon Act, and Buy American Provisions). Moreover, the costs of compliance with the numerous clauses (found in Section I of the Uniform Contract Format) incorporated into the solicitation need to be adequately addressed.

This close examination should lead to questions for which you need answers or to continuing issues that were not resolved while the RFP was in the drafting stages. Many times the government places its draft RFPs on its Web site for comment by prospective offerors. Serious vendors avail themselves of this opportunity to influence the procurement in an ethical manner.

Unfettered access to government officials (e.g., operational, technical, procurement, quality, and budgeting users) by prospective offerors, including their business development teams, at varying stages of the acquisition cycle can lead to an unfair competitive advantage or the appearance of impropriety among offerors. Hence the FAR has established rules related to the professional and ethical conduct of "information exchanges" with government buyers at critical stages in the source selection process:

1. Prior to the release of the solicitation for bidding
2. After the release of the final solicitation to the public
3. While considering award on initial proposals submitted by sellers
4. While establishing which proposals will be allowed into the competitive range
5. While conducting discussions (negotiations) with selected offerors in the competitive range
6. While determining whether or not to allow revisions to the proposals that made it into the competitive range and, if so, which ones

Under the procurement regulations, awards are frequently made on the basis of timely submitted initial proposals without any discussions or negotiations.

The solicitations will place prospective bidders on notice that an award may be made by the contracting officer on "initial proposals." Hence it behooves a trader to offer its best technical product or services at the lowest price. No revisions are allowed to the baseline "initial proposal" submitted to the government, and an award is made only after limited exchanges serving as clarifications of the written or electronic initial timely submittals. These exchanges are summarized in figure 4-2 and are consistent with procurement integrity requirements.

The purpose of exchanging information is to improve the understanding of government requirements and industry capabilities, thereby allowing potential offerors to judge whether or how they can satisfy the government's requirements and enhancing the government's ability to obtain quality supplies and services at reasonable prices and increase the efficiency in proposal preparation, evaluation, negotiation, and contract award. As a government policy, therefore, early exchanges are encouraged.

After the final RFP is publicly released, no firm or potential offeror can have direct contact with the user of the product or services or the procurement staff who finalized, coordinated, and released the final RFP for public access and bidding. Access to such contracting officials during the drafting stage could allow you to persuade the contracting officials to make revisions

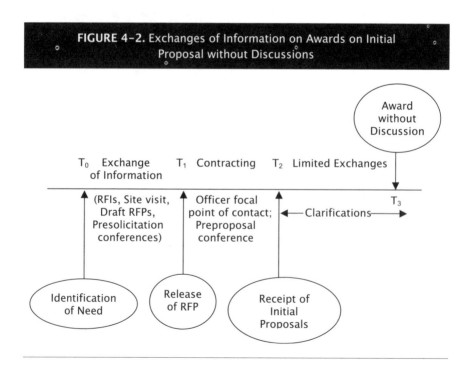

FIGURE 4–2. Exchanges of Information on Awards on Initial Proposal without Discussions

to the requirement, allowing your firm to profitably submit a proposal and at the same time provide a best value proposal to the government.

However, once the RFP has been released to the public, time is generally at a premium. If you are going to try to persuade the contracting officer to make changes to the solicitation at this late date by pointing out improvements or problems with the RFP, you can do it only by e-mail or written communications to the contracting officer or contract specialist.

You are not allowed to communicate with any other person, save the agency's competition advocate, who may intercede on your firm's behalf. Each major acquisition center has appointed a competition advocate who is an experienced procurement official and has the ear of the head of procurement. This position was created by Congress in its Competition in Contracting Act of 1984 to assist in removing obstacles to "full and open" competition. In some instances, the duties of the competition advocate and the duties of the ombudsman, which involve complaints in the award of MAC tasking and delivery orders, have been combined in one official.

An experienced contracting officer will respond to your request because he realizes that a prospective bidder can file more than an agency protest against the solicitation. In such an event the trader assumes the role of a protestor, pointing out deficiencies and other issues that make the requirement for procurement being proposed anticompetitive, too restrictive, and not open to small business, thus restricting competition.

In fact the trader may want to skip the contracting officer of the agency responsible for the procurement and proceed to lodge a bid protest directly with the General Accountability Office at www.gao.gov/legal.htm. To avoid this, precluding a matter of urgency, the contracting officer will have to take the time to resolve the issues before the submission date and time set for the receipt of the traders' proposals in response to the RFP. Therefore, at your urging, the requirements in the statement of work and related specification requirements, to include the weighting of the factors and related subfactors, could be amended. The proposal preparation period would of course be extended if the amendments were substantive so that the amendments to the solicitation could be addressed by all the prospective offerors.

This opportunity to correct RFP errors or defects becomes extinguished when the required date and time passes when the initial proposal was required to be submitted. Repeatedly the GAO has denied protests about matters that should have been addressed prior to bid opening or proposal submission time.

War Game?

Engage in a "What if?" session with your team to find possible alternate solutions to the need that is advertised. The government will use functional or performance-based acquisition (PBA) specifications in lieu of design or build-to specifications at every opportunity. Hence the opportunity exists to propose innovative but proven approaches to a procurement, each with its benefits, price, timetable, and risks, from which the government may pick. Offering alternatives, such as technology-growth, enhanced reliability, robust performance, ease of inserting future capabilities, provided each meets the solicitation's "core" requirements, will actually improve one's chances on being selected in a best value source selection procedure.

Make the Conscious Decision to Bid or Not to Bid

Again engage in some Q&A. Is it in your firm's interest to submit a proposal? Its cost and the risks may not be acceptable. What is your firm's annual overhead budget for B&P costs in relation to the amount of business that must be bid on to arrive at a preestablished gross win level? Playing the bidding game does not come cheap.

You may want to submit a proposal for the benefit of the experience once you set your mind to get your feet wet. You can never be a loser because regardless of the outcome, you can learn a lot. As a near-winner or interested party you may be eligible to ask for a debriefing in which the government highlights your weaknesses and deficiencies so they are not repeated again. You will get the chance, perhaps, of meeting the buyer, which could allow you the opportunity at a future date to meet again to explain your products or services. It sets you up for the next round. Do not consider yourself a loser even if you don't win the bid.

How Do You Prepare the Proposal Economically yet Effectively?

Set up your outline for your response to the RFP as follows:

1. Open the RFP in Microsoft Word (convert the RFP from PDF format to Word).
2. Cut and paste any RFP information that is pertinent into a blank Word document using the proposal format and content explained in Section L, Instructions, Conditions, and Notices to Offerors, found

in the Uniform Contract Format used in SF 33, Solicitation, Offer and Award. Competitive proposals generally follow a similar format, calling for separate volumes by title that correlate to the factors for evaluation required by a typical solicitation. These are management, technical, cost, small business participation, past performance, and other identified factors and related subfactors to be evaluated (see fig. 4-3).

3. Now, although not creative or tailored to your firm but merely administrative at this point in time, the tedious culling of a solicitation (which may consist of some seventy-five to two hundred pages) to identify, sort, and paste government-provided information into blank Word documents is a vital step. Sort the information into volumes that are related to a key evaluation factor. This process, known as "peeling" an RFP, reduces the risk of missing or failing to address a key requirement in the solicitation. The documents you create collectively for submission or evaluation will become known as your "Initial Proposal."

4. Identify and paste the "clauses" either verbatim or by reference in the RFP (Section I in the Uniform Contract Format) under the response submission heading related to each requirement. You will in essence create a draft "strawman" response that includes "requirements and instructions" by cutting and pasting from the Word RFP. Some RFP information can easily be moved into several different sections. Color code this pasted information in red or whatever color you select to distinguish it from your own proposal library database and from your own sales notes. Make sure to color code the RFP information used to create the sections you have cut and pasted because you will eventually have your own wording and compelling themes. The original RFP data you pasted then will be deleted.

You are now ready to write to your outline and explode your response in each volume and refine it. You may want to describe your solution to the requirement in multiple locations in your initial proposal or fit it into one of the headings only. In a different color enter your own wording and sales information. Then delete the initial strawman wording in red. Remember that you eventually need to slant the information to fit your company's style.

FIGURE 4-3. Six Typical Components to an Initial Proposal

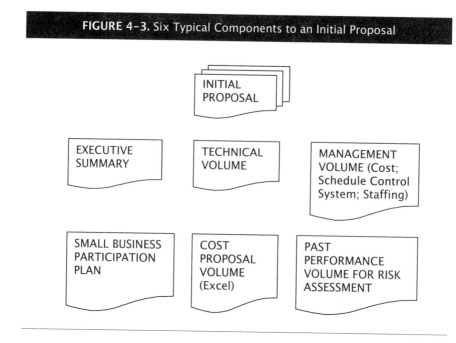

Is the Proposal's Content "Responsive"?

Sealed bids, generally used for commercial items and services that have government design specifications, are offers that must be "responsive" to the solicitation. In the case of a submitted bid, lack of responsiveness to the solicitation (IFB) at the time of submission into the "electronic bid box" causes the bid to literally be scrolled into the trash. Lack of responsiveness is fatal. There are a number of issues that cause the bid to be materially unresponsive. Some examples are failing to acknowledge amendments to the solicitation that change a material part of the statement of work or change portions of the testing requirements, omitting a bid bond or providing one in an insufficient amount, failing to provide a product sample as required, and failing to provide a required certification.

Competitive proposals resulting from an RFP or an RFQ are submitted when the simplicity of the sealed bid procedure is not adequate owing to the complexity of the acquisition. However, in order for it to win, a competitive proposal also must have "responsive content" in keeping with the requirements of the solicitation's Performance Work Statement (PWS) or Statement of Objectives (SOO) and its Section L, Instructions, Conditions, and Notices to Offerors.

Such a written proposal that contains the content and information requested in a concise manner and demonstrates how your proposed solution solves the user's problem. Writing a compelling technical approach is the foundation to such a proposal. An effective technical approach can be accomplished using traditional outlining techniques, storyboards, tables, and the development of themes. These provide the jumping-off point for developing the detailed technical approach with its defined and interrelated tasks/subtasks, timetables, staffing requirements, and solution concepts.

Do not delegate the writing of your core proposal to consultants or "out of house" hired technical writers because it is easy to tell when that is done. Proposal writing is tedious and costly in resources (both manpower and dollars). It requires a disciplined process, standardized content, and tight quality control. You and your engineers know better than anyone your service capabilities and product. Be clear as to why your proposal should be selected. Do not be timid. Ask for bonus points.

In contrast to the sealed bid, if you have omitted some key item at the time the initial proposal had to be submitted, it is not fatal as long as you submit the proposal on time. However when the source selection evaluation commences, you may lose points that could lead to your firm not making the cut into the competitive range.

A firm may not revise its submitted initial proposal unless specifically authorized by the contracting officer through an offeror's answers to items for negotiation (IFN) or a Final Proposal Revision (FPR) when discussions are being closed with the offerors who still remain in the competitive range of a source selection. All such requests are approved by the contracting officer. It is in the competitive range that you really have the opportunity during discussions to revise your initial proposal at the request of the contracting officer.

What If the Solicitation's Acquisition Requires a Performance-based Preference?

Since most recent acquisitions require the evaluation of proposals that meet performance-based criteria, take the time to write and deliver such a submission in your initial proposal. It is anticipated that in the years to come a majority of the contracts offered throughout the federal government will be performance-based acquisitions. Rather than micromanaging the details of how contractors operate, in other words, the government will set the standards, set the results, and give the contractor the freedom to achieve them in the best way.

Performance-based acquisition contracting is a collective responsibility that involves representatives from budget, technical, contracting, logistics, legal, and program offices. The idea behind PBA, which is applicable to both products and services, is to shift the paradigm from traditional acquisition thinking into one of collaborative, performance-oriented teamwork, with a focus on program performance and improvement, not simply contract compliance. Performance-based acquisition can be daunting, with its discussion of work breakdown structures, quality assurance plans, and contractor surveillance. Hence the process for PBA has been broken down into seven steps (see fig. 4-4).

The contract statement of work—the PWS or the SOO—is the foundation of performance-based contracts. The performance work statement describes the effort in terms of measurable performance standards (outputs). These standards should include such elements as what, when, where, how many, and how well the work is to be performed. In essence the work is described in terms of the purpose of the work to be performed rather than either the "how" of it or the number of hours to be provided. The PWS is the statement

---

FIGURE 4–4. Seven Steps to Performance–based Contracting (PBC)

1. Establish an integrated solutions team.

    ↓

2. Decide what problem needs solving.

    ↓

3. Examine private-sector and public-sector solutions.

    ↓

4. Develop a Performance Work Statement (PWS) or Statement of Objectives (SOO).

    ↓

5. Decide how to measure and manage performance.

    ↓

6. Select the right contractor.

    ↓

7. Manage performance.

in the solicitation that identifies the technical, functional, and performance characteristics of an agency's requirements.

The SOO is an alternative to the PWS. It is a summary of key agency goals, outcomes, or both that are incorporated into performance-based acquisitions so that competitors may propose their solutions, including a technical approach, performance standards, and a quality assurance surveillance plan based upon commercial business practices. It opens the competition to a wide range of solutions.

The recent Air Force KC-X Tanker Replacement Program was a performance-based, best-value source selection competition. The Air Force solicitation for the KC-X Systems Development and Demonstration and the KC-X Low Rate Initial Production and Full-rate Production statements of work were each described using SOOs. The Air Force selected on February 29, 2008, a team composed of U.S. Northrop Grumman and European Aeronautic Defence and Space (EADS), the parent of Airbus, to supply the first 179 aerial refueling tankers of some 500, an upset over the favored Boeing bid.

A Quality Assurance Surveillance Plan (QASP) that directly corresponds to the performance standards and measures contractor performance is needed to determine if contractor services and/or products meet contract PWS requirements. Positive and negative performance incentives, based on QASP measurements, should be included.

The PWS performance standards, QASP, and incentives are interdependent; they must be compatible in form, style, and substance and should be cross-referenced. For a procurement to be a true performance-based contract, it should contain a PWS or SOO, a QASP, and the appropriate financial or term incentives or both. Training and assistance in understanding PBAs can be obtained at www.acqnet.gov/comp/seven_steps/introduction.html.

Remove Skeletons that May Have Crept into the Closet

Past performance records can really hurt a business, so make sure that you are cognizant of all your firm's filed performance reports. Attempt to remove incorrect or incomplete statements or unjustified performance reports that bear the fruit for surprises. Use your MPIN to enter the Past Performance Information Retrieval System at www.ppirs.gov. Remember that the government cannot preclude you from checking your own past "report cards." The comments on these records may surprise you.

Verify each personnel resume you are planning to submit, whether it is contingent on your winning the bid or not, to ensure it is truthful and the background, experience, training, and schooling described in it meet the buyer's requirements.

Check your subcontracting plans carefully and verify that none of your proposed subcontractors are excluded parties, barred from selling to the government owing to criminal records of officers at the company, having been debarred, or being proposed for debarment. The Excluded Parties Listing System is maintained by the GSA at www.epls.arnet.gov. (See chapter 10 for more information on debarment and PPIRS.)

Have You Indentified and Marked Your Intellectual Property?

You do not want to give away your intellectual property (IP) rights (see chapter 9). Identify your intellectual data rights with proper notices and protective markings that you have developed or obtained ownership with your private funds, internal R&D, or through previous government contracts. Make it clear to the buyer what you are willing to license. Identify whether the government will be given the normal commercial license or a negotiated special license if required.

Identify the competitive proposal you submit with a legend on the front cover and with a protective marking on each key technical and financial page to indicate that it is being provided only for evaluation purposes. These markings are the same whether the proposal is solicited or unsolicited.

To protect one's technical and cost data the title page of the proposal should be marked (in capital letters):

> USE AND DISCLOSURE OF DATA. This proposal includes data that shall not be disclosed outside the government and shall not be duplicated, used, or disclosed—in whole or in part—for any purpose other than to evaluate the proposal. However if a contract is awarded to this offeror as a result of, or in connection with, the submission of these data, the government has the right to duplicate, use, or disclose the data to the extent provided in the resulting contract. This restriction does not limit the government's right to use information contained in these data if they are obtained from another source without restriction. The data subject to this restriction are contained in sheets [insert page numbers or other identification of sheets].

Then the offeror should also mark each sheet of data that contains technical information and financial data it wishes to restrict with the following legend: "Use or disclosure of data contained on this sheet is subject to the restriction on the title page of this proposal."

Such markings will go a long way toward protecting financial and technical information as an exemption against the public's access right to records, precluding a competitor from obtaining a copy of the unsolicited proposal under the Freedom of Information Act.

Do You Need a Red Team?

You need an independent team—a Red Team—to scrub your proposal by reviewing it before its submission. The size and professional composition of this team will depend on the importance of the solicitation and your time and resources. Part of this review should be to verify that each paragraph in the government's work statement is addressed in your proposal.

Keep in mind that the government evaluation team has no obligation to search through the various volumes of your initial proposal (see fig. 4-3) to correlate essential proposal information among the various submittals. Each component of your initial proposal must stand on its own. As but one example, do not include material in the cost volume alone that would also be needed by an evaluator in the technical and management volumes.

How to Manage the Production and Delivery of your Initial Proposal

Remember that all the above work may be for naught if the initial proposal is not submitted on time. Untimely proposals are, as general rule, discarded. It helps to practice well in advance to submit the proposal via the media designated in Section L of the Uniform Contract Form. In most cases expect the transmission media to be electronic—over the Internet—or a mix of electronic and hand-delivered or mailed means (e.g., CDs and paper volumes). Regardless, fully comply with the delivery instructions in Section L.

THE UNSOLICITED PROPOSAL

An unsolicited proposal is a smart way to get your company in front of a government buyer. It works only if what you have to offer solves a problem that no one else has been able to solve, a buyer has not formally placed the need into an acquisition program, or it has not been authorized funds for acquisition. It is worth talking to an agency's technical or other appropriate personnel before preparing a detailed unsolicited proposal. The government prefers that innovative ideas be submitted in a response to an announcement or solicited program.

For a firm to be successful in submitting such a proposal, it needs to have done its homework "scouting" out what the government user needs and who that user's purchasing agent is. Public searches in congressional or agency records should reveal the availability of funds or the ability and even, perhaps, the willingness of the procurement official to reprogram monies to fund the unsolicited proposal.

An example of an unsolicited proposal is the evolution of the U.S. soldier's belt quart canteen, carried by millions of soldiers since World War I. In Iraq, the plastic belt quart canteen has been supplanted by a camouflaged, water-filled, 3.2-quart backpack hydration unit with a tube that fits under a bulletproof vest and extends to the soldier's mouth. The soldier's backpack also can have a reservoir liner to protect water in a chemical attack. The backpack hydration unit frees the soldiers' arms, while drinking water, to use a rifle or radio while involved in critical military activity. What was once a biker's cycling accessory has become the canteen of choice for soldiers, especially those in desert operations or in countries with high temperatures. A small business firm in the commercial recreational cycling arena saw this need and today has become a leader in hydration systems, selling thousands of its products to the Pentagon. A soldier can drink through a drinking nozzle or "bite valve" without reaching for a water bottle or canteen on his belt. The backpack canteen demonstrates how an innovative nondefense firm can fuel its growth by pivoting between two markets, promoting and helping product development.

The beauty of such an arrangement is that military requirements can further drive innovation and durability. The militarized version of the backpack canteen was developed with sturdier, non-infrared-detectable materials and a silver-based, antigerm lining to keep water clean. It was then adapted for a less-expensive retail version to serve the recreational market. The trader in the above case solved an important military need, transforming the "Camel-Bak" from an accessory for cyclists and by mountain climbers to a personal hydration system widely recognized today for police, first responders, and warfighters throughout the world.

In essence, an unsolicited proposal is a "smart" paper that solves a problem in a unique manner, saves a lot of money, is innovative, and is not being solicited by the government in any other forum or by any other means. It carries the indicia of being independently created and developed by the trader without any government involvement, endorsement, supervision, or direction.

An unsolicited proposal is neither a value engineering proposal nor a response to a Small Business Innovation Research topic, Small Business Technology Transfer Research topic, Program Research and Development Announcement, or Broad Agency Announcement. It is not a process to attempt to circumvent the full and open competition policy by using the submittal of an advance proposal for a known agency requirement that can be acquired by competitive methods.

An unsolicited proposal must be in sufficient detail to reflect its scientific, technical, or socioeconomic merit to permit an evaluation leading to a determination that government support would be worthwhile. The proposed work must benefit the buying agency's R&D or other mission responsibilities. Moreover, the proposal must contain sufficient cost-related or price-related information for a meaningful evaluation. With such characteristics one hopes that the unsolicited proposal will pass its initial screening so it may be considered meritorious enough to undergo a comprehensive evaluation.

A summary of the recommended content and format of the unsolicited proposal is described below. Keep in mind there is no required format, nor is there an IFB with its instructions to bidders, nor an RFP with a performance work statement normally provided by the government. A particular agency may want to dictate its own tailored format. The following model format should also work well for an application for a federal grant:

1. Begin with a concise title and a two-hundred-word or so abstract.
2. Next include a complete description stating the objectives of the effort or activity, the method of approach and extent of effort to be employed, the nature and extent of the anticipated results, and the manner in which the work will help to support the agency's mission. A work breakdown structure would be useful, and a section on environmental impacts may be appropriate.
3. Insert a cost proposal section that links the effort with the cost of

each major piece of work in the work breakdown structure and describes the proposed duration of the funded effort. This section should include any requirements for government-furnished equipment (GFE), supplies, or government-owned facilities (GOF). The last and most important part of this section is to recommend to the government the appropriate type of contract (Cost-Reimbursement or Fixed-Price).

4. List the names of and biographical information on the offeror's key personnel who would be involved with the project, with alternatives that include the names and details of any independent subcontractors that may be used. If you have some key investigators who will come on board once the proposal is funded, then provide the written contingent employment contracts that commit these key personnel. Whether or not key personnel have had security clearances in the past is an important point to emphasize.

5. Include a detailed description of the organization, its previous experience, its relevant past performance, and the facilities to be used. If the organization is new, then emphasis should be placed on the experiences and work of the key investigators, with their biographies and contingent commitment agreements to join the team, if not already on board.

6. List the names and telephone numbers of agency technical or other agency points of contact already contacted regarding the proposal. Nothing is lost by mentioning the government contacts related to this independently, privately derived unsolicited proposal. Moreover, if the offeror plans to provide, or has already done so, the proposal to several other organizations, it should be so stated, along with the names of said organizations.

7. Finally, state the name and signature of the person authorized to represent and contractually bind the offeror. In this part there should be also a self-attestation of the offeror's type of organization (e.g., small business, profit, nonprofit, educational), along with the firm's TIN.

A close look at this format for an unsolicited proposal should reveal a resemblance to the elements associated with an initial proposal submitted in response to an RFP (as described in figures 3-3 and 4-3).

POSTSUBMISSION ACTIVITIES

Once a firm has submitted its solicited proposal to the government, the initiative lays with the government for any type of communications. An offeror can always withdraw a proposal, whether solicited or unsolicited, that was submitted at any time prior to contract award.

An offeror is expected to communicate only with the contracting officer or his agents if it is necessary. It is the contracting officer who may want to initiate "limited exchanges" for the purpose of seeking clarifications prior to an award decision on the basis of initial proposals. Moreover, the contracting officer may want to have communication in assisting his evaluation team to determine which proposals are to be included in the competitive range. If such communications occur, one will not be allowed to revise the initial proposal. Moreover, there is no obligation on the government's part to communicate with all the offerors at this time. Those proposals that do not make it into the competitive range are dropped and will receive rejection notices.

If your offer has been included in the competitive range, you can expect negotiations (discussions) leading to possible revisions of your initial proposal. At any time, even if you are in the competitive range with a highly rated proposal, your firm may be dropped from the competition for purposes of "efficiency." If you are not the winner or you are dropped, then you may ask for a debriefing, which should serve as a learning experience for the next RFP response your firm submits. Chapter 6 has more details on competitive proposals.

Remember that your proposal, even if you are one of the losers who has submitted a competitive proposal, will not be released to any other party to review. A proposal in the possession or control of the government submitted in response to a competitive solicitation is not to be made available to any person under the Freedom of Information Act. The only exception would be the proposal of the winner who was awarded the contract, but only if the winning proposal was set forth or incorporated by reference in the contract with the United States. For public policy reasons, awarded federal contracts are made available to the public at large. The FOIA request would have to be forwarded to the contracting officer who is responsible for the government's contract file (see chapter 11). Moreover, FOIA has an exemption precluding the release of cost or pricing data submitted as part of a competitive proposal used in the government's conduct of cost or price analyses.

If your unsolicited proposal does not pass muster during its initial review, a prompt letter of rejection with reasons for that rejection will be sent to the submitting firm by the agency's contact point. If it is not rejected, a comprehensive review will be undertaken by the contracting officer. The contracting officer may initiate discussions only if the unsolicited proposal received a favorable comprehensive evaluation. Remember that because your unsolicited proposal received a favorable comprehensive review does not mean that a contract award is justified without providing full and open competition or obtaining an exception thereto (see fig. 2-2).

PRACTICING BUSINESS TIPS

Whether one prepares a solicited or unsolicited proposal, the effort and expense are significant. However, even if one does not snag a win, the potential to learn from the submission looms large. The lessons learned will have primed you for the next one, so go for it!

CHAPTER 5

Simplified Acquisitions, Sealed Bidding, and Acquisition of Commercial Items

nce market research is completed and the type of contract to be used determined in accordance with the acquisition plan, there are four procurement methods that government-authorized officials use for source selection to purchase services, products, supplies, and construction (see fig. 5-1).

If a product or service is classified as a commercial item, the source selection procedures to be discussed in this chapter are to be applied, but these can be even further streamlined. Of the four procedures, the two most important, especially for high-value procurements (in excess of one hundred thousand dollars), are the use of sealed bidding and contracting by negotiation for the award of Firm-Fixed-Price Contracts or Fixed-Price with Economic Price Adjustment Contracts when some flexibility is necessary and feasible.

These two procedures are used for high-cost commercial items and services as well as products and services that are customized to meet particular needs. Remember that sealed bidding equates to Firm-Fixed-Price Contracts in which the risk of performance and cost are on the shoulders of the contractor.

FIGURE 5–1. Procurement Procedures

- Micropurchase Procedures (government credit card)
- Simplified Acquisition Procedures (SAP)
- Sealed Bidding
- Contracting by Negotiation (Competitive Proposals)

MICROPURCHASE PROCEDURES

The simplest procedure is the use of the government-wide credit card to the full extent of the micropurchase threshold (normally under three thousand dollars or as may be adjusted upward temporarily in the event of emergency). This procedure allows the authorized buyer with the minimum of paperwork, if any, to purchase in an unrestricted manner from any source in the local trade area with only one quote or through the use of a previously established BPA. It is an effective, swift acquisition procedure provided proper oversight is exercised, especially under emergency circumstances.

SIMPLIFIED ACQUISITION PROCEDURES

Simplified acquisition procedures for acquisitions above three thousand dollars and normally under one hundred thousand dollars, the simplified acquisition threshold unless increased owing to contingencies, allow the procurement officer to use innovative approaches to the maximum extent in awarding contracts only to small business. Under SAP, numerous substantive statutory and regulatory clauses that are applicable for sealed bidding and competitive proposal procedures are inapplicable, as directed under the Federal Acquisition Streamlining Act of 1994.

In exercising SAP, the government buyer is instructed to use the procedures for sealed bidding and contracting by negotiation to the extent necessary for a particular procurement. This process accelerates the procurement cycle time in the event of emergencies or based upon the size of the acquisition. Under SAP, quotations, written as well as oral, are used extensively. A submitted quote in response to an RFQ is not an offer and consequently cannot be accepted by the government to form a binding contract. Rather, the government issues an offer in the form of a purchase order in response to a supplier's quote and then the contract is established when the supplier accepts the offer or commences actual performance.

When appropriate, the contracting officer may ask the supplier to indicate acceptance of a purchase order by notification to the government, preferably in writing or electronically. In other circumstances, the supplier may indicate acceptance by furnishing the supplies or services ordered or by proceeding with the work to the point where substantial performance has occurred.

When SAP are used contracting officers are mandated to promote competition to the extent practicable to various types of small business, but there is no requirement to obtain full and open competition. Overall SAP accelerate the procurement cycle time in the event of emergencies or based upon the size of the acquisition. For a review of the monetary acquisition thresholds between micropurchase and simplified acquisition procedures, refer to the Source Selection Procedure Matrix in figure 2-3.

SEALED BIDDING PROCEDURES

The sealed bidding process for the award of government contracts, although rigid, has become standardized through years of wars and major conflicts, not to mention federal laws and agency procurement regulations. It is the "workhorse" procurement method of the United States for acquisitions in excess of the SAT.

At the end of my Small Business Innovative Research contract, I received one check from the U.S. Treasury for $42,782—the fixed price in the contract. I had left on the table some $7,218. The proposal that I had submitted to win the award did not ask for the full $50,000 allowed by the SBIR program in Phase I in that year.

Prior to my receipt of the contract no one called me to discuss or negotiate the price. Although I had submitted a proposal with technical information that included a cost breakdown, work schedule, and biographical information, the award was treated in a manner similar to a solicited sealed bid based upon an invitation restricted to small business vendors for offers. The contract was awarded on what is called in the trade and regulations the "initial proposal." The Air Force asked for no clarifications to my submitted initial proposal. No competitive range was established to eliminate those offers that did not make the cut. No discussions as part of negotiations were conducted. No best and final price was requested. No revisions to my initial proposal were requested. Not one penny more or less was paid, and there were no change orders to the scope of work increasing or decreasing the contract price. No one—defense contract auditor or regional contract management administrator—examined my books. No one cared if I had worked one hundred hours or two thousand hours. Nor did they care what my computer supplies had cost me. The contracting officer just wanted the job done right and on time.

I had no wage rate schedule attached to the solicitation from the government requiring me to pay specific minimum hourly wages with fringe benefits for particular skills or tradesmen mandated by the Department of Labor in coordination with my state's labor department and local unions. There was no requirement for me to submit weekly payroll reports or to develop an affirmative action plan. Of course, I kept my records for three years as required from the date of last performance on the contract. I had paid at least minimum wages as required by federal law and paid my taxes on the profit. The IRS did not audit me.

It is important to look at sealed bidding as the classic acquisition process for the procurement of supplies, services, and construction before looking at using the procedures for negotiated acquisitions. Both procedures are acceptable under current federal laws for obtaining full and open competition, meaning that all responsible sources are permitted to submit bids or proposals for a proposed procurement. The requirement for such competition is mandated by law.

When my clients complain to me that they "left a pot of money on the table," I now understand better what they mean. Although one client, for example, won a contract at $265,000 as the lowest-priced, responsive, responsible bidder, the next lowest bid was $300,000, leaving $35,000 on the table. The client included a nice profit in its bid but still could have won the contract if the originally submitted sealed bid was $299,999.99. After a public bid opening with such results, one needs to perhaps visit a local pub—not only to celebrate the win in a low-key manner but also to reflect on how to refine the cost estimate on the next project.

Sealed bidding has since World War II, and continues to be, the preferred acquisition strategy for obtaining products and services by the government, especially commercial products, services, and construction. Periodically during election periods you hear members of Congress threatening to sponsor legislation mandating the use of only sealed bids as a defense against negotiated Cost-Plus-Fixed-Fee Contracts. Current law allows and treats sealed bidding and competitive proposals, the latter of which implies the need for negotiations, on an equal footing for their inherent benefits.

The sealed bidding process lends itself well to the purchase of commodities, commercial products, and even services that can be quantified before soliciting responses from a vendor. It allows for market forces to set the price and allows for full and open competition consistent with the congressional intent. Sealed bidding employs competitive bids, public opening of bids, and awards. There are six elements to this source selection procedure (see fig. 5-2).

FIGURE 5-2. Elements of Sealed Bidding

1. Preparation of Invitations for Bids (IFB)
2. Publicizing the Invitation for Bids
3. Submission of Bids
4. Public Bid Opening (in person or via the Internet)
5. Evaluation of Bids
6. Contract Award

Preparation of the Invitation for Bids

The IFB describes the terms upon which the government will contract and invites bids for the supplies in accordance with those conditions. It includes all documents (whether attached or incorporated by reference) furnished to prospective bidders by the purchasing agency for the purpose of bidding through the government point of entry Web site, www.fedbizopps.gov.

For a construction project one would find or be able to gain access to the government's architectural, mechanical, site, and engineering drawings. For a build–to drawings project the government would provide the production drawings and specifications from the last competitive procurement. In other cases a detail specification will be provided so that the price estimate can be developed by a bidder. If the government requirement cannot be specified with particularity in the solicitation, then sealed bidding is not the correct acquisition procedure and contracting by negotiation should be used instead.

To the maximum extent practicable IFBs for contract prices estimated to exceed twenty-five thousand dollars follow the Uniform Contract Format (see fig. 3-3), which is reproduced on SF 33. Bidders submit their bids on the government provided schedules. The government will tailor the uniform format if simplified procedures are used or for other reasons. Those sections of the Uniform Contract Format that do not apply will be annotated as such in the solicitation's table of contents. One must remember that at this point the submitted bid, despite the fact that it is on a government-provided form, is only an offer.

Publicizing the Invitation for Bids

Invitations must be publicized through distribution to prospective bidders, posting in public places, and such other means as may be appropriate. Publicizing must occur a sufficient time before the public opening of bids to enable prospective bidders to prepare and submit bids. Placing the solicitation on the GPE achieves this requirement. (See figure 2-4 for public notice requirements of such contract actions.)

Once a solicitation has been released "on the street," through the GPE or other authorized transmission means, a prospective offeror must channel all of its communications to the contracting officer.

Submission of the Bid

When one submits a timely, compliant offer into the "electronic bid box" in response to a federal IFB, that bid is considered to be firm and cannot be withdrawn after the bid opening occurs. This is known as the "firm bid rule," which is unique to federal contracts. To be timely, the bid must be in the specific electronic bid box by the time directed in the IFB. Timeliness is determined by the clock being used by the government contracting officer at the designated office, not by your own watch. A model of the sealed bidding process is depicted in figure 5-3.

As an offeror be mindful of the instructions to bidders for transmission, which may require that your bid be submitted in a manner (fax, telegraph, or hand delivery) different from electronic commerce (computer to computer via the Internet, electronic data interchange, or electronic mail). To not conform could mean that your bid may very well be rejected.

Remember that at the public bid opening your bid price may be placed on the Internet for viewing by the general public as part of the abstract of bids.

As a bidder you may withdraw or amend your bid (counteroffer) prior to the bid opening time. Upon withdrawal of an electronically transmitted

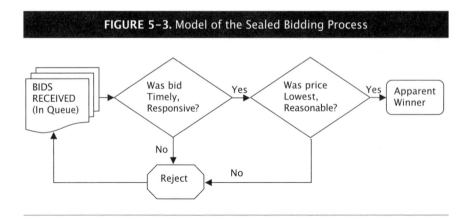

FIGURE 5–3. Model of the Sealed Bidding Process

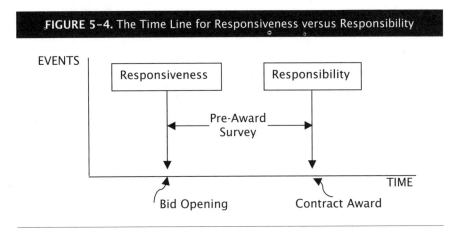

FIGURE 5-4. The Time Line for Responsiveness versus Responsibility

EVENTS

Responsiveness   Responsibility

Pre-Award
Survey

TIME

Bid Opening   Contract Award

bid, the data received is not viewed and is purged from primary and backup government data storage systems.

Bid Responsiveness

It is not sufficient to have submitted the lowest, timely bid. The bid on its face must be responsive to be considered at the time of submission (see fig. 5-3). It is important to distinguish responsibility from responsiveness. The former is not ascertained until the time of award, while the responsiveness of the bid is determined at bid opening and must be ascertained from the bid itself, not extrinsic evidence. To constitute proper responsiveness, the information must be an essential element of the promise to perform as required by the specifications, not the ability to carry out that promise, which is responsibility. Many factors may change a bidder's responsibility after bid opening prior to award, but the bid must be responsive when opened (see figure 5-4).

To be responsive, the sealed bid must be in the correct form and conform to all the material requirements in the solicitation (the IFB) at bid opening. Some solicitations recommend attendance at pre-bid conferences. Others make such attendance at these conferences mandatory as an eligibility gate for a bid to be considered responsive. This especially occurs where construction is the heart of the proposed solicitation.

In some cases a bid bond, performance bond, or a performance and payment bond may be required to be submitted with the bid, depending on the nature of the solicitation: supply, service, or construction. Such bonds, provided by corporate or individual sureties and paid by a bidder (the principal), attached to a submitted bid serve as insurance to the public agency (the obligee or government) and others that may be affected in the event a duly awarded contract either fails to be performed or is not properly performed by the bidder once the contract is awarded. A bid bond attached to a bid demonstrates to the government that that particular bidder has a qualified surety backing up the offer; since the surety is guaranteeing that it will issue the payment and performance bonds before the notice to proceed on any contract work occurs in a timely manner.

The Miller Act requires performance and payment bonds for any construction contract exceeding one hundred thousand dollars, except this requirement may be waived by the contracting officer for as much of the work as is to be performed in a foreign country (e.g., reconstruction in a war zone of power generator systems, water plants, etc.) upon a finding that it is not practical for the contractor to furnish the bond. Generally, the penal amount of the performance bond will be 100 percent of the original contract price; for requirements contracts, it is the price payable for the estimated quantity; or for Indefinite-Quantity Contracts, it is the price payable for the minimum specified quantity. The penal amount of payment bonds in the event of default by the prime contractor to pay all persons supplying labor or material in the prosecution of work provided for in the contract varies as a function of the amount of the contract price.

Such bonds issued upon payment of the premium to sureties are separate from insurance coverages for work such as builder's risk insurance, liability insurance, architect's and engineer's errors and omissions, and overseas workers' compensation and war-hazard insurance policy coverages provided after contract award and consistent with the requirements of the terms of the awarded contract.

The absence of a required bond guarantee called out by the IFB or even an RFP from the offeror or bidder could be fatal, causing one's offer to be rejected on the basis of nonresponsiveness. Such a call is not curable after bid opening if an IFB is involved and if the award is made strictly on initial proposals without any opportunity for discussions based upon an RFP.

In some cases a working model or samples of a product must be submitted. Absence of such requested items, as with the case of a missing bond, is fatal, unless the omitted item is not material. Such absences may cause your bid to be labeled nonresponsive.

Follow closely Section L—Instructions, Conditions, and Notices to Offerors—in Part IV of the Uniform Contract Format. The three major causes leading to a defective bid are failing to acknowledge in writing or electronically any issued solicitation amendments that have a material impact on the scope and price of the project, the late submission of a bid, and incomplete or unauthorized signatures on a bid itself. In the latter case the contracting officer at the time of the public bid opening is not able to correlate the electronic signature with the firm's authorized signatures for binding a firm prepositioned in the firm's filed Trading Partner Profile through the Central Contractor Registration database (see fig. 2-11). Once determined nonresponsive, a bid may not be made responsive after the public bid opening, notwithstanding the reason for the failure to conform.

Evaluation of Bids

At the public bid opening, an abstract of bids is prepared by the contracting officer and is available to the public in paper or on the Internet. From the abstract one can determine which is the lowest "apparent" winner just by examining which firm's offer is the lowest (see fig. 5-3). However, to determine the lowest bid the government conducts a price analysis (discussed in chapter 8) using all the timely bids to determine the responsible bid that will be most advantageous to the government, considering only price and price-related factors included in the solicitation. The contracting officer must make a determination the prices offered are reasonable before award.

This price analysis considers also whether the prices of the line items in a bid are materially unbalanced; if so, what risks are posed by such bidding; and how the government's economic interest can be protected. Unbalanced pricing exists when despite an acceptable total evaluated price, the price of one or more contract line items is significantly over- or understated. Such unbalancing is not only found in sealed bidding but also in the evaluation of competitive proposals. Unbalanced bids may occur in contracts with options where the offeror's prices for the base period are higher (allegedly owing to start-up costs) than the option year prices.

Some of the price-related factors that may be considered are foreseeable inspection costs, locations of supplies, and transportation costs or delays to the government; advantages or disadvantages (administrative costs) to the government from making multiple awards; federal, state, and local taxes; origin of supplies; and if the origin of supplies is foreign, application of the Buy American Act. If a basis other than price is to be used in the evaluation, that basis and its effect must be stated in the IFB.

What remains, even today, so desirable about a sealed bid is that the winning firm does not have to explain how it came up with lowest price, whether it be fifty thousand dollars for several computer terminals or five million dollars for the construction of a new post office. No negotiations are allowed to transpire. No cost and pricing data breakdowns are required to allow for any cost analysis. No certification of your costs is mandated. The emphasis rests on whether or not your price is "reasonable" in comparison to the other bids or the government's own price analysis, estimate, and past procurement history, if any.

This raises the issue of how much profit you should include in your sealed bid. The more profit you place on top of your estimated costs (labor, benefits, subcontracts, material, and overhead), the greater will be your bid price and hence the less chance you have in winning the project. If you need work, you bid low to get the job. If you have a lot of work, you bid high and maybe you will be lucky. But make sure you can do the work on time. The government will not tolerate a nonperformer. You will not win the next job that you really need even if you are the lowest bidder, because it will find you nonresponsible on the issue of past performance. If you are a small business you can, in such a case, run to the SBA for a Certificate of Competency (COC) to override the contracting officer. The risk one runs in such an event, however, is that the SBA may side with the contracting officer.

Without some profit your firm will not be able to survive. Just think how angry shareholders would be if the firm in which they had invested their savings did not earn any profit to pay dividends or reinvest for growth in capital improvements. They would not be able to recover their investment, much less earn a respectable return on investment. Thus in a sealed bid, your risk is that you have won the project but have underbid the job. You may not make any profit. On top of that you may place your firm at risk of not being able to complete the project as a result of unforeseen cost overruns. The government will not bail you out. (See chapter 11.)

If you feel the project's risk is high, do not bid on it. Let it go. No business, without reviewing current architectural and engineering site plans, would bid a firm-fixed price on the repairs and reconstruction of the New Orleans levee system after Hurricane Katrina. The extent of the damaged levee network and the site conditions one may run into are unknown; it would be impossible to provide a reasonable price by sealed bid for such a project.

Rejection of All Bids

An IFB does not impart any obligation to accept any of the bids received, and all bids may be rejected by the contracting officer if it is determined to be in the government's interest to do so. The authority to reject all bids is not ordinarily subject to the review by the General Accountability Office. This broad authority to reject all bids after bid opening has been restricted by regulation to certain situations in which the agency determines in writing any of the following:

- Inadequate or ambiguous specifications were cited.
- Specifications have been revised.
- The supplies or service being contracted for are no longer required.
- The invitation did not provide for consideration of all factors of cost to the government, such as transporting government furnished property to bidder's plants.
- Bids received indicate that the needs of the government can be satisfied by a less expensive article differing from that for which the bids were invited.
- All otherwise acceptable bids received are at unreasonable prices, only one bid is received and the contracting officer cannot determine the reasonableness of the bid price, or no responsive bid has been received from a responsible bidder.
- The bids were not independently arrived at in open competition, were collusive, or were submitted in bad faith.
- A cost comparison as prescribed by the Office of Management and Budget shows the performance of the government is more economical.
- For other reasons cancellation is clearly in the public's interest.

These limitations on the discretion of the contracting officer were imposed in the interest of preserving the integrity of the competitive bidding system and avoiding the prejudice to bidders at having their prices publicly disclosed at bid opening. In essence, there must be cogent and compelling reasons for the rejection of all the bids after bid opening.

The Responsibility of Bidders

Once the responsive, lowest reasonable bidder (apparent winner) is selected to be the winner based only on price and price-related factors, this offeror is evaluated to determine if it is responsible (past performance record, accounting-cost control system, available resources, integrity, etc.) using extrinsic data and information outside the bidding documents (see fig. 5-5).

Your firm has to have a sufficiently good history of past performance and the resources to do the project so that the firm can jump the hurdle of being found to be responsible. In the event your firm is a new start-up with little or no past history, the government may assess the performance histories and qualifications of its key managers in relation to the products or services being solicited and the proposed subcontractors committed to the project.

Before the government awards the Firm-Fixed-Price Contract resulting from a sealed bidding competition, the buyer needs assurances that the apparent winner is "capable," in fact, of doing what it says or is promising and that this bidder will be around to complete the project. There is nothing worse from the government's point of view than to select a bidder for a project only to find that this winning contractor has to abandon the project because of a lack of resources, an inability to overcome technical roadblocks, or a low-balled price that was not backed up by sufficiently deep pockets to cover unexpected cost overruns.

Federal regulations require the contracting officer to make an affirmative determination on the lowest, responsive bidder as to its responsibility.

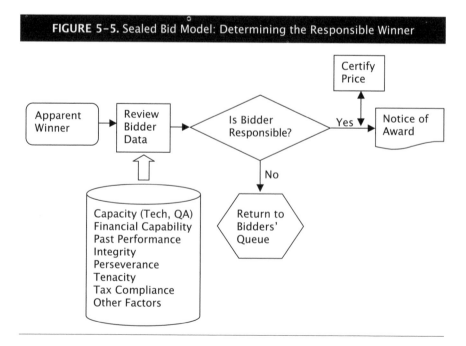

FIGURE 5-5. Sealed Bid Model: Determining the Responsible Winner

This has long been understood to permit a contract award to other than the low bidder when the bidder is found incapable of performing satisfactorily. Before the release of the required Notice of Award to the winner, the buyer is required to rule in writing in the official contract file on whether the winner is "responsible" for the project under contract. If not, the contracting officer moves up the rung to the next lowest responsive bidder and repeats his evaluation as shown in figure 5-3.

The contracting officer may elicit the assistance of an on-site pre-award survey (see fig. 5-4) by a government team to conduct an in-plant inspection of facilities and equipment, review past performance reports on similar projects, and examine the financial risk (perhaps finding that a prospective winner is teetering on bankruptcy). Moreover, a firm that refuses to pay delinquent federal taxes may be deemed not responsible. This issue, tax evasion, has been added to the standards for contractor responsibility. In determining the responsibility of prospective contractors, a contracting officer should request a pre-award survey only if sufficient relevant information is unavailable from other sources, including information from commercial sources.

If the contract has a fixed price at or below the simplified acquisition threshold (see fig. 2-3) or will involve the acquisition of commercial items, the contracting officer should not request a pre-award survey unless circumstances justify its cost. The contracting officer may check a bidder's past history reports through the Past Performance Information Retrieval System (www.ppirs.gov).

If you are a small business and are considered not responsible, you can get another bite at the apple to try to jump the hurdle on the second run by calling for the assistance of the Small Business Administration under its statutory authority to issue on your behalf a COC. In such a case the contracting officer has the obligation to refer the responsibility issue to the SBA (see chapter 7).

Except for small business, the determination of responsibility is left primarily to the contracting officer and is not questioned by the U.S. comptroller general or the courts in the absence of a showing of bad faith or lack of a reasonable basis. This rule is followed even though the same contractor may be given opposite findings by different contracting officers for separate contracts. Moreover, the GAO no longer considers challenges against a contracting officer's affirmative determination of responsibility, except when the actions of the procurement officials are tantamount to fraud or where the IFB itself sets forth objective criteria.

The contracting officer may also request the lowest bidder under consideration for award to certify in writing its bid. Such a request may be considered by the contracting officer when the bid appears to the procurement official to be too low; when it appears to contain a mistake, especially when compared to the other bids and to the official independent government cost estimate (IGCE) for the product or services; or as a matter of prudent practice by a particular contracting officer. When an offeror receives such a request it should be treated seriously and the bidder is required to reply confirming its bid by certification or providing an explanation of any mistakes. See the discussion below on mistakes.

One must remember that the lowest-priced bidder may be responsive at the time of bid opening but may not be responsible at that very instant. Such a predicament may not be fatal. If that bidding firm becomes responsible by the date of award, it may be granted the contract. Figure 5-4 depicts the time gap that generally occurs between the time of bid opening, when responsiveness is determined, and the time of award, when a firm's responsibility can be brought up to a level of acceptance.

Conversely the time gap also provides a time when a bidder's responsibility may turn from being acceptable at the time of bid opening but is not found responsible at the time of award (e.g., a criminal indictment is issued against the firm or its principals, a firm files for bankruptcy during the intervening time, the IRS reports tax evasion, etc.).

Contract Award

The contract award is made with reasonable promptness by giving written notice (Notice of Award) or by electronic commerce to the "responsible" bidder whose bid conforms to the invitation and will be most advantageous to the United States, considering only price and price-related factors included in the invitation. This action must be taken within the time specified for acceptance of the bid or any extension of the bid acceptance period. For awards in excess of three million dollars, a public notice is required on the government point of entry.

Two-Step Sealed Bidding

Sealed bidding may be undertaken in two steps in acquisitions requiring a technical proposal, particularly those for complex items. Such bidding is a combination of competitive procedures designed to obtain the benefits of sealed bidding.

The first step consists of the request for submission, evaluation, and, if necessary, discussion of technical proposals from each bidder. No pricing is involved. The objective is to determine the acceptability of the supplies or services offered. This step obtains clarification of questions relating to technical requirements. The second step involves the submission of sealed bids only by those who submitted acceptable technical proposals in step one. Bids submitted in step two are evaluated and awards made in accordance with the sealed bidding procedures discussed above.

Reverse Auctioning

It is in this second step of the two-step sealed bidding procedure, after technical proposals have been received and evaluated, that online "private" reverse auctioning might be appropriate provided all the invited bidders agree that their prices can be publicly disclosed.

Such a technique is merely another pricing tool that the contracting officer may exercise if appropriate. A separate user name and password are assigned to each invited bidder. Under these conditions the practice of anonymous auctioning is allowable and not prohibited by the Federal Acquisition Regulation. Reverse auctioning is an acquisition technique that allows prospective buyers to list item(s) they wish to purchase and the vendors bid to provide the best price. The intent is to have prices spiral down rather than up. The risk here, as a buyer, is to get caught up in price and lose sight of quality.

In essence the sellers bid down the price through a series of quotes that descend in price during a specified period of time as they compete for the work. The format for the auction may be unit price or total net price; price only for multiple line items, formatted for the winner to take all or multiple awards for the lowest price per line item; or part of a best value source selection once the competitive range has been established (as discussed in chapter 6) for negotiated acquisitions using competitive proposals.

To use this procedure the government must select its product candidates for procurement carefully (commercial items fully and accurately specified, IT products, military-specified items, technically acceptable low price items) and have a good handle as to what the "starting" price, to include the bid increments, for the auction for the whole procurement or for each line item should be. The government will have an assigned auction manager, the instructions for the auction must have been placed in the solicitation under Section L in an IFB/RFP, and time will have to be set aside to train the invited bidders/offerors on the auctioning online software system.

Such auctioning is not intended to take the place of simplified or sealed bidding procedures as discussed herein, unless the projected savings offsets the cost of conducting the procurement using reverse auctioning. It is more intended to be used during the source selection procedures for RFQ/RFP. Two-step sealed bidding does, however, provide our first opportunity to use this pricing tool. The details for the conduct of a reverse auction, including the designated Web site/auction operator under contract, will be spelled out by the government buyer in its solicitation.

Bid Mistakes

We all make mistakes. The issue is to gracefully recover from such a mistake, especially if you as a trader have bid a project too low or forgot to price a major piece of the project work. The solution to the mistake problem may be complex, however, depending on when and who discovers the mistake.

If the bid closing time and date have not passed, the firm can withdraw its bid up to the time for bid opening regardless of whether it is a paper bid or an electronic bid. With enough time still left one can make corrections and submit a revised bid. The government does need to know that an error occurred. No explanation is required. The government does not need to know what your intended bid was or what mistake you made.

If the bid opening time or proposal submission date and time have closed but the contract has not been formally awarded, mistakes of both omissions and mistakes of price can be made. Mistakes of omission that are material could make you nonresponsive to the solicitation. That means that the bid was dead upon arrival because it was missing some required item that cannot be corrected or provided after bid opening no matter how much you plead. The fact that your bid was the lowest price does not matter. Examples of such omissions are not signing the bid, not acknowledging a material amendment to the solicitation that impacts price, or failing to provide a sample or surety bond as instructed.

With mistakes of price the buyer has had a chance to review the bids and in all likelihood has prepared an abstract of bids recording the name of each bidder and the bid amount for each line item. Since each buyer has a budget or an estimate of what the cost or price should be, the government buyer is in a position to form an opinion as to which bids are high and which bids are low. In fact some of the bids may be so low or high that the impulse would be to "trash" those that seem to be way out in left field. Although the high bids can just be disregarded, the low bids cannot if the buyer is doing his job.

The reason low bids are treated carefully is because the government, like any other buyer, is looking for a bargain. So if the buyer notes a bid below the official government estimate or historical purchasing prices, the buyer will probably issue a request that the offeror "verify" its bid. When a trader receives such a request it serves as a flagging action, putting the bidder on alert that perhaps its bid is too low. Something is wrong. The scramble then starts in the trader's estimating "back room." At this point the vendor's response to the buyer may follow one of the three scenarios illustrated in figure 5-6.

Under Scenario 1, the trader has made a conscious decision to bid low for his or her own purposes. The government will award contracts to low bids even if it projects that the work to be performed as bid could not be performed with the submitted price. The contracting officer has done his duty by sending out the request for bid verification.

The trader may want to buy into the work, perhaps the trader has surplus supplies purchased on another project, allowing the trader to underbid and

FIGURE 5-6. Bid Mistake Response Scenarios

1. "We have verified our calculations and specifications, and we stand by our bid price as submitted."

OR

2. "We have gone back and reviewed our submitted bid and find that we are not able to perform the project based upon the submitted bid. We want out!"

OR

3. "We checked our bid price and all the sheets of pricing on which we built our sealed bid and found several mistakes that can be clearly seen on the face of the original work papers. Our actual intended bid should have been $xxx,xxx. This figure includes the increase in bid price or requested correction of $yy,yyy. When you look at our bid you will find that our intended bid is still the lowest responsive bid and the submitted mistaken bid price plus the requested correction, when added, does not displace any other bidder. Attached are the originals of all our paperwork, which are authenticated and have not been tampered with. Notarized statements by our estimator and others involved in the bid's preparation are attached."

perform the work to completion. You can be assured that the government will take a close look at the past performance history of this bidder on similar projects. A thorough responsibility assessment will be conducted, including the bidder's current audited financial statements. If the trader is a small business the contracting officer may request that the SBA provide a COC confirming that the trader is responsible.

Under Scenario 2, the government buyer will in all probability allow the bidding firm to withdraw its firm bid gracefully, especially in the event that there were more than two bidders. No buyer wants to award a contract to a trader who may default on the project by not making progress on the work and/or abandoning the project after the contract is awarded or the work gets started. A contracting officer's horror scenario would be for the trader to default on the project or delivery of supplies and claim damages because the government "overreached" awarding the contract. The claimant would allege that the contracting officer knew the government was getting such a good deal despite superior knowledge that the project could not be performed for the bid price.

Under Scenario 3, the contracting officer may approve an upward bid revision to the bidder's "intended bid" based upon clear and convincing proofs and certifications that the bidder submits. The decision of the contracting officer will generally stand, especially if it does not displace a lower bidder and if the actually intended bid is still the lowest after the correction. The existence of the mistake must be both clear and convincing from the bidding records and any authenticating supporting statements as to how the error occurred. The government has the power through its chartered contracting officers to revise upward a submitted sealed bid under the limited conditions explained herein.

ACQUISITION OF COMMERCIAL ITEMS

When the government buyers conduct their market search a determination must be made as to whether commercial items or nondevelopmental items are available that could meet agency requirements. The description of the need is an agency responsibility as well as the market search and classification of a product as a commercial item. It is not a trader's decision as to whether or not an item is a commercial item. Certainly, a trader has an interest in providing information on its product lines and nondevelopmental items via unsolicited proposals, existing product literature, brochures, or catalogues in an ethical manner.

A commercial item, under FAR 2.101, means any item, including services other than realty, customarily used by the general public and

1. has a core configuration whose baseline has been sold, leased, or licensed to the general public or has been offered for sale, lease, or license to the general public;
2. has evolved from an item described in number 1 above through advances in technology or performance that is not yet available to the marketplace but will be available in the commercial market place in time to satisfy the delivery requirements under a government solicitation;
3. involving a minor modification(s) to any of the items at (1) or (2) above of a type not customarily available in the commercial marketplace made to meet federal government requirements (special frequency, special tires, etc.) that do not significantly alter the nongovernmental function or essential physical characteristics of an item or component, or change the purpose of a process. Factors to consider when deciding whether a modification is minor include the value and size of the modification and the comparable value and size of the final product. Dollar values and percentages may be used as guideposts, but are not conclusive evidence that a modification is minor; or
4. developed exclusively at private expense and sold in substantial quantities, on a competitive basis to multiple state and local governments. The regulations do not mention third party foreign governments or foreign commercial entities.

Now services are considered to be commercial if they are of a type offered and sold competitively in substantial quantities in the commercial marketplace based on established catalog or market prices for specific tasks performed or specific outcomes to be achieved and under standard commercial terms and conditions. This does not include services that are sold based on hourly rates without an established catalog or market price for a specific service performed or a specific outcome to be achieved. Moreover, the contracting officer may use FAR Part 12 for any acquisition for services that does not meet the definition of commercial item in FAR 2.101, if the contract or task order

1. is entered into before November 24, 2013;
2. has a value of $27 million or less;
3. meets the definition of performance-based acquisition at FAR 2.101;
4. uses a Quality Assurance Service Plan;
5. includes performance incentives where applicable;
6. specifies a firm-fixed price for specific tasks to be performed or outcomes to be achieved; and
7. is awarded to an entity that provides similar services to the general public under terms and conditions to those in the contract or task order.

Once a product (or service) is classified as a commercial item to meet a "need," it allows for streamlining the acquisition procedure selected, moving it from SAP (FAR Part 13), Sealed Bidding (FAR Part 14), and even Contracting by Negotiation (FAR Part 15) to Acquisition of Commercial Items (FAR Part 12), which implements the government's preference for commercial items by establishing acquisition policies more resembling those of the commercial marketplace. Once in FAR Part 12, then FAR Parts 13, 14, and 15 still are used and "tailored" for the solicitation, evaluation, and award as appropriate for a particular acquisition.

FAR Subpart 13.5 allows as a test program for the acquisition of commercial items exceeding the simplified acquisition threshold ($100,000) but not exceeding $5.5 million to be treated as if the $100,000 threshold for simplified acquisition procedures has not been exceeded—allowing solicitation and award to be restricted only to small businesses, provided there are at least two responsible small business sources.

In a commercial item acquisition, past performance must be evaluated in any award decision; Firm-Fixed-Price Contracts or Fixed-Price with Economic Price Adjustment Contracts are mandated, even in IDIQ-type contracts where a firm-fixed price must be used. Time-and-Materials or Labor-Hour Contracts may be used under limited conditions as discussed in chapter 3. All other types of contracts are prohibited. Technical data is presumed by the government to have been developed at private expense. Cost accounting standards do not apply.

PRACTICING BUSINESS TIPS

If a product or service can be classified as a commercial item, its purchase with the preference being toward fixed-price-type contracting will be streamlined under any of the selected source selection procedures.

Despite alleged abuses expect to employ and plan for the use of the micropurchase (credit card) procedure for source selection as the government gains experience and confidence in exercising and policing the use of variable micropurchase thresholds process.

SAPs are increasingly popular for contract award based on offers or quotes under one hundred thousand dollars owing to their flexibility, reduction in "red tape," and focus on awards only to small business. SAPs also may be authorized variable dollar thresholds depending on the exigency.

Sealed bidding has for years been and remains the preferred source selection acquisition vehicle for the government for those acquisitions (commercial items and tailored procurements) that lend themselves to definitive statements of work, design specifications, and drawings. When sealed bidding does not fit the procurement, the preferred source selection procedure is contracting by negotiation using competitive proposals. The Competition in Contracting Act (CICA) allows for the use of sealed bids as well as competitive proposals (chapter 6) to promote competition—either to be used as determined applicable at the discretion of the contracting officer.

CHAPTER 6

Contracting by Negotiation
Taking the Mystery Out of Best Value
Source Selections

The Competition in Contracting Act of 1984 established competitive negotiation as a legitimate form of competition. It allows for sealed bidding if four conditions are met:

1. There must be ample time for all the necessary actions, from solicitation through evaluation.
2. The award will be based on price and price-related factors.
3. Discussions with offerors about their bids will not be necessary.
4. There is reasonable expectation of receiving more than one bid.

If those four conditions are not met the agency "shall request competitive proposals." Contracting officers need not explain in writing their rationale for choosing to use competitive proposals rather than sealed bidding, as was required in the past.

With competitive proposals the government has restored a large degree of the element of bargaining. Moreover, the auctioning technique or practice of disclosing prices to competitors to obtain price reduction from an offeror under controlled conditions is allowed provided the offeror grants its permission to reveal its price. This authority when granted by participants allows reverse auctions to occur (as discussed in chapter 5).

Competitive proposal procedures may be used to award contracts based upon full and open competition; on less than full and open competition, including the use of simplified acquisition procedures that restrict the procedure to small business or set-asides pursuant to the Small Business Act; and in situations other than competitive procedures or what is known in the trade as "sole-source negotiated acquisitions" (see fig. 2-2).

THE SOURCE SELECTION PROCESSES FOR BEST VALUE

The evaluation and negotiation of competitive proposals submitted in response to an RFP, as well as the procurement strategy for an RFQ, is undertaken by applying the best value continuum processes discussed in this chapter. The results are intended to lead to the award of the contract to the offeror whose proposal is most advantageous to the United States considering only price and the other factors included in the solicitation. This standard has been interpreted to be the proposal with the best value. "Best value" means, in the estimation of the government, that the expected outcome of the acquisition provides the greatest overall benefit in response to the requirement.

An agency can obtain the best value in negotiated acquisitions by using any one of or a combination of source selection processes and techniques, depending on the extent of the definition of the requirement, the risk of successful performance, and the variation of the relative importance of cost or price. The two source selection techniques for RFPs most used for obtaining the "best value" are the trade-off process and the lowest price technically acceptable process. The two comprise the spread of the "best value continuum."

The trade-off process is appropriate when it may be in the best interest of the government to consider award to other than the lowest priced offeror or other than the highest technically rated offeror. This process permits trade-offs among cost or price and noncost factors. It allows the government to accept other than the lowest-priced proposal. The perceived benefits of the higher-priced proposal must merit the additional cost, and the rationale for tradeoffs must be documented with attention to detail in a price negotiation memorandum (PNM).

The lowest price technically acceptable process is used when the best value is expected to result from selection of the technically acceptable proposal with the lowest evaluated price. It is known more commonly as the "pass/fail" selection option.

The solicitation specifies that award will be made on the basis of the lowest evaluated price of proposals meeting or exceeding the acceptability standards of the noncost factors. Past performance need not be an evaluation factor in this process. However, responsibility will be assessed before award of any selected offeror as is always required regardless of the source selection process. Trade-offs are not permitted.

Proposals are evaluated for acceptability but not ranked using the non-cost/price factors. This process inherently allows even reverse auctioning to be used (chapter 5), especially if the competitor's concepts, products, or services meet performance-based acquisition specifications with price being the discriminator.

THE COMPETITIVE PROPOSAL SOURCE SELECTION PROCESS

Source Selection Plan, Integrated Product Team

Once the market research has been completed and the type of contract selected, the contracting office is ready to prepare the source selection plan that evolves around the solicitation package using an integrated product team. In this regard the integrated product team will follow the solicitation format of the Uniform Contract Format. An integrated product team is composed of representatives from all appropriate government buying organizations, contract administrative services, and audit offices working together in full and open discussions to build successful and balanced procurement programs.

The first major action for the team is the development of the source selection plan based upon the user's requirement before the solicitation is released. The user has the funds appropriated for the acquisition; hence the intended user is critical to an efficient procurement. The source selection plan (see fig. 6-1) guides the team in preparing the solicitation and evaluating the received proposals. It is the key document that describes the source selection strategy, including but not limited to the type of contract contemplated, the extent of any restrictions to competition, what instructions in preparing proposals will be provided for the offerors in the solicitation, the evaluation factors and related significant subfactors to include their relative weights in order of importance, how the evaluation will be conducted, and other fundamental acquisition-related strategies, including how cost/pricing analysis should be conducted as well as the assessment of reasonable profit. Furthermore, the source selection plan can provide guidance as to the need for the submission of cost or pricing data and its certification.

The source selection plan will identify what professionals should be on the Source Selection Evaluation Board (SSEB), depending on the nature of

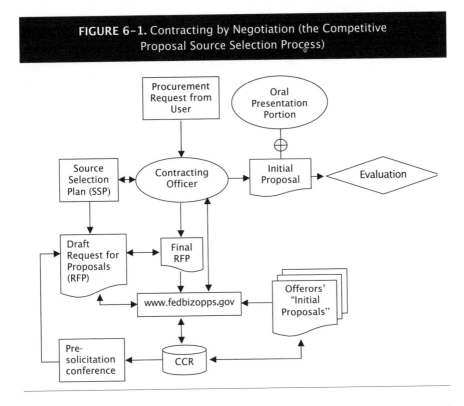

FIGURE 6-1. Contracting by Negotiation (the Competitive Proposal Source Selection Process)

the acquisition, and the members of the Source Selection Advisory Council (SSAC), if any, which reviews the technical, management, performance risks, and cost evaluations conducted by the SSEB. It is the SSAC that prepares recommendations for the Source Selection Authority (SSA); if it is not the contracting officer, the procurement official appointed by the agency head will be the SSA owing to the particular nature of the acquisition. The SSA will make the final decision for the award to the source or sources whose proposal is the best value to the government.

The major objectives of the an integrated product team is a better RFP, better proposals, reduced acquisition cycle time between issuance of the RFP and contract award, and better understanding by all interested parties of the contract requirements. The team will begin work to develop the RFP and continue to work together through the acquisition cycle's steps for advertisement, evaluation, audit, negotiation, contract award, and contract administration and compliance. The intent of the team approach is to avoid rework at the end of the process and to find potential solutions at the earliest possible point in the procurement cycle.

Figure 6-1 depicts the interaction of the various activities leading to the complete receipt of those timely responses to the RFP known as an offeror's "initial proposal," allowing thereafter the evaluation to commence to ascertain if an award can be made on just initial proposals or whether a ranking will have to be established and discussions undertaken only with those offerors included in the competitive range.

Public Notices

Once the RFP has been finalized through several iterative cycles, it is placed onto the GPE to serve as the request for the submission of proposals (www. fedbizopps.gov). Depending on the level of urgency, industry should have been given the opportunity to provide inputs (exchanges) through the use of government-released RFIs, a presolicitation conference, and comments on a draft RFP before the final version was released (see fig. 4-2).

Oral Presentations

In support of the need for streamlining the source selection process, the government may request oral presentations (fig. 6-1) on the part of offerors. Such presentations may substitute for or augment written information. They may occur at any time in the acquisition process and are subject to the same restrictions as written information regarding timing and content.

The use of oral presentations as a substitute for portions of a proposal can be effective in streamlining the source selection process. The solicitation may require each offeror to submit a part of its initial proposal through oral presentations. However, a signed offer sheet (including any exceptions to the government's terms and conditions) must be in writing. The representations and certifications of the offeror would have been transmitted through the use of ORCA (www.orca.bpn.gov), the primary online repository for such data required for the conduct of business with the government. Information pertaining to areas such as offeror's capability, past performance, work plans, approaches, staffing resources, transition plans, or sample tasks may be suitable for oral presentations.

These presentations require substantial effort on the part of an offeror. They provide significant benefits because they allow an excellent opportunity for dialogue among the parties. Oral presentations are not to be used to conduct discussions with the government unless so stated in the instructions to offerors in the solicitation, which direct the content and nature of the oral presentation.

Proposal Evaluation

After the proposals have been received and any questions resolved regarding acceptance of any late proposals, the procurement authority must determine by evaluation which proposals merit negotiations by commencing written and oral discussions. The government may undertake limited exchanges (fig. 6-2; also refer to fig. 4-2) in the form of requesting selected clarifications to an offeror's submitted initial proposal. No revisions to the submitted proposal are allowed in such an event.

Upon the complete evaluation of all the submitted proposals and their rankings, the first decision generally made is whether or not an award is possible based upon initial proposals. In such a case no further exchanges (oral or written) with offerors are necessary. If the decision is made to award on initial proposals, the winner is designated and that offeror's responsibility review is conducted to include any necessary on-site surveys.

Once the contracting officer confirms that the best value offeror is responsible and the necessary advance notices to Congress and executive offices are completed, the contract award is publically announced. The award can be made without discussions if the solicitation places on notice all prospective offerors that the government intends to evaluate proposals and make an award decision without discussions.

The Competitive Range

On the other hand, once having decided that award is not possible on the basis of the initial proposals or through various limited exchanges (see fig. 6-2) or was not applicable owing to the nature of the acquisition, the government must undertake whatever communications are warranted with each offeror, if necessary, to establish the competitive range (see fig. 6-3).

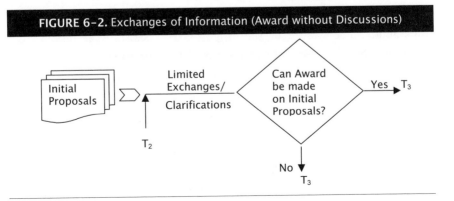

FIGURE 6-2. Exchanges of Information (Award without Discussions)

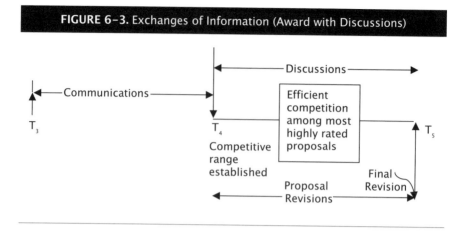

FIGURE 6-3. Exchanges of Information (Award with Discussions)

The competitive range consists of those proposals having the greatest likelihood of award based on the factors and significant subfactors in the solicitation. This statutory requirement has been translated by regulation into a competitive range comprised of "all of the most highly rated" proposals, unless the range is further reduced "for purposes of efficiency." A notice in the solicitation is required in the event that after evaluating the offers, the contracting officer needs to reduce the number of the proposals in the competitive range for efficiency in conducting the competition.

An executive agency has flexibility in making the determination of which proposals are within the competitive range. An agency determination will not be overturned unless it is shown that the agency has abused its discretion. Figure 6-4 depicts the evaluation model for competitive proposals with negotiations, which generally comprise discussions with the offerors and possible revisions to their submitted initial proposals.

Proposal evaluation is an assessment of both the proposal and the offeror's ability, as conveyed by the proposal, to successfully accomplish the prospective contract work. Evaluation may be conducted using any rating method or combination of methods, including color or adjectival ratings, numerical weights, and ordinal rankings. If numerical weights are to be used in proposal evaluation, they may be disclosed in the solicitation on a case-by-case basis.

There is no requirement that all of the factors considered in the evaluation must be price related. Although price must be one of the factors considered, there is no statutory requirement that it be accorded the greatest weight

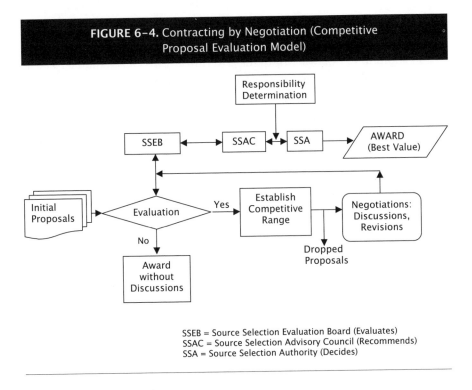

FIGURE 6-4. Contracting by Negotiation (Competitive Proposal Evaluation Model)

SSEB = Source Selection Evaluation Board (Evaluates)
SSAC = Source Selection Advisory Council (Recommends)
SSA = Source Selection Authority (Decides)

in the evaluation. An agency may evaluate such factors as life-cycle cost, survivability, technical excellence, human factors, quality control programs, past performance, management prior experience, and subcontracting plan, including therein the small business subcontracting participation.

Currently, past performance on prior similar projects is required to be evaluated in all source selections for negotiated acquisitions expected to exceed one hundred thousand dollars. Moreover, past performance evaluation now includes a contractor's record of integrity and business ethics. This evaluation results in a risk assessment assigned to each particular offeror in executing the proposed new work described in the RFP and reflected in an offeror's overall proposal. It is distinct from the responsibility determination that is conducted once the apparent winner is selected just prior to the announcement of the award.

The evaluation factors and significant subfactors that apply to an acquisition and their relative importance are within the broad discretion of the agency acquisition officials. When the contracting is to be in a sole-source environment, the RFP should be tailored to remove unnecessary information and requirements (e.g., evaluation criteria and voluminous proposal preparation instructions).

In addition to price or cost to the government, which is required to be an evaluation factor in every source selection, quality also is addressed in every source selection. In evaluation factors, quality may be expressed in terms of technical capability, management capability, personnel qualifications, prior experience, past performance, and schedule compliance. Any other relevant factors, such as cost realism, also may be included, depending on the type of contract to be awarded (e.g., cost-reimbursement types).

The solicitation must state whether all evaluation factors other than cost or price, when combined, are

1. significantly more important than cost or price;
2. approximately equal to cost or price; or
3. significantly less important than cost or price.

The solicitation shall inform offerors of minimum requirements that apply to evaluation factors and significant subfactors. If numerical weights are used in proposal evaluation, they may be disclosed in the solicitation on a case-by-case basis. Further, the factors set out in the solicitation must be factors actually used in the evaluation. However, subcriteria that were not listed in the solicitation may be considered in the evaluation if they are reasonably related to or encompassed by the main evaluation factors.

In the event of protest to an award by an aggrieved offeror, the selection decision's consistency with the evaluation factors will be considered by the Government Accountability Office. But where an agency reasonably determines that two competing proposals are essentially equal technically, price or cost properly becomes the determining factor in making the award.

Once the competitive range is determined the contracting officer generally conducts discussions with the offerors of those proposals. In these discussions the contracting officer is responsible for

1. advising the offeror of deficiencies, significant weaknesses, and adverse past performance information to which the offeror has not yet had an opportunity to respond in its proposal;
2. calling apparent mistakes to the offeror's attention without disclosing information about competing proposals;

3. resolving any uncertainties concerning the proposal itself; and

4. providing an opportunity for the offeror to submit proposal revisions that may result from the discussions.

The contracting officer is not required to discuss every area where a proposal could have been improved. The scope and extent of the discussions are matter of the contracting officer's judgment. Also, it must be understood that the contracting officer has no obligation to conduct discussions with each offeror in the competitive range unless there is some meaningful reason to initiate discussions. The contracting officer may just feel comfortable with a proposal and see no need to initiate discussions on any subject. There is no legal obligation on the part of the contracting officer to undertake any discussions to improve an offeror's proposal from the grade of C to a B or A.

If the contracting officer determines that an offeror's proposal is no longer in the competitive range, the proposal will no longer be considered for award. Written notice of this decision will be provided to the unsuccessful offeror at the earliest practical time. Offerors excluded from the competitive range may request a debriefing.

Closing the Negotiations

At the conclusion of the discussions, all remaining participants are notified. The notification generally states that all discussions have been concluded; each offeror has the opportunity to submit any remaining final revisions to its proposal; a common cut-off date is set for the submission of any final revisions; and further notice that the revisions, if submitted, should be timely or they will be treated as late proposals and modifications, which could cause them not to be included in the final rating (see fig. 6-3).

Gone is the misused concept of the call for "best and finals" issued by the government that was used by offerors to hold back on their lowest prices to the very last minute and then submit a dramatic change in their cost proposals. The new procedure is that as discussions progress, the contracting officer expects and allows by invitation an offeror to submit revisions to the initial proposal consistent with the progress of the discussions. Thus you may expect to make a number of substantive revisions before discussions are concluded. There should not be any surprises. Extreme variants to what was presented during negotiations could have a detrimental effect on a prospective contractor's evaluation scores in the areas of its credibility and cost risk.

Contract Award

An SSEB, comprising various (see fig. 6-4) members of the technical and cost-integrated product team (IPT) who have been conducting the evaluations of the proposals generally over an extended period of time, concludes its efforts by ranking each proposal remaining in the competitive range. The results are provided to the SSAC, which will examine the results and provide its recommendation and advice to the SSA. The top proposals are selected for responsibility reviews so that award may be able to be made upon the selection of one of them as the best value winner.

The results of all the evaluations are provided to the SSA, who generally is the contracting officer, depending on the size of the procurement and its importance. The greater these two factors are, the higher the level of the decision maker appointed as the SSA. Keep in mind that the SSA is not bound by the order of the rankings proposed by the SSEB or the recommendations of the SSEC. The SSA's objective is to decide which offeror's proposal provides the "best value" to the armed service or agency.

Decisions by the GAO over the years have set the precedent that the SSA's disagreement with the majority of the evaluators and acceptance of the minority's recommendation in favor of another awardee has been found to be unobjectionable under certain conditions. Such a reversal by the SSA has been found not to constitute evidence of a lack of impartiality where the SSA reached a reasoned conclusion, supported by the record, that the awardee's lower-priced, lower-rated proposal deserved a higher technical rating than was assigned by the majority and represented best value to the government.

Decision makers realize that in most major procurements, the losers will request debriefings; they therefore are diligent in their review of the evaluations. The SSA will memorialize the basis of the final source selection. The record will contain the reasons the selected offeror provides the best value to the government even if a higher price premium has to be paid. Once the selection is made the winner is sent a Notice of Award and the losers are notified within three calendar days. A losing offeror should request a debriefing within three days of the received notice that an award has been made. The debriefings of the losers then can commence, if requested, followed by any bid protests by the interested losers to the agency or the Govenment Accountability Office.

Protests

On occasion an interested bidder or offeror has reason to believe that a contract has been or is about to be awarded improperly or illegally or that he or she has been unfairly denied a contract or an opportunity to compete for a contract. A major avenue for prompt, economical relief in comparison to other forums for those concerned about the propriety of the award has been the GAO. The GAO is an independent, nonpartisan agency that works for Congress.

An offeror has the choice of a number of forums (see fig. 6-5). One can start by filing a procuring agency-level protest and then proceed to the GAO within ten calendar days from the date the offeror receives notice of an adverse decision. An alternative would be to proceed to the U.S. Court of Federal Claims sitting in the District of Columbia, which in 2001 was granted by legislation the exclusive judicial forum for bid protest litigation. However, the preferred avenue is to file with the GAO. The GAO is organized and is the foremost expert on protest matters, being recognized as such by all the federal courts.

Protests of proposed or just awarded procurements by agencies such as the Federal Aviation Administration, U.S. Postal Service, the Federal Deposit Insurance Corporation, and nonappropriated fund activities are beyond the GAO's bid protest jurisdiction (31 U.S.C. 3551-3356).

However, such procurements by DoD, NASA, and executive agencies such as the Department of Homeland Security, to include the Transportation Security Administration (TSA), which use FAR-based procurements fall under GAO's jurisdiction. Selected exceptions are primarily those associated with small business size determinations or (8)a program awards whose jurisdiction rests with the SBA.

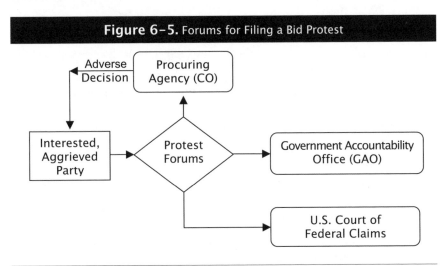

Figure 6-5. Forums for Filing a Bid Protest

Timely GAO protests have the effect of stopping awards in their track by triggering an automatic stay of award or performance until a review and decision is rendered on the protest. GAO protests have been instrumental in unseating the apparent winner or requiring the procuring agency to withdraw the solicitation and resolicit the project. Winning the award should be paramount, despite one's initial hesitancy to file for fear of antagonizing a contracting officer. Such fears are not only for the most part unfounded but also detrimental to sound business practices with Uncle Sam. Please do not opt to pass and wait three or more years for the resolicitation to occur before trying again to unseat the incumbent.

If you have been dealt with unfairly or the government has indeed violated the procurement laws, then you owe it to yourself, your employees, and stockholders to file a protest. At the GAO's Web site, www.gao.gov, click "Legal Decisions" and then on the left-side menu click on "Bid Protests" (www.gao.gov/legal/bidprotest.html), where one will find useful information in the filing and prosecution of a protest. The GAO protest-filing process is user friendly and does not require an attorney.

Only an interested party—an actual or prospective bidder or offeror with a direct economic interest in the procurement—may file the necessary written or online protest. The interested party is generally an offeror who would potentially be in line for an award if the protest was sustained. There is no prescribed format for filing a protest, except that it must be in writing. The protest may be filed using hand delivery, the mail, a commercial carrier, fax (202-512-9749), or e-mail (Protests@gao.gov). Microsoft Word is recommended, especially for the submission of attachments. Coincident with the protest filing a protestor may request document discovery of all the documents received and evaluated by the agency's SSEB. In such cases a protective order between counsels will in all probability be agreed on by all the parties and issued by the GAO. For more information on how to prepare a protest, consult the GAO Web site. A copy must be filed with the procuring agency's individual or the location identified for that purpose in the solicitation within one day after the protest is filed at the GAO. Within one day of the receipt of the protest the GAO will telephone the contracting agency to advise it that a protest has been filed. That telephone call is important because it is the official notice that may trigger a statutory stay of the award or performance of a contract pending GAO's decision.

Although most protests challenge the acceptance or rejection of a bid or proposal and the award or proposed award of a contract, the GAO also considers protests of defective specifications (e.g., restrictive specifications, omission of required provisions, ambiguous or indefinite evaluation factors, and the cancellation of a solicitation). In deciding bid protests the GAO considers whether federal agencies have complied with statutes and regulations controlling government procurements.

Protests alleging improprieties in a solicitation must be filed before bid opening or the time set for receipt of initial proposals if the improprieties were apparent prior to that time. In all other cases, a protest must be filed not later than ten calendar days after the protester knew or should have known the basis of the protest (whichever is earlier). There is an exception for a protest challenging a procurement conducted on the basis of competitive proposals under which a "debriefing" is requested and, when requested, is required by law.

In such cases the initial protest must be filed not later than ten calendar days after the date on which the debriefing was held. The rationale is that after a losing offeror attends the government's debriefing with its proposal team, a more rational decision can be made as to the merits of filing a GAO protest. The office recognizes that the North American Free Trade Agreement (NAFTA) contains a ten-working-day timeliness requirement, which is inconsistent with the GAO's timeliness rules. The GAO in such cases will afford a NAFTA protestor or any other U.S. free trade agreement member all treaty rights for purposes of the timely filing of a protest.

Once the procuring agency is notified of the protest you can rest assured that it will oppose the challenger and will provide its agency report within thirty days or sooner for comment. The protestor must promptly review the agency report and within ten calendar days comment on its merits substantively. Protests are rarely sustained when the protestor does not file substantive comments on the agency report. Thereafter the GAO may or may not conduct a hearing on the issues at its main office.

After the record is complete, the GAO will consider the facts and legal issues raised and will issue a decision, a copy of which will be sent to all parties participating in the protest. The GAO will sustain the protest (e.g., find that the agency violated a procurement statute or regulation and that the violation prejudiced the protestor) and case-appropriate corrective action will be recommended. Alternatively the GAO may deny the protest or may dismiss the protest without reviewing the matter. The office will render a decision well within one hundred days from the date the protest was filed unless a decision is rendered under an express option of within sixty-five days requested by any of the parties. The exact date will depend upon the complexity of the issues raised in the protest and GAO's workload.

An example of a protest decided just within the one-hundred-day deadline because of its complexity, high dollar value, and the importance of the acquisition to national defense was the Boeing Company protest associated with the aerial refueling tanker program. The issues are summarized below.

On March 11, 2008, the Boeing Company protested the award of a contract to Northrop Grumman Systems Corporation, whose winning contractor team arrangement included Airbus parent European Aeronautic Defence and Space Company, under RFP No. FA8625-07-R-6470, issued by the Department of the Air Force. The acquisition was for the first procurement of 80 out of 179 KC-X aerial refueling tankers to replace the aging (forty-six years old) tanker fleet of KC-135 aircraft. Aerial refueling is a key element supporting the effectiveness of the Department of Defense's airpower in military operations and is, as such, an important component of national security.

Boeing challenged the Air Force's technical and cost evaluations, conduct of discussions, and source selection decision.

The GAO found that the Air Force's selection of Northrop Grumman's proposal as reflecting the best value to the government was undermined by a number of prejudicial errors that called into question the Air Force's decision that Northrop Grumman's proposal was technically acceptable and its judgment concerning the comparative technical advantages accorded Northrop Grumman's proposal. In addition the GAO found a number of errors in the agency's cost evaluation that resulted in Boeing displacing Northrop Grumman as the offeror with the lowest evaluated most probable life-cycle costs to the government. Although the GAO sustained Boeing's protest on grounds related to these errors, the GAO also denied many of Boeing's challenges to the award.

Specifically, the GAO sustained the protest on June 18, 2008, some ninety-nine days after the protest was lodged, because it found that (1) the Air Force did not evaluate the offerors' technical proposals under the key system requirements subfactor of the mission capability factor in accordance with the weighting established in the RFP's evaluation criteria, (2) a key technical discriminator relied upon in the selection decision in favor of Northrop Grumman relating to the aerial refueling area of the key system requirements subfactor was contrary to the RFP, (3) the Air Force did not reasonably evaluate the capability of Northrop Grumman's proposed aircraft to refuel all current Air Force fixed-wing, tanker-compatible aircraft using current Air Force procedures as required by the RFP, (4) the Air Force conducted misleading and unequal discussions with Boeing with respect to whether it had satisfied an RFP objective under the operational utility area of the key system requirements subfactor, (5) Northrop Grumman's proposal took exception to a material solicitation requirement related to the product support subfactor, (6) the Air Force did not reasonably evaluate military construction costs associated with the offerors' proposed aircraft consistent with the RFP, and (7) the Air Force unreasonably evaluated Boeing's estimated nonrecurring engineering costs associated with its proposed system development and demonstration.

In summary the GAO found a number of errors in the Air Force's conduct of this procurement, including the failure to evaluate proposals in accordance with the RFP criteria and requirements and to conduct discussions in a fair and equal manner. But for these errors the GAO believed that Boeing would have had a substantial chance of being selected for award. Accordingly the GAO sustained Boeing's protest of the Air Force's award of a contract to Northrop Grumman for the aerial refueling tankers.

The GAO recommended that the Air Force reopen discussions with the offerors, obtain revised proposals, reevaluate the revised proposals, and make a new source selection decision consistent with this decision. If the Air Force believed that the RFP, as reasonably interpreted, does not adequately state its needs, the agency should amend the solicitation prior to conducting further discussions with the offerors. If Boeing's proposal is selected for award, the Air Force should terminate the contract awarded to Northrop Grumman. The GAO also recommended that Boeing be reimbursed the reasonable costs of filing and pursuing the protest, including reasonable attorneys' fees.

A CASE STUDY OF A COMPETITIVE PROPOSAL PROCESS

After some three years in Germany I was notified of my transfer by Washington to a project office located at Fort Monmouth, New Jersey. I had been to Fort Monmouth only as a cadet during the summer rotation, when junior cadets visit various branch schools in an effort to decide which branch of the army one will select at graduation. Going to the home of the Signal Corps was not what I had in mind, despite the pleasant memories of the nearby Jersey Shore and the dance populated with the New Jersey debutantes we met that summer as cadets.

But I was told they needed an artillery officer who understood communications and had a master's degree in electrical engineering. The Pentagon decided that as an electrical engineer, artillery commander, and prior member of the Army General Staff, I could best represent the Artillery Corps in the development and acquisition of a new family of tactical FM radios.

The DoD needed a new combat radio to replace the diverse assortment of FM manpack, vehicular, and airborne sets that had entered the armed services through the Army inventory during the 1960s. The older family of radios (e.g., PRC manpack and VRC-12 vehicular) were bulky, subject to enemy electronic jamming, needed considerable frequency spectrum space, and used obsolete components that were expensive and increasingly hard to procure.

I had spent two grueling years as executive officer to two major generals who sequentially occupied the seat of the deputy chief of staff for operations of the Army's European Command, located in Heidelberg, Germany. For me it was a prime staff position coming from my recent battalion command in the West German town of Aschaffenburg during a challenging time for the Army. We had focused on South Vietnam and allowed our forces in Europe to reach low levels of combat readiness. Morale was indeed low as the draft was still in force. Among other qualified officers I was one of the combat officers who had served in Vietnam and on the Army General Staff in the Pentagon. I was sent to Germany to bolster the readiness of U.S. forces.

Earlier at Aschaffenburg I had been the commander of an artillery battalion as well as the custodian of a special weapons site that stored primarily artillery nuclear munitions and engineer nuclear demolitions. I commanded a nuclear-tipped Honest John missile battalion that was retired some time ago and replaced with the then-new Lance missile. Last time I checked an inert missile stood as a museum piece of antiquated missile technology at Fort Sill, Oklahoma, the home of Army missiles and artillery. The European land-based tactical nuclear weapons were expatriated some thirty years ago back to the United States, after the Greek-Turkish crisis in Cyprus, the fall of the Berlin Wall, and the rise of terrorism.

I was exhausted as I departed Rhein-Main Air Base for the flight to Dover Air Force Base, Delaware, and Fort Monmouth. My main consolation was that I had given this staff assignment my best, from participating in the closing of major U.S. facilities (hospital, PX warehouses, etc.) to the drama of avoiding a full-blown Greek-Turkish conflict over Cyprus.

Not only were the U.S. Army's warfighters exhausted, but so was the state of readiness, from deficits in unit team training, obsolescent weapons, outdated communications, and aging armored fighting transports to low stocks of munitions. In many respects the Army is now facing the same challenges because of the ongoing wars in Iraq and Afghanistan.

It was now time to rebuild and modernize the Army. I recognized that I had been chosen for a key part in that effort. The Army had not replaced its combat net radios (used at all fighting echelons from tank commanders to brigade commanders) for some thirty years. In fact, the Army was using the same radio used by infantrymen not only in Vietnam but also in Korea. The new radio was to be used throughout the Army and the Marine Corps and on all army helicopters and be compatible for use by Air Force forward air controllers providing close air support.

The warfighters' need for the radio led its proponents down a winding path that started with the Army's Signal Corps at Fort Monmouth, New Jersey, and later Fort Gordon, Georgia, through U.S. Army Communications Electronics Command at Fort Monmouth in New Jersey, through the Army Material Command in Alexandria, Virginia, into the Pentagon by the Army Staff, then with the Army secretariat to the Office of the Secretary of Defense for approval of funding. On the way stops were made to brief the Joint Chiefs of Staff, followed by staffers on both congressional Armed Service committees. Hence I found myself and family assigned to Fort Monmouth, New Jersey, the Garden State, on the Jersey Shore. However, I was going to be camping in Virginia inside the Pentagon's E-ring on many occasions.

On arrival in the project office the first objective was to review the draft performance specification for the new radio assembled by the Command's Tactical Radio Branch of the Research Center of the Communications Electronics Command. This document was to translate the combat performance needs of the modern warrior into technical performance requirements to assist contractors in their bids.

Specifications tend to be classified as either a performance specification or a design specification. In the latter the buyer is provided detail specifications and design requirements, including, in the applicable cases, engineering design drawings, built-to specification drawings, or construction architectural drawings. The trader reviews the government provided detail specifications and drawings. Then the prospective contractor responds in its proposal on how it is going to manage, build, and manufacture the requisite systems or product or deliver the services and at what cost.

In a performance-based specification, which is preferred by the government, the contrary occurs. An offeror must take the performance specification and return with a proposal of how the offeror's team will design and build a product or render a service that meets the performance criteria.

If a new building were being built, design specifications, including construction drawings (architectural, electrical, mechanical, structural, and site) from an architectural firm, would be the preferred procurement package to bid. If one needed a new laser-guided missile system, a performance specification would be preferred, specifying range, lethality, and launch systems as well as logistic criteria but leaving the offerors to come in with their designs as to how to meet the performance and quality parameters. The government would not be responsible for the design. The offeror would be the responsible body because it is its design. (Refer to chapter 4 for more information on specifications.)

We were looking for novel approaches for an FM radio for the handling of both voice and data traffic. In addition we wanted offerors to propose novel electronic countermeasure defenses that would allow the radio to work through an electronic jamming environment. We also wanted a secure radio that could handle encryption. All of these capabilities were essential, but at the same time we required the radio to be light and durable, possess a maximum range, have a long battery life, and be highly reliable.

The Single Channel Ground and Airborne Radio Subsystem (SINC-GARS-V) program was approved in 1976, and the Army became the executive agent for development and acquisition. That program was to be planned to provide the armed services with the next generation of combat net radios. The new radios were to be lighter, capable of both voice and data transmission, and have antijamming features. By using the greatest possible number of common components, the Army would be able to cut down on logistic support. A draft performance specification was developed in-house and then released for comment to firms such as ITT, Motorola, and Cincinnati Electronics Corporation. Ethical standards had changed from when the first government technical definition of the HAWK Air Defense System was written by Raytheon's retired military business development representatives at Fort Bliss, Texas, with input from the home office engineering team. Raytheon then went on to win the contract. Such actions today would not be tolerated and would border on unethical conduct just on the basis of fairness to the other offerors, who would not have the chance to influence the development. If a support contractor today provides such assistance to a government agency under its contract, it would be required to recuse itself from participating in the competitive bidding process of the new system or services. The importance of getting in on the ground floor of a program either as a prime contractor, subcontractor, or supplier cannot be understated. It gives one a chance to influence the technical requirements to match its capabilities, technology, and resources. Moreover, it provides an entry to gain legitimate industrial intelligence. With the use of the Internet many more firms have the option of commenting on draft solicitations. Contracting officers today seek to encourage exchanges with industry. Concurrent with the development of the specification well before the release of its draft for the radio, exchanges had commenced on the acquisition strategy for these radios. The engineering development phase would be by negotiated acquisition using competitive proposals.

The radio program was divided into phases to involve engineering development of prototypes to reduce the technical risk before entering limited and then full-scale production. We struggled with various issues, including: Was the project to be awarded to just one of the offerors or would it be prudent to have multiple contract awards for innovative concepts and to accommodate wartime production surge requirements? What technology growth should be built into a prototype? What would be the criteria (factors and significant subfactors) for evaluation? What technical data did we want industry to include in their proposals for delivery? How much weight would each evaluation factor and significant subfactor be given? How would the winning proposal or proposals be determined? What would be the organization and composition of the technical evaluation team? What would be the composition of the SSEB and SSAC? Which SSA would make the final selection decision? What would be the relation and importance of cost to technical performance? How important would past performance be in the evaluation?

As always happens, once you help develop an acquisition plan you get picked to participate in its execution. That is what happened to me. I was sequestered on what is called temporary duty for some six months along with some twenty other professionals—engineers, cryptologists, radio experts, testers, quality assurance types, and cost analysts—to conduct the technical and cost evaluations and to rank the competitive proposals. The proposals were color coded when they were received so that we as the evaluators would not know with whom the proposals had originated.

The paper proposals along with their demonstration models arrived on the due date by flatbed truck, and the tedious evaluation started. Today such proposals, except for any working prototypes for testing, arrive through the Internet in electronic format or through the government point of entry and by the delivery of computer disks. Technology has allowed us to move from spiraled notebook to computer terminals, where we can view the same text and graphics and make comments simultaneously. The Integrated Acquisition Environment allows both the government and public concurrent access to multiple databases (see figs. 2-7, 2-10, 2-11, and 4-1), which promotes the speed and efficiency of the acquisition process.

In essence we are approaching a paperless electronic acquisition process. The submission of the competitive proposal has become electronic; however the evaluation process was then and remains today human-intensive, depending on the user and technical and cost specialists. The issue always comes down to this: When can the parties talk with one another? As a general rule before a solicitation is released, the parties can talk as much as they want. After the solicitation hits the street (Internet), then industry should only talk with the appointed contracting officer or the assigned contract specialists.

After one submits the proposal to the government, the offeror must wait to be contacted by the government. Now the government has two major choices. First, it can proceed to do its evaluation and not talk with anyone, except for limited exchanges for clarifications on the submitted initial proposal of an offeror, if warranted, thus awarding the contract on initial proposals. Or second, it may conduct communications with each offeror to establish a competitive range of those proposals that have the greatest chance for selection. All others would be notified of their being dropped from consideration for reasons of efficiency (too many better proposals) or for material deficiencies in their proposals.

Of course those interested parties dropped may have a right to receive a debriefing and if not satisfied as to why they were dropped to proceed to file a protest to the Government Accountability Office or to the headquarters of the agency that was conducting the evaluation.

Discussions (face to face and written) are then conducted with those offerors remaining in the competitive range and revisions are requested by the contracting officer until discussions are concluded and final revisions received. These discussions are the negotiations associated with the contracting by negotiation using the competitive proposal acquisition process.

As an evaluator we prepared numerous items for negotiation (IFN) that were mainly questions sent to or orally discussed with an offeror of its proposal as part of our discussions during negotiations. The IFNs were intended to obtain an understanding of the submitted proposal as related to the government's statement of work and to seek revisions in the nature of the product or services to be delivered in quality, performance, and/or price in order to conform with the Army's solicited need.

Once the winning proposal is selected from among the most highly rated proposals, the government conducts debriefing conferences of the losers, if requested, and awaits the outcome of any lodged protests.

Contracts were awarded in fiscal year 1978 for the design and fabrication of prototypes of two SINCGARS-V radio sets, one with a slow frequency change ("hopping") and the other with a fast frequency change capability—characteristics that would make enemy interception or jamming extremely difficult.

PRACTICING BUSINESS TIPS

Although I was sequestered for six months, I really got to bond with my civil servant engineers, testers, and cost analysts. Despite our different views on each proposal, we were able to argue the pros and cons of each offeror's concept, especially their costs and the innovations that were presented by each industry proposal, and reach a consensus.

Best value contracting using competitive proposals may consider contractor past performance, logistical support costs, surge capability, the industrial base, technology insertion, proposal risk, performance risk, concurrent engineering, contractor technical capability, contractor management ability, and other salient—measurable and intangible—factors. The FM VHF combat radio, regardless of what generation, next to the rifle and helicopter, is a lifeline for the American warfighter—in any branch of the armed services. We had to get it right.

The timely protest of an award of a contract to the GAO is a key policing element in the U.S. procurement system. An interested party should not be inhibited in using this avenue for relief because of material errors caused by the procurement agency in its evaluation of proposals. The protest process is relatively quick and cost effective. A notable case of national interest was the GAO decision to sustain the Boeing Company protest against the award of the Aerial Refueling Tankers to the CTA of Northrop Grumman Systems Corporation and the European Aeronautic Defense and Space Company.

CHAPTER 7

My Small Business Is Special
Using Contracts for Socioeconomic Programs

Socioeconomic programs and policies are part of the U.S. government procurement experience. Figure 7-1 outlines the socioeconomic areas of interests in federal procurements—including issues regarding labor, small businesses and equal employment, and free trade—that dominate the business and political landscapes. This chapter focuses on selected subjects on the list.

PROMOTION OF SMALL BUSINESS (SET-ASIDES)

Possibly the most extensive and complex social policy in government procurement is that which favors small business, primarily because most new jobs and new ideas are generated by small businesses. The Small Business Act of 1953 states that it is the policy of Congress that a fair proportion of government procurement be placed with small businesses. Out of this act came the creation of the Small Business Administration to aid, assist, counsel, and protect insofar as possible the interests of small businesses.

The process first requires a determination as to whether or not a firm is eligible for participation in any small business program. A small business for the purpose of government procurement is a concern, including its affiliates, which is independently owned and operated, is not dominant in the field of operation in which it is bidding on government contracts, and does not have employees or annual receipts exceeding the published size standards on an industry-by-industry basis included in the solicitation. If it qualifies it may

FIGURE 7-1. Socioeconomic Policies and Federal Procurement

PROMOTION OF SMALL BUSINESS (SET-ASIDES)
Small Business including Women-Owned
Small Disadvantaged 8(a) Program
Service-Disabled Veteran-Owned

ECONOMICALLY DISTRESSED URBAN AND RURAL COMMUNITIES
Historically Underutilized Business Zone (HUBZone)

LABOR
Equal Employment Opportunity
Affirmative Action
Minimum wage hourly rates

SERVICE CONTRACT ACT (SERVICES)

WALSH-HEALEY PUBLIC CONTRACTS ACT (SUPPLIES)

DAVIS-BACON ACT (CONSTRUCTION)

BUY AMERICAN ACT, FREE TRADE AGREEMENTS

ENVIRONMENT, ENERGY, WATER EFFICIENCY

---

have the opportunity to participate in one or more of the following types of acquisition programs:

1. Competing only among one's own peers for set-aside acquisitions by firms that are similarly classified, including small business, Historically Underutilized Business Zone (HUBZone) small business, small disadvantaged business (SDB), women-owned small business (WOSB), veteran-owned small business, and service-disabled veteran-owned small business (SDVOSB) concerns. Keep in mind that a contracting officer is required to set aside an individual acquisition for competition among small business when it is in the interest of maintaining or mobilizing the nation's full productive capacity or national defenses and to ensure that a fair proportion of government contracts in each industry category are placed with small business. In fact, each acquisition of supplies or services that has an anticipated value exceeding three thousand dollars but not the SAT of one hundred dollars is automatically reserved for small business

unless there is no reasonable expectation of obtaining competitive offers from two responsible small business firms.

2. The competency program, which allows you to call upon the SBA. The SBA is empowered to certify your competency to be awarded a contract by issuing a Certificate of Competency with regard to all elements of responsibility (capability, competency, capacity, credit, integrity, perseverance, tenacity, etc.) as a small business overriding a contracting officer's decision that your firm is not responsible for an award.

3. Being matriculated into the 8(a) Program under which agencies contract with the Small Business Administration for goods and services to be furnished under a subcontract awarded by the SBA to an SDB concern, more commonly known as an 8(a) contractor. The contracts may be awarded by SBA for performance by eligible 8(a) firms on either a sole or competitive basis. WOSBs and SDVOSBs may be able to qualify not only as SDBs but also as 8(a) firms.

4. The Subcontracting Assistance Program.

5. The Small Disadvantaged Business Program.

6. Sole-source awards to HUBZone small business and SDVOSB concerns. Under the Service-Disabled Veteran-Owned Small Business procurement program a contracting officer may restrict competition to SDVOSBs if (a) the contracting officer has a reasonable expectation that no fewer than two such firms will submit offers, and (b) the award can be made at a fair market price. Both prongs must be met. Measures such as prior procurement history, market surveys, and advice from the agency's business specialist may all constitute grounds for a contracting officer's decision to set aside or not to set aside a procurement. It is difficult to fault the assessment of the contracting officer on the reasonable expectation that award will be made at a fair market price, since this is a matter of business judgment. To award a contract on a sole-source basis to an SDVOSB, four conditions must be met: (a) only one SDVOSB can satisfy the requirement, (b) the anticipated award price of the contract (including options) will not exceed five million dollars for a requirement using the NAICS codes for manufacturing or three million dollars for a requirement using any other NAICS code, (c) the SDVOSB has been determined responsible with respect to performance, and (d) the award can be made at a fair and reasonable price.

7. Using a price evaluation adjustment for SDB concerns and the use of a price evaluation preference for HUBZone small business concerns. One has to check periodically whether or not this price evaluation adjustment is suspended or in force for each fiscal year by calling on the SBA. When the price evaluation adjustment is active, a price factor is added to all other offers except those from SDBs. The factor to be added is determined by the Department of Commerce. The only restriction is that the award price is not allowed to exceed fair market value by more than the factor determined by the Department of Commerce. These SDB procurement mechanisms determined by the Commerce Department are posted by the General Services Administration on its Web site at www.gsa.gov/portal. Go to "search," type in "price evaluation adjustment small business." The Acquisition Central Web site at www.arnet.gov/References/sdbadjustments.htm contains a list of industries eligible for price evaluation adjustment published by the Commerce Department that should be correlated to the previously referenced GSA Web site.

Your business size and corporate social classification is an important designation to distinguish you from the competition. The SBA, Department of Commerce, and GSA are advocates for Section 8(a) small business development, SDBs, HUBZone businesses, SDVOSBs, and WOSBs. The SBA offers assistance and certification in preference programs to small business (http://app1.sba.gov/faqs/; www.sba.gov/smallbusinessplanner/index.html).

Procurement agencies for most small business programs have set-asides for acquisitions that are reserved for competition among small businesses or SDBs. However, remember that the recent legal advantages granted to such small businesses do not guarantee government work.

Your first query must be whether or not your firm is a small business. Small business size standards generally are determined by the SBA on an industry-by-industry basis dependent on sales averaged over a three-year period and by the number of employees. The criteria are published by the SBA. The contracting officer specifies the size standard in the solicitation for the product or services being acquired so that offerors can appropriately represent themselves as small or large.

A trader should classify the product or service that it is selling using the descriptions that most closely resemble one or more of the codes found in the

North American Industry Classification System Manual. This manual best describes the principal nature of the product or services and their associated codes. The manual is available on line at www.census.gov/epcd/www/naics.html.

Determining your business size can begin with your entry at the SBA Web site on the page at www.sba.gov/services/contractingopportunities/sizestandardstopics/index.html, which contains the size standards published by the SBA. Then, as necessary, visit the Office of Small and Disadvantaged Business Utilization (SADBU) in the agency you want to do business. Each procurement agency has such an office, where a trader may consult with its director or one or more of its small business technical advisers. In addition, at this office there will be one or more assigned SBA procurement center representatives from the regional SBA office. These officials from the procurement agency and SBA can help you to do the following:

1. Classify the type of small business your firm is and apply and obtain a written certification of your firm's advantaged status. One can self-attest as to the firm's status, but self-attestation can be challenged by the contracting officer checking with the SBA or the Central Contractor Registry, which includes SBA's PRO-Net.
2. Obtain the names of the end users of your products and services and arrange for a meeting.

An offeror may represent that it is a small business concern in connection with a specific solicitation if it meets the definition of a small business concern applicable to the solicitation and has not been determined by the SBA to be other than a small business. Such self-certification is accepted by the contracting officer unless another offeror or interested party challenges in a timely manner (generally within five business days after bid opening in writing) the concern's small business representation or the contracting officer has reason to challenge it. In such cases the matter is referred to the SBA for a ruling.

By accessing the CCR database or by contacting the SBA by e-mail at hubzone@sba.gov, prime contractors have the responsibility to confirm that a subcontractor representing itself as a HUBZone small business is certified consistent with legal requirements. Such responsibility is expected to increase subcontracting opportunities and ensure accurate reporting of awards to HUBZone small business concerns under government contracts.

Contractors are required to rerepresent their size status for the NAICS codes in their existing contracts

1. prior to exercising any option thereafter;
2. following the execution of a novation agreement; or
3. following a merger or acquisition of the contractor, regardless of whether there is a novation agreement.
   This should be accomplished online through ORCA 60 to 120 days prior to the end of the fifth year of a contract that is more than five years in duration (a long-term contract).

The change in size status will not change the terms and conditions of the contract, but the purchasing agency may no longer include the value of options exercised or orders issued against the contract in its small business prime contracting goal achievements.

The bottom line is that an end user does not care whether or not you are a small business. However, the sourcing procurement manager does care, especially if he or she has a goal to fill. For example, if the Pentagon has set a goal that 0.5 percent of its total contracting dollars will go to SDVOSBs, then such businesses have a good chance of receiving their part of the pie. But to be able to do so, the small businesses must

1. develop relations with the buying agents and the users they serve by getting in front of the customers with their capabilities and products then getting to know its government customer;
2. arrange for an industrial product demonstration through an agency's technical industrial liaison office if applicable;
3. develop a solution that solves a problem or a need the agency or user has that the seller can bring before them to gain their trust and respect;
4. submit an unsolicited proposal of your unique and innovative ideas, suggestions, and concepts that relate to a particular agency's mission; and
5. move to close the deal by using your special status as a designated small business.

CONTRACTOR TEAM ARRANGEMENTS (CTA)

In recent years teaming arrangements have become popular owing to the need for past experience on particular projects, the need for special equipment or the special technology one partner possesses, the need to use the intellectual property (patents and technical data) owned by one party to the team, the availability of skilled personnel, and for purely economic considerations, such as efficiency, allowing for the sharing of business risks.

Depending on the phase of the acquisition process one may develop a teaming agreement for the bid and proposal phase so that the resources to win a program are shared. As part of such an effort the responsibilities of each team member would be delineated also for the performance phase once the project is won. The teaming parties can assume a prime contractor-subcontractor relationship for portions of the project as shown in figure 7-2. The government, acting through its agent, the contracting officer, establishes privity of contract with one entity as the prime contractor, who in turn establishes multiple subcontracts with various entities, such as raw material and parts suppliers, specialists, manufacturers, and other subcontractors. In this classic arrangement, responsibility for the performance of the contract rests with the prime contractor.

The other approach is to undertake the work as a joint venture, a legal entity in the nature of a partnership engaged in the joint undertaking of a specific commercial transaction for mutual profit. In our case it could be the submission of a competitive proposal or bid and the associated performance of an awarded government contract. Generally it involves a one-time group-

FIGURE 7–2. Classic Contractor–Subcontractor Team Arrangement

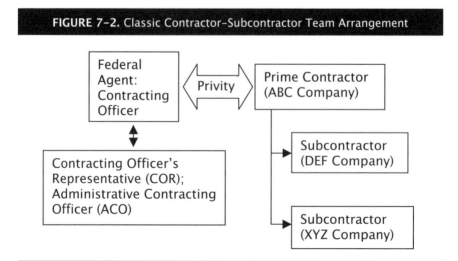

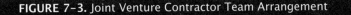

FIGURE 7-3. Joint Venture Contractor Team Arrangement

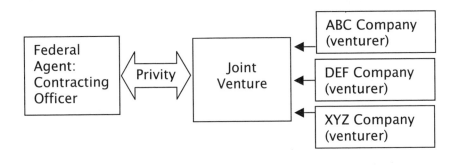

ing of two or more persons or firms of disparate size and resources in a business undertaking.

Unlike a partnership a joint venture does not entail a continuing relationship among the parties. A joint venture has a community interest in the performance of a particular subject matter. The right to direct and govern the policy of the joint venture and duties of its members are defined by written agreement. Profit and loss are shared in a pro rata manner to the extent of each member's invested interest in the venture. For tax accounting and reporting purposes, a joint venture is treated like a partnership. The principals are known as joint venturers or members, and they in turn appoint a committee or board of directors to direct the overall policy management of the venture. The committee or board in turn appoints the common general manager and other officers of the joint venture (see fig. 7-3).

The CTA is coupled to a public relations effort targeted to the procuring agency, including the formal agreement, which would be provided to the contracting officer as part of a proposal for information and evaluation. The DoD allows and recognizes, as matter of policy, the integrity and validity of a teaming arrangement provided the arrangement is as a matter of policy identified and company relationships are fully disclosed in an offer or, for arrangements entered into after submission of an offer, before the arrangement becomes effective.

Contractor teaming is not only for large defense firms (e.g., Boeing, General Dynamic, General Electric) that may be competing for a new Navy destroyer or fighter plane. Teaming can occur between two small businesses—one established and the other an 8(a) SDB, SDVOSB, or WOSB—for services or products or both.

Figure 7-4 presents a matrix of allowable joint venture arrangements that preserve the special status of the small business or small disadvantaged business.

An SDB joint venture is a smart business arrangement in which all of the following apply:

1. Each company in the venture is small, at least one of the companies is small disadvantaged, and the joint venture as a whole is small pursuant to the implementing regulations of the Small Business Act and the implementing regulations. By law the joint venture takes on the aspect of an SDB despite the fact that one of the firms is just a small business. Therefore, the entire venture takes on the appearance of an SDB and can reap the contracting advantage in being awarded a set-aside project for a disadvantaged business or may be allowed to compete for the project only against other disadvantaged business regardless if they have teamed up or not.

2. The majority of the venture's earnings accrue directly to the socially and economically disadvantaged individuals in the SDB concern in the joint venture.

3. The management and daily business operations are controlled by the SDB in the venture.

4. A signed agreement is executed by the eligible concerns for the purpose of performing a specific contract prior to the submission of

FIGURE 7–4. Small Business Joint Venture Teaming Matrix			
Socioeconomic Status	Small Disadvantaged Business (includes Women-Owned Small Business and Service-Disabled Veteran-Owned Small Business)	SBA 8(a)	Large Business
Small Business	Yes	Yes	No
Small Disadvantaged Business	Yes	Yes	No

offers, which specifies the responsibilities of the parties with regard to the contract performance, source of labor, itemization of major equipment and facilities to be committed by each member, and negotiation of the contract and any subcontracts to the small disadvantaged joint venture.

Businesses entering into a joint venture to compete for government contracts are faced with issues unique to federal procurement. A common matter is that joint venture agreements are the product of negotiation between the prospective venturers or members. The longer the intended duration of the venture and the more projects it involves, the more defined the relationship will need to be to address the various issues. These include issues of responsibility (whether the responsibility of one of the venturers may be imputed to the joint venture), time of formation, safeguarding of proprietary data, and cost accounting, to mention but a few.

The Federal Acquisition Regulation states the standards of responsibility that a potential contractor must meet by the time of award. These include standards regarding financial resources, tax compliance organization, experience, technical skills, production capabilities, technical equipment and facilities, integrity, performance record, and ability to comply with the performance schedule. Certain of these standards will be judged on the basis of the joint venture's combined abilities: financial resources, technical equipment and facilities, skills in technology, and organization. Others, however, will be judged on the basis of the members' separate abilities.

For example, one venturer's lack of integrity is sufficient to support a determination that the joint venture is not a responsible bidder. In one instance, when the controlling shareholder of a corporate venture had been convicted for tax evasion, the lack of integrity was imputed to both the shareholder's company and the venture. One member's lack of integrity, unlike a single member's lack of capacity or ability, cannot be cured by association with another member. This is especially true when the members' obligations are equal. Under such circumstances a finding of lack of integrity in one venturer may be considered a sufficient basis to support a determination that the joint venture is not responsible.

Another qualifying issue is whether the joint venture partakes of its creator's small business status. The SBA considers each venturer's size in determining whether the joint venture is a small business eligible for participation in certain programs. Thus a small business that forms a joint venture will have its size status assessed when both firms are combined because the size determination takes into consideration the size of all parties to the joint venture.

Another unique issue is the timing of the joint venture formation. A joint venture may be formed before or after an offer is submitted to the government and may even be formed after contract award. The joint venture relationship must be fully disclosed in the offer, or for joint ventures formed after award, the joint venture must be disclosed before the relationship becomes effective. This means at least informing the SBA that a joint venture is contemplated if the offeror is a small business low bidder.

A joint venture must comply with the pertinent cost accounting standards (CAS) requirements, such as preparing its own CAS disclosure statement. At the least the venture must maintain an accounting system that is adequate for government cost-accounting purposes. The members also must agree on an acceptable allocation of corporate general and administrative costs to the joint venture.

Joint ventures have to give consideration to the antitrust violation risk inasmuch as the combination of two companies engaged in the same business or a similar business may decrease competition by monopolizing the market or eliminating would-be competitors. In addition the joint venture's business activity may reduce competition. The Justice Department treats R&D joint ventures more permissively than production joint ventures in recognition of the obvious efficiencies obtained by having two parties researching the same subject through joint efforts.

It is possible that contributions to a joint venture in return for a share of the profits may be viewed as a security; in such cases federal securities regulations would apply requiring possible registration and disclosure requirements. This can be avoided if each member of the joint venture exercises some managerial control, has power to control joint venture expenditures through capital withdrawals, and makes a substantial and necessary contribution to the joint venture.

Lastly, if the joint venture is incorporated, it will be taxed as a corporation; if not, the joint venture will be treated as a partnership for tax purposes. The most noticeable differences between the two treatments is that in a partnership the profit and loss flow directly to the partners (venturers) to be individually reported, while a corporation generally must file its own tax return and is treated as separate entity. The desired tax features of a partnership can be combined with the limited liability of a corporate structure if the members are set up as separate incorporated subsidiaries that then participate in a partnership.

In summary CTAs are in, especially in a globalized economy. Teaming allows for access to complementary skills and resources. It provides the opportunity to convert fixed costs to variable costs and to develop even superior continuity and increased responsiveness. The bottom line: More competitive offers and better performance can be delivered to the government, and national security concerns can be met, regardless of the venturers' location. Teaming enhances the chances of winning a procurement, especially if the team's organizations, specialties, and past performance are presented effectively in a competitive proposal.

The surge in outsourcing ongoing in the United States and globalization in recent years and for the foreseeable future means traders need to manage a complex web of supplier relations to ensure timely and quality performance in the delivery of supplies and services. Teaming is essential. Moreover the execution of free trade agreements and the exceptions to the Buy American Act is supporting this economic phenomenon. Without teaming the needs of the warfighter will not be met owing to increasingly scarce commodities and the risks of disruptions to supply lines posed by terrorists, striking dock workers, or other uncontrolled causes. Therefore, choose teammates who are dependable, and make your choice consistent with security requirements.

THE SMALL BUSINESS SUBCONTRACTING PROGRAM

Under current statutory law any contractor receiving a contract for more than the simplified acquisition threshold must agree in the contract that small business, veteran-owned small business, SDVOSB, HUBZone small business, SDB, and WOSB concerns will have the maximum practicable opportunity to participate in contract performance consistent with efficient performance. It is also the policy of the United States that such socially designated firms be paid in a timely manner amounts due by the prime contractors pursuant to the terms of their subcontracts.

In negotiated acquisitions or even sealed bidding acquisitions, wherein a prime contractor's contract is to exceed $550,000 ($1 million for construction at any public facility), a large business is required to submit a small business subcontracting plan to the government for approval as a precondition for the award of the contract. (One should verify each year if this threshold has increased.) This requirement applies only to large businesses. Small business contractors are exempt, as are contracts that will be performed outside the United States.

A small business subcontracting plan, preferably covering the offeror's fiscal year and applying to the entire production of commercial items sold by the firm, should include

1. separate percentage goals for using small business as subcontractors and a description of the method used to develop the subcontracting goals;

2. a statement of the total dollars planned to be subcontracted and a statement of the total dollars planned to be subcontracted to small business;

3. a description of the principal types of supplies and services to be subcontracted and an identification of the types planned for subcontracting to small business;

4. a description of the method used to identify potential sources for solicitation purposes;

5. a description of the method used to determine indirect costs to be incurred with small business if indirect costs were included in establishing the subcontracting goals; and

6. various assurances by the offeror associated with the sound management of the subcontracting plan to ensure that small business has an equitable opportunity to compete for subcontracts; a good faith effort to comply with the plan, including ensuring that all of its subcontractors who receive subcontracts or modifications in excess of the $550,000 threshold also implement similar subcontracting plans and providing the necessary reporting and maintaining of the requisite records on the execution of the small business subcontracting plan.

Wherever the phrase "small business" is mentioned it includes not only small business but also veteran-owned small business, SDVOSB, HUBZone, SDB, and WOSB concerns. The above plan should not be confused with the call in a solicitation for the submission of a small business "participation" plan to be evaluated as one of the factors of a best value source selection competition for a contract award by negotiation. The contents of such a plan as it applies to the performance work statement in the solicitation and how it will be evaluated in relation to all the other factors will be addressed in the RFP's instructions to offerors. This "participation" plan generally provides any information substantiating the offeror's track record of using small business on past contracts.

Thus prime contractors have a continuous need for many small business contacts and options. Most would prefer a small business that already has a reputation and contacts with the government buyers. Why not team with a firm that can bring more to the table than just a good product?

The Department of Defense maintains a list of all major DoD prime contractors by state and provides a point of contact (the small business liaison officer) within each firm on its "Office of Small Business Programs" Web page (www.acq.osd.mil/osbp/doing_business/index.htm). Click on the heading titled "Subcontracting Opportunities with DoD Major Prime Contractors." Concurrently, many firms also have their own Web sites, which may be useful in promoting teaming relationships.

The next generation of tools to collect subcontracting accomplishments government wide is known as the Electronic Subcontractor Reporting System (eSRS), part of the Federal Procurement Data System–New Generation, Integrated Acquisition Environment discussed in chapters 2 and 4. This Internet-based tool (www.esrs.gov) is intended to streamline the process of reporting on subcontracting plans and to provide agencies with access to analytical data on subcontracting performance. Specifically the eSRS eliminates the need for paper submissions and processing of SF 294, Individual Subcontracting Reports, and SF 295, Summary Subcontracting Report, and replaces the paper with an easy-to-use electronic process to collect the data. Contractors and their business associates will report data through their Web browser of choice, visiting this site and logging on to report accomplishments using an easy data entry process. The eSRS promises to provide an easier process for federal contractors and their business associates to report subcontracting activity.

LABOR

The social policy of equal employment opportunity, which has been the subject of many laws and judicial decisions, has been required in government contracts principally by a series of executive orders, currently Executive Order 11246, as amended. These orders delegate to the secretary of labor the overall responsibility for administering this policy. This is carried out by the Office of Federal Contract Compliance. Executive Order 11246 assigns to the contracting agencies the responsibility for seeing that contractors comply with race-conscious procurement policies as described by mandatory clauses in each contract.

Such clauses forbid discriminatory hiring practices and require the contractor to undertake affirmative action to recruit employees without regard to race, color, religion, sex, or national origin. An exemption is granted to religious entities, which are permitted to consider employment of individuals of a particular religion to perform work connected with carrying on the entity's activities. In addition contractors and subcontractors with contracts in excess of fifty thousand dollars and fifty or more employees are required to develop a written affirmative action program prior to the award of any contract.

The Walsh-Healey Public Contracts Act requires by contract clause that contractors for supplies in excess of ten thousand dollars pay the prevailing minimum wages, not work their employees in excess of the maximum daily or weekly hours, observe certain minimum wages for employment, and not permit performance of the contract under unsanitary, hazardous, or dangerous working conditions. The act provides for liquidated damages, contract termination, and a three-year debarment from government contracts for violations.

The Service Contract Act (SCA) of 1965 covers all service contracts in excess of twenty-five hundred dollars, whether advertised or negotiated, and requires the contractor to pay wages not less than those determined by the secretary of labor to prevail in the area for the type of work; to provide certain fringe benefits, such as hospital care, or the equivalent payment; and to see the contract is not performed under unsanitary or unsafe conditions. The act exempts contracts for maintenance, calibration, or repairs of certain equipments.

Violations of the act may result in debarment from government contracts, contract termination, and withholding of contract funds. Under this act the contractor bears the responsibility for classifying unlisted positions so that there is a reasonable relationship, in terms of skill level, between the unlisted classification and the classifications listed in the wage determination.

The Davis-Bacon Act (DBA) was enacted to provide for payment of prevailing minimum wages for the county in which the work site is situated, as determined by the secretary of labor, to laborers under construction contracts in excess of two thousand dollars. Provisions similar to those under the Walsh-Healey Act are provided in the event of violations. Davis-Bacon Act wage-determination decisions published by the Department of Labor are requirements mandated by the statute that are incorporated in contracts by operation of law. Lack of knowledge of these requirements does not extinguish a contractor's obligation to comply with the law. The same extension applies to the Service Contract Act. The act further requires prime contractors and subcontractors to maintain and submit appropriate certified payrolls and related records and to disburse proper overtime payments to the employees for all time in excess of an eight-hour day.

THE BUY AMERICAN ACT

The Buy American Act restricts the purchase of supplies that are not domestic end products for use within the United States. A foreign end product may be purchased if the contracting officer determines that the price of the lowest domestic offer is unreasonable or if another exception applies as discussed below; and the act requires, with some exceptions, the use of only domestic construction materials in contracts for construction in the United States.

The restrictions in the Buy American Act are not applicable in acquisitions subject to certain trade agreements. In these acquisitions end products and construction materials from certain countries receive nondiscriminatory treatment in evaluation with domestic offers. Generally the dollar value of the acquisition determines which of the trade agreements applies. There are exceptions to the applicability of the trade agreements. The Buy American Act also applies to small business set-asides. A manufactured product of a small business concern is a U.S-made end product but is not a domestic end product unless it meets the component test in item number 2 in the list below. The test to determine the country of origin for an end product under the Buy American Act is different from the test to determine the country of origin for an end product under the trade agreements, or the criteria for the report on end products manufactured outside the United States. The Buy American Act uses a two-part test to define a "domestic end product"—manufacture in the United States and a formula based on cost of domestic components. In particular,

1. the article must be manufactured in the United States; and
2. the cost of domestic components must exceed 50 percent of the cost of all the components.

Under the trade agreements the test to determine country of origin is "substantial transformation" (i.e., transforming an article into a new and different article of commerce, with a name, character, or use distinct from the original article). For the reporting requirement the only criterion is whether the place of manufacture of an end product is in the United States or outside the United States, without regard to the origin of the components. When one of the following exceptions applies, the contracting officer may acquire a foreign end product without regard to the restrictions of the Buy American Act.

The head of the government agency may make a determination that domestic preference would be inconsistent with the public interest. This exception applies when an executive agency has an agreement with a foreign government that provides a blanket exception to the Buy American Act.

A non-availability determination can be made based on the list of articles found at FAR 25.104 (e.g., bauxite, bananas, cocoa beans, chrome ore, industrial diamonds, nickel, tungsten, cobalt); the fact that the article is not mined, produced, or manufactured in the United Sates in sufficient and reasonably available commercial quantities of a satisfactory quality; or that the non-availability of an article is likely to affect future acquisitions. Written determinations are not necessary if the acquisition was conducted through full and open competition, the acquisition was synopsized publicly, and no offer for a domestic end product was received.

Lastly, the contacting officer may make the determination that the cost of a domestic end product would be unreasonable or may decide to purchase foreign end products specifically for commissary resale.

FREE TRADE AGREEMENTS

The Trade Agreements Act provides the authority for the president to waive the Buy American Act and other national discriminatory provisions for eligible end products from countries that have signed a reciprocating international trade agreement with the United States or that meet certain other criteria, such as being a least developed country. The president has delegated this waiver authority to the U.S. Trade Representative (USTR). In acquisitions covered by the World Trade Organization Government Procurement Act (WTO GPA), free trade agreements, or the Israeli Trade Act, the USTR has waived the Buy American Act and other discriminatory provisions for eligible products. Offers of eligible products receive equal consideration with domestic offers. The contracting officer determines the origin of services by the country in which the firm providing the services or products is established. The value of an acquisition is a determining factor in the applicability of trade agreements. Most of these dollar thresholds are subject to revision by the USTR approximately every two years. The various thresholds are found in the FAR. The Free Trade Agreements Act does not apply to

1. acquisitions set-aside for small businesses;
2. acquisitions of arms, ammunition, or war materials or purchases indispensable for national security or for national defense purposes;
3. acquisitions of end products for resale;
4. acquisitions from Federal Prison Industries, Inc. and nonprofit agencies employing people who are blind or severely disabled; and
5. other acquisitions not using full and open competition, if authorized, when the limitation of competition would preclude use of the procedures of this subpart or justified-sole source acquisitions are involved.

The above policies and procedures apply to acquisitions that are covered under any of the following laws and agreements:

1. The World Trade Organization Government Procurement Agreement (WTO GPA) as approved by Congress in the Uruguay Round Agreements Act (Public Law 103-465)
2. Free trade agreements consisting of the (a) North American Free Trade Agreement Implementation Act of 1993 (19 U.S.C. 3301); (b) United States–Chile Free Trade Agreement Implementation Act (Public Law 108-77); (c) United States–Singapore Free Trade Agreement Implementation Act (Public Law 108-78); (d) United States–Australia Free Trade Agreement Implementation Act (Public Law 108-286); (e) United States–Morocco Free Trade Agreement Implementation Act (Public Law 108-302); (f) Dominican Republic–Central America–United States Free Trade Agreement Implementation Act (Pub. L. 109-53); and (g) United States–Bahrain Free Trade Agreement Implementation Act (Public Law 109-169)
3. The least-developed-country designation made by the USTR and pursuant to the Trade Agreements Act (19 U.S.C. 2511[b][4]) in acquisitions covered by the WTO GPA

4. The Caribbean Basin Trade Initiative determination by the USTR that end products or construction material granted duty-free entry from countries designated as beneficiaries under the Caribbean Basin Economic Recovery Act (19 U.S.C. 2701, et seq.), with the exception of Panama, must be treated as eligible products in acquisitions covered by the WTO GPA

5. United States–Israel Free Trade Area Implementation Act of 1985 (19 U.S.C. 2112)

6. The Agreement on Trade in Civil Aircraft, a USTR waiver of the Buy American Act for signatories of the Agreement on Trade in Civil Aircraft as implemented in the Trade Agreements Act of 1979 (19 U.S.C. 2513)

In the World Trade Organization Government Procurement Agreement and each respective free trade agreement, there is a U.S. schedule that lists services that are excluded from that agreement in acquisitions by the United States. Acquisitions of products or services in the areas of automatic data processing, telecommunications, teleprocessing, telecommunications network management, R&D, transportation, nonnuclear ship repair, and DoD and NASA operations are just some excluded from coverage by the U.S. schedule of the WTO GPA or a free trade agreement.

ENVIRONMENT, ENERGY, AND WATER EFFICIENCY

It is government policy to support acquisition procedures for ensuring a drug-free workplace and for protecting and improving the quality of the environment by controlling pollution, managing energy and water use in government facilities efficiently, and using renewable energy and renewable energy technologies.

Among other ends, the government attempts to acquire energy- and water-efficient products and services that use renewable energy technology and use energy-savings performance contracts, when life-cycle cost effective, to obtain energy-efficient technologies at government facilities without capital expense to the U.S. Treasury. The Farm Security and Rural Investment Act of 2002 as amended by the Energy Policy Act of 2005 requires that a procurement preference be afforded bio-based products within items designated by the secretary of agriculture (see www.usda.gov/biopreferred). This program applies to acquisitions by federal agencies using federal funds for procurement as well as government contractors that use USDA-designated items in the performance of government contracts.

The reader is directed to FAR Part 23 for details of programs, both individual and related, regarding the environment, energy, and water efficiency, including purchasing products that contain recovered materials or services. Recovered materials means waste materials and by-products recovered or diverted from solid waste. There you will find that the applicability of regulations in the above-referenced subject areas are excepted from contracts

1. at or below the simplified acquisition threshold (under one hundred thousand dollars) other than contracts awarded to individuals;
2. for the acquisition of commercial items;
3. performed outside the United States and its outlying areas or in such places as Iraq;
4. by law enforcement agencies in connection with undercover operations; or
5. where application would be inconsistent with the international obligations of the United States or with the laws and regulations of a foreign country.

PRACTICING BUSINESS TIPS

A small business under the U.S. procurement system is able to receive preferential treatment through specific entitlements for program set-asides, depending on its self-certified status in the 8(a) small business development, SDB, WOSB, SDVOSB, and HUBZone programs.

If you overreach in your self-certification be assured that the government will find out when it verifies your company's small business certification or a competitor challenges your status. Do not allow your firm to be embarrassed and be subject to financial or even criminal penalties. Coordinate closely with the Small Business Administration nearest you.

Remember that the director of SADBU makes recommendations to the contracting activities of the agency as to whether a particular procurement should be awarded as a small business set-aside, an 8(a) award, a HUBZone set-aside, or an SDVOSB set-aside.

There are plenty of other entities available to help a small business owner. The Procurement Technical Assistance Centers (PTAC) located in most states (www.dla.mil/db/procurem.htm) provide services at minimal or no costs.

However, you should first do your homework by reading and developing your preliminary business plan.

It is in the interest of each small business to pay a courtesy call to its nearest Small Business Administration office, your SBA procurement center representative, and agency small business specialists. Such branches and satellite offices exist to assist small firms to obtain government contracts, team with a major contractor as a subcontractor, or be included in a joint venture.

The acquisition laws and regulations push large firms to meet or exceed small business utilization objectives. Incentives are created within contracts for such large firms to develop associations with small business as mentors or because the small business has essential technology, skills, or labor that promote contract performance.

If you are working on putting together a teaming arrangement, protect your flank by insisting that the agreement be placed in writing. After all the government will want to read a copy of the teaming agreement in the prime contractor's proposal. There is nothing more demoralizing to a small business than being "paraded" as a partner with the prime contractor only to never do the work. If the prime contractor plans to market the teaming arrangement, one must insist that it be set in writing and that the relationship be tied down with money.

One must not forget that your contract carries with it wage requirements found in the statement of work and in the contract's incorporated clauses. One must be sensitive to the applicable minimum wage determination. Ensure compliance to avoid serious consequences.

Finally, be attentive to any clauses referenced in the solicitation or your contract that require environmental actions, energy efficient products, pollution control, or water efficiency compliance; these could surprise you and lead to unexpected performance costs.

CHAPTER 8

Show Me the Estimate
Government Accounting

Staying in business is all about wise cost estimating as reflected in your bids or cost proposals. You need to master a few basic relationships, which are presented below, to understand the basic elements of a cost or pricing system that is compliant with the Federal Acquisition Regulations and government audits.

It is great to win a government contract, but you must adjust the variables of the following equation to meet the specification requirements and still wind up with a profit for your shareholders:

EQUATION E-1:
$$\text{Proposed total price or submitted bid} = \text{Proposed total costs} + \text{profit/fee} + \text{facilities capital cost of money}$$

Lowball your submitted bid and you may be able to snag a project. However, you may never complete it. The worse feeling is to be working on a project that, at the end of the tunnel, is unprofitable. You cannot take on too many such projects before you go bankrupt. Moreover, the government will rate your performance unsatisfactory, thus creating a hurdle every time you attempt to obtain another government contract. So competent project estimating is a must. It will help avoid audit problems and possible accusations of fraud owing to incurred or proposed cost manipulations. How you do it, whether using Excel spreadsheets, manual spreadsheets, or commercial pricing software systems, and who your teammates, subcontractors, and suppliers are, are your trade secrets.

Whether you are a project engineer or the proposal cost estimator, you should finish reading this chapter before you purchase an expensive proposal-pricing software program. This chapter lays out the minimum cost-estimating pricing techniques a successful firm must understand before it prepares a bid or cost proposal for submission in response to an IFB, RFQ, or RFP, whether it is done with a tablet of spreadsheets or a cost-estimating program.

Spreadsheets or commercial government contract pricing software should incorporate the principles described herein and allow a user to quickly and easily summarize data, make changes, and fix errors to cost proposals. You must have total confidence that the data you have entered is calculating accurately with the selected pricing tool. When changes are needed, you should be able to make them quickly. The proposal-pricing software or spreadsheets should allow you to easily correct an error, and the pricing system then should be able to automatically reflect the change throughout the entire proposal . . . in just seconds.

That said, regardless of the type of contract, at some point the bid or your initial cost proposal you present to the government for a project will be compared with others by the contracting officer. In many cases the contracting officer may have prepared an independent government cost estimate for use in the conduct of price or cost analysis and subsequent negotiations. By law, the final price offered is to be considered in every contract action.

COST OR PRICING DATA

As a general rule contracting officers are not to obtain more information than is necessary for determining the reasonableness of the contract price or evaluating for cost realism. Contracting officers are in fact prohibited from obtaining cost or pricing data if an exception to the cost or pricing data submission requirement applies under the Truth in Negotiations Act and pertinent regulations. (The exceptions are listed in figure 8-1.)

Minor modifications made to existing commercial items that are of a type not customarily available in the commercial marketplace made to meet federal requirements that do not significantly alter the nongovernmental function or essential physical characteristics of an item or component or change purpose of the process fall within the exception subparagraph 3 of figure 8-1.

FIGURE 8-1. Exceptions to Cost or Pricing Data

1. Based upon adequate competition, if two or more responsible offerors, competing Independently, submit priced offers that satisfy the government
2. Set by law or regulations in the form of periodic rulings, reviews, or similar actions of a governmental body, which are sufficient to set price
3. When a commercial item that meets the commercial item definition in FAR 2.101 or any modification that does not change the item from a commercial item to a noncommercial item is being acquired
4. By waiver of the requirement in exceptional call by the head of the contracting activity, without power of delegation (e.g., sufficiant cost or pricing data furnished on previous buys)

The commercial item exception above does not apply to noncommercial modifications of a commercial item that are expected to cost in the aggregate more than five hundred thousand dollars or 5 percent of the total price of the contract, whichever is greater. This policy applies only to contracts, delivery orders, and tasking orders funded by the DoD, NASA, and Coast Guard or contract actions awarded or placed on behalf of the DoD, NASA, and Coast Guard by an official of the U.S. government outside of these agencies. The threshold in this rule applies to an instant contract action, not to the total value of all contract actions, and as applicable to subcontractors, the threshold applies to the value of the subcontract, not the value of the prime contract.

Otherwise, without any exception, statutes require the submission and certification of cost or pricing data in conjunction with the pricing of negotiated prime contracts and subcontracts exceeding $650,000. This threshold is subject to adjustment every five years. However, if a fair and reasonable price cannot be determined, the head of the contracting activity may require cost or pricing data for procurements below the cost or pricing data threshold, but not for those below the simplified acquisition threshold ($100,000).

The statutory requirements also apply to modifications of negotiated or advertised contracts or subcontracts, contract terminations, and final pricing actions under price redeterminable contracts that exceed $650,000. Contract and subcontract changes or modifications are subject to the requirements if the total amount of both the related increases and decreases exceeds $650,000, even though the net change in price is less than $650,000.

As an offeror you need not wonder if cost-pricing data will be required as part of your initial proposal. The contracting officer has the obligation of making that determination and plainly placing such a notice and the requisite form required for submission within the solicitation with the instructions to prospective offerors.

Requirements for Submission

There are many situations in which cost or pricing data must be obtained. Contracting officers may (1) require proposal submission of cost or pricing data in the format prescribed in FAR 15.408, Table 15-2, (2) specify an alternate format, or (3) permit submission in the contractor's own format. Some contractors still elect to use SF 1411, Contract Pricing Proposal Cover Sheet, even though it has been eliminated from the FAR and declared obsolete by the GSA.

There is a clear distinction between submitting cost or pricing data and merely making available books, records, and other documents without identification. The requirement for submission of cost or pricing data is met when all accurate cost or pricing data reasonably available to the offeror have been submitted, either actually or by specific identification, to the contracting officer or an authorized representative.

As subsequent information comes into an offeror's possession, it should be submitted promptly to the contracting officer in a manner that clearly shows how the information relates to the price proposal. The requirement for submission of cost or pricing data continues up to the time of agreement on price, or an earlier date agreed upon between the parties. Figure 8-2 depicts the various cost or pricing documents involved in the process of negotiations where discussions of cost take place and lead to an agreed final revised cost and profit.

Cost or pricing data require certification (see fig. 8-2). Such data are factual, not judgmental, and are verifiable. While they do not indicate the accuracy of the prospective contractor's judgment about future estimated costs or projections, they do include data forming the basis for that judgment. Cost or pricing data are more than historical accounting data. They are all the facts that can be reasonably expected to contribute to the soundness of estimates of future costs and to the validity of determinations of costs already incurred.

Such data also include factors such as vendor quotations, nonrecurring costs, information on changes in production methods and in production or purchasing volume, data supporting projections of business prospects and objectives and related operations costs, unit-cost trends such as those associated with labor efficiency, make-or-buy decisions, estimated resources to attain business goals, and information on management decisions that could have a significant bearing on costs. Cost or pricing data may include parametric estimates of elements of cost or price from the appropriate validated calibrated parametric models.

The Truth in Negotiations Act, particularly its cost or pricing data provisions, has generated much controversy and litigation. If after award cost or pricing data are found to be inaccurate, incomplete, or noncurrent as of the date of final agreement on price given on the contractor's or subcontractor's Certificate of Current Cost or Pricing Data, the government is entitled to a price adjustment, including profit or fee, of any significant amount by which the price was increased because of defective data. This entitlement is ensured by the Price Reduction for Defective Cost or Pricing Data clauses in the contract. Price reductions have been upheld for failure to disclose lower vendor quotes even though the contract price was not negotiated on the basis of those quotes.

By submitting your proposal you grant the contracting officer the right to examine records that formed the basis for the cost or pricing proposal. That examination can take place at any time before award. It may include those books, records, documents, and other types of factual information (regardless of form or whether this information is specifically referenced or included

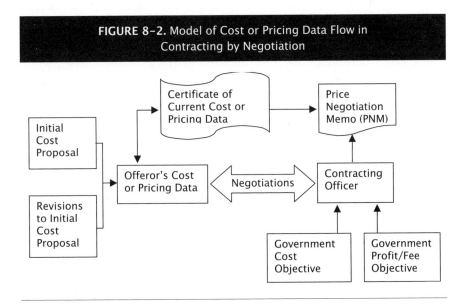

FIGURE 8-2. Model of Cost or Pricing Data Flow in Contracting by Negotiation

in the proposal as the basis of pricing) that will permit an adequate evaluation of the proposed price. Information other than cost or pricing data may be submitted in the offeror's own format unless the contracting officer decides that use of a specific format is essential and the format has been described in the solicitation.

Therefore you will find yourself submitting fixed prices in response to IFBs that are just numerical figures for which only your firm has the worksheets of how that cumulative bid entered in the bid's schedule of prices was derived. On such occasions the government has no right to receive your estimate's built-out work papers. On the other hand, you may in many cases be required to submit a cost proposal to an RFP, RFQ, grant for a BAA, or SBIR justifying each cost element that comprises your contract price.

To be prudent you need to discipline your team to maintain neat records of how a bid or a project cost proposal was "built" along with all its backup, including your suppliers' and subcontractors' submissions (e-mail quotes, oral quotes, contingent subcontracts) to your estimating office. The accounting method used in estimating proposed costs should be the same as the method used to accumulate incurred costs. The proposal and supporting data should be provided in electronic format since it conserves resources and is more efficient to both parties.

Figure 8-3 is an extract from the Model Cost Proposal prepared by the Defense Contract Audit Agency (go to www.dcaa.mil, then "Publications" in the menu, then click on "Information for Contractors"). The cost proposal reflects the price for the hypothetical production of fifty prototypes of a new heavy-duty shock absorber for the armored personnel carrier, which was designed previously on another Army contract over a period of seven months.

The contractor and government should work to resolve any software compatibility issues well before a cost proposal's date and time for submission of an offer. Testing should include practicing trial runs of a proposal sample to ensure compatibility. An electronically received late cost proposal carries the high risk of being discarded unless fault can be placed on the government's information network infrastructure.

The estimated cost (total cost objective) of $938,241 plus profit (total profit objective) of $93,824 could be used for submission in a sealed bid of $1,032,065 without any requirement for a breakdown of the estimated cost elements that make up the bid. In this case the Model Cost Proposal is in

FIGURE 8-3. Model Cost Proposal: Advanced Tank Technologies

Proposal Submitted in Response to RFP DAAH01-02-R-0001

ELEMENT OF COST	AMOUNT ($)	REFERENCE
Engineering Labor	$ 452,151	Schedule 1
Manufacturing Labor	26,412	Schedule 1
Direct Labor Overhead @ 56.7%	271,345	Schedule 3
Material	113,175	Schedule 2
Material Handling Overhead @ 5%	5,659	Schedule 5
Subtotal	868,742	
General and administrative @ 8%	69,499	Schedule 4
Estimated Cost	938,241	
Profit @ 10%	93,824	
Total Price	$1,032,065	

Information for Contractors, DCAAP 7641.90,
Figure 3-5-1, (Jan. 2005) pp.3-1

response to an RFP and reflects the offeror's breakdown of cost elements. At the end of discussions with the government the submitted total price would be revised as agreed by the two parties. The offeror would then submit a final revision to its initial proposal, reflecting the contract price to be awarded. Since the offeror in response to the RFP has provided cost or pricing data, it may be asked to certify such data, including all supporting schedules, unless an exception (see fig. 8-1) exists. You can view Reference Schedules 1–5 of the Model Cost Proposal at http://www.dcaa.mil/dcaap7641.90.pdf.

Price Analysis

If the solicitation is an IFB and the contract vehicle is to be a Firm-Fixed-Price Contract, the government will perform "price analysis" to determine the lowest offer based on price and any other price-related factors only. It will basically compare your contract price bid with that of the other offerors and examine the past cost procurement history perhaps using some cost-estimating formulas.

Price analysis is the process of examining and evaluating a proposed price without evaluating its separate cost elements and proposed profit to determine if it is fair and reasonable. Some of the techniques that the government uses to evaluate your offered price, in order of preference, with techniques 1 and 2 preferred, are

1. comparison of proposed prices received in response to the solicitation;
2. comparison of previously proposed prices and previous government and commercial contract prices with current proposed prices for the same or similar items;
3. use of parametric estimating methods/application of rough yard-sticks (such as dollars per pound or per horsepower, or other unit) to highlight significant inconsistencies that warrant additional pricing inquiry;
4. comparisons with competitive published price lists, published market prices of commodities, similar indexes, and discount or rebate arrangements;
5. comparison of proposed prices with independent government cost estimates;
6. comparisons of proposed prices with prices obtained through market research for the same or similar items; and
7. analysis of pricing information provided by the very offeror.

Cost Analysis

If the solicitation is an RFP and the contract vehicle could be a Firm-Fixed-Price, Cost-Reimbursement, or Indefinite-Delivery Contract, the government will probably ask for cost or pricing information so that it can conduct a "cost analysis" of your submitted cost proposal to assess whether or not the costs are reasonable and realistic.

Unless award is done on initial proposals, without any discussions, the contracting officer will want to enter discussions with your firm. Keep in mind that the contracting officer has in mind his own cost objective and profit objective for the contract. At the end of negotiations be assured that the contracting officer will ask you to certify your cost and pricing data as being accurate, complete, and current as of the date the negotiated final contract price is agreed upon.

Cost analysis is the review and evaluation by the government of separate cost elements and profit in an offeror's or contractor's proposal, using the cost and pricing data provided by the offeror. The contracting officer applies his or her judgment to this data to determine how well the proposed costs represent what the cost of the contract should be, assuming reasonable economy and efficiency. The government may use a variety of techniques in performing its analysis, some of which are listed below:

- Verifying cost or pricing data and evaluation of cost elements
- Evaluating the effect of the offeror's current practices on future costs
- Comparing costs proposed by the offeror for individual cost elements with actual costs previously incurred by the same offeror, previous cost estimates from the offeror on the same or similar items, other cost estimates received in response to the government's request for proposals, independent government cost estimates by technical personnel, and forecasts for planned expenditures
- Verifying that the offeror's cost submissions are in accordance with the contract cost principles and procedures in the FAR and according to cost accounting standards (certain factors must be considered in determining whether a projected or incurred cost may go into the cost objective bin as illustrated in figure 8-4)

To go into the final cost objective bin as allowable, a cost first must be reasonable in its nature and amount as measured by an amount that does not exceed that which would be incurred by a prudent person conducting a competitive business. Then a cost, to be allowable further, must not be precluded by the contract cost principles described by FAR Part 31 (e.g., bad debts, donations, entertainment costs, lobbying, marketing, goodwill, alcoholic beverages, etc.). Finally, a cost must be allocable to a government contract if it is incurred specifically for that contract, benefits both the contract and other work, and can be distributed to them in reasonable proportion to the benefits received or is necessary to the overall operation of the business though a direct relationship to any particular cost objective cannot be drawn.

Review the proposal to determine whether any cost or pricing data necessary to make the contractor's proposal accurate, complete, and current

---

FIGURE 8-4. Factors for Allowability of a Cost

- Reasonableness
- Standards promulgated by the Cost Accounting Standards Board, if applicable, otherwise generally accepted accounting principles and contract cost principles (FAR Part 31)
- Terms of the contract
- Allocability

have not been submitted or identified in writing by the contractor. Analyze the results of any make-or-buy program reviews in evaluating subcontractor costs. Keep in mind that the government will expect an offeror to have conducted and provided proof of its own cost analysis on each of its intended subcontractors' submitted cost proposals.

The steps discussed above for determining allowability as depicted in figure 8-4 will be repeated in Cost-Reimbursement Contracts each time a payment request is submitted to justify payment for services performed and supplies delivered or installed.

Cost Realism Analysis (Cost–Reimbursement Contracts)

Cost realism analysis is the process of independently reviewing and evaluating specific elements of each offeror's proposed cost estimate to determine whether the estimated cost elements are realistic for the work to be performed, reflect a clear understanding of the requirements, and are consistent with the unique methods of performance and materials described in the offeror's technical proposal. The goal of the analysis is to ensure that the proposed costs are not significantly understated.

Such an analysis normally is required to be performed on Cost-Reimbursement Contracts to determine the probable cost of performance for each trader. The probable cost is determined by adjusting each offeror's proposed cost, and fee when appropriate, to reflect any additions or reductions in cost elements to realistic levels based on the results of the cost realism analysis.

The probable cost should reflect the government's best estimate of the cost of any contract that is most likely to result from the offeror's proposal. This cost is then used for purposes of the evaluation to determine best value.

This type of analysis may be used also in performance risk assessments and for responsibility determinations. In such cases, the offered prices are not adjusted as a result of such analysis. Therefore, regardless of whether one (government or trader) is involved with an IFB, RFQ, or RFP, pricing and costing are involved.

Cost Estimating

Step 1 (Creating the Work Breakdown Structure)
The first step in cost estimating is to determine the pieces of work that need to be performed to fulfill the stated and implied requirements of a project.

This should lead you to develop a contract work breakdown structure (WBS) comprised of a number of levels, from the product itself, to major elements, to elements subordinate to elements subordinate to level 3 (L3) major elements. In so doing one winds up with building blocks of hardware, software, data, or services, which when put together and completed deliver a completed project by a realistic completion date, the subject of the contract. Such methodology minimizes the risk of forgetting or omitting to estimate a parcel of work described in the specification or performance work statement.

To this end one may want to follow Military Handbook 881A, which addresses mandatory procedures for those programs subject to DoD Instruction 5000.2, "Operation of the Defense Acquisition System," and provides guidance to industry in extending contract WBSs. This handbook is approved for use by all departments and agencies of the DoD. It is for guidance only and should not be included as a contract requirement. The handbook is an update to Military Handbook 881, Work Breakdown Structures for Defense Matériel Items. Military Handbook 881A is based on the cooperative efforts of the military services with assistance from industrial associations. Changes to the handbook specifically address the advances in technology, modification of the acquisition process, and incorporation of new developmental concepts and approaches.

In essence you are performing during the bidding phase the duties of a wise project/systems engineer by developing a product-oriented family tree composed of hardware, services, and data coupled with estimated times for completion of each block of work, which during the development and production of a defense matériel or software item completely defines the project under contract. It also serves as the specification tree that structures the performance parameters of the systems or components to be developed. It subdivides the system into its component elements and identifies the performance algorithms of the systems elements. Use of the WBS such as shown in figure 8-5 for cost estimating facilitates program and contract management. The WBS aids the program office in planning, coordinating, controlling, and estimating the various program activities.

For example, if compliance is required to implement a Personal Identity Verification System for employees and subcontractor personnel who require routine access to a federal-controlled facility or federal-controlled information system, the cost of such implementation should be included in the cost estimating for that contract. The WBS provides a common framework for

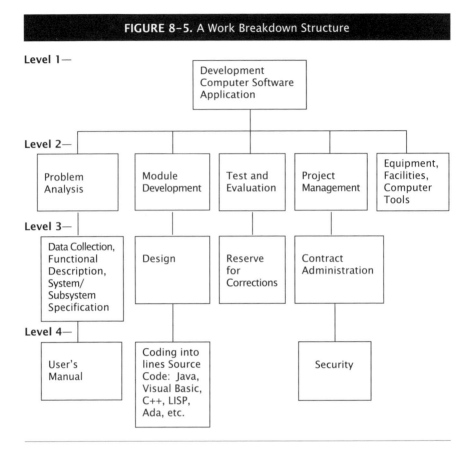

FIGURE 8-5. A Work Breakdown Structure

tracking the estimated and actual costs during the performance of each contract. The data from the various program contracts support the DoD program manager in evaluating contractor performance, preparing budgets, and preparing program life-cycle costs.

Cost information collected by the WBS element can be used not only for pricing and negotiating contracts but also for contract changes and follow-on procurement. The DoD is accumulating a growing cost database of similar work breakdown structure elements from different programs. This historical cost data can be used for regression analysis, developing learning curves, and with other techniques for estimating the cost requirements for like elements of new programs. Actual cost data collected by the DoD on each program when compared to the original estimates can identify trends and establish the validity of estimating techniques. Contractors will similarly benefit from such databases. The cost history accumulated on their programs can assist them in estimating and bidding future contracts and in budgeting new work.

The contract WBSs are not intended to be standardized. Any logical product-oriented WBS developed by the contractor will meet DoD needs for reasonably consistent program data. The structure was never intended to be enforced verbatim; rather, it was to be used as a starting point for continued tailoring. Rigidity of task procedures and superfluity of data are issues to be resolved before solicitation release, or at least before contract award.

After contract award, at each point in the acquisition cycle, the contract WBS provides the framework for delineating the areas of responsibility regarding funding, schedules, and future contract performance, as well as for integrating total program requirements.

Estimating costs for any project can be daunting. A storm can damage a building during construction or a supplier can go out of business. Sometimes a project is more complicated than originally thought and takes longer to finish. Time is often the biggest reason projects go over budget.

Estimators talk to project managers to learn what they want to build or manufacture. Estimators read bid proposals and look at blueprints and drawings. They may research costs for projects such as dams, highways, bridges, factories, transportation equipment, computer chips, or software. Estimators research how long it takes workers to finish tasks. They determine pay levels, calculate that cost, and add amounts for insurance and taxes. They check prices for supplies, equipment, and parts. They estimate delays that can arise from bad weather or late deliveries. Cost estimators make a complete list of all the tasks, time, supplies, equipment, parts, and labor the project will need.

Step 2 (Conduct of Estimating Costs by Element)
Once you have each building box of the WBS in a logical tree that comprises the project, the second step in cost estimating is to estimate the cost of the work horizontally or vertically in each box to determine the bare costs of providing the required services or product over various periods or stages of time. The base period could be one year plus three or more years, which the government may exercise because of the yearly priced options proposed.

Each block of the contract work breakdown structure was developed so that all costs (both direct and indirect) of producing the products or providing the services can be identified in a final cost objective for the proposed contract. A cost objective (see Equation E-2 below) means a function, contract, or other work unit for which cost data are desired and for which provision is made to accumulate and measure the cost of processes, products, and jobs. A computer program can assist you in this effort.

Do not forget that the government is also automated and should be expected to have its technical-estimating staff using its own published software-pricing programs, proprietary or off-the-shelf trade-related (e.g., ProPricer from Executive Business Services, Inc., or the Means Costworks Building Construction Cost Data CD-ROM 2008, 11th edition, to develop its independent estimate of the cost objective.

In some instances it is an accepted practice, especially in construction IDIQ fixed-price contracts, for the government to provide its estimated costs for multiple line items, for example, for a line item package of work such as installation of a particular size or type of water boiler. The solicitation there ask offerors to bid on that work line item or a group of such work packages by multiplying the pre-priced packages by a percentage coefficient that could vary, as an example, from 0.90 or less to 1.25 or greater. If the bidder's coefficient is under 1.0, then the bidder is underbidding the government estimate. If the bidder's coefficient is over 1.0, then the bidder is bidding a price higher than the government baseline estimate.

Regardless of your estimating resource system, to accomplish this step one needs to be able to define the basic cost elements that will comprise your total costs for the contract being sought. The costs of a contract primarily comprise direct costs and the contract's allocable share of indirect costs as defined by the following relationships:

EQUATION E-2:
$$\text{total costs} = \text{allowable direct costs} + \text{allocable indirect cost}$$

EQUATION E-3:
$$\text{indirect rate} = \text{net allowable expenses} \div \text{allocation base}$$

EQUATION E-4:
$$\text{allocable indirect costs} = \text{allowable contract expenses} \times \text{indirect rate}$$

In government contracting the elements in the above equations are fairly well established. Accordingly, accounting for costs in government contracts involves the classification of costs as either direct or indirect costs so that they can be placed in the correct "pool" for accumulation. In doing accounting one must never forget to apply the factors to first establish that a cost is allowable as described in figure 8-4.

DIRECT COST ELEMENT

The first elements to consider are direct costs. "Direct costs" means any costs that are identified specifically with a particular final cost objective. They are not limited to items that are incorporated in the end product as material or labor. Costs identified specifically with a contract, including subcontract costs, are direct costs of that contract. All costs identified specifically with other final cost objectives of the contractor are direct costs of those cost objectives. A discussion of the components of direct costs follows.

A. Materials and Subcontracts

Provide a consolidated priced summary of individual material quantities included in the various tasks, orders, or contract line items being proposed and the basis for the pricing (vendor quotes, invoice prices, etc.). Include raw materials, parts, components, assemblies, and services to be produced or performed by others. For all items proposed, identify the item, and show the source, quantity and price. Conduct price analysis of all subcontractor proposals. Conduct cost analysis for all subcontracts when cost or pricing data are submitted by the subcontractor.

B. Direct Labor

Provide a time-phased (monthly or quarterly) breakdown of labor hours, rates, and cost by appropriate category, and furnish bases for estimates. Ensure the labor rates, including the fringe benefits, meet or exceed the minimums required by the solicitation's project wage determination to be incorporated as part of the awarded contract subject to the Service Contract Act or Davis-Bacon Act. For example, if you are preparing a bid or cost proposal for a construction project, the specified rates found in the solicitation's Department of Labor wage determination under the Davis-Bacon Act must be used.

If the classification of a craftsman to be employed cannot be found in the wage decision, then you must query and provide the requisite information to the contracting officer so that the job can be classified and a wage rate determination issued. The same process applies to service contracts in which the Service Contract Act requires minimum wages to be paid in accordance with the applicable wage rate decision for the locality where the work site is situated. If you are using a software program to estimate your direct or indirect labor costs, then you will have to input at least the minimum wage rates for laborers, secretaries, draftsmen, software engineers, construction trade craftsmen, computer programmers, and so on required by the applicable wage determination specifically incorporated as part of the statement of work and specification, aside from the critical estimated hours projected for each category of employee.

The Department of Labor Wage Determinations Online (WDOL) Web site, at www.wdol.gov, is the source for federal contracting agencies to obtain general wage determinations issued by the Department of Labor for service contracts subject to the McNamara-O'Hara Service Contract Act and for construction contracts subject to the Davis-Bacon Act.

The contracting officer will be able to check the WDOL Web site to find the applicable wage determination for a contract action subject to the Service Contract Act or Davis-Bacon Act. If this database does not contain the applicable wage determination the contracting officer must use the e98 process to request an SCA wage determination, which is a Department of Labor–approved electronic application whereby the contracting officer submits pertinent information to the Department of Labor and requests a wage determination directly from the Wage and Hour Division of the department.

With regard to Davis-Bacon Act requirement, if the WDOL database does not contain the applicable wage determination for a contract action, the contracting officer must request a wage determination by submitting SF-308, Request for Wage Determination and Response to Request, to the Department of Labor for the specific construction project.

INDIRECT COST ELEMENT

Indicate in your proposal how you have computed and applied your indirect costs, including cost breakdowns. Trends and budgetary data are shown to provide the basis of how the indirect cost rates are computed and for evaluating the reasonableness of proposed costs. Appropriate explanations are provided to support the indirect rates applied.

And "indirect cost" is any cost not directly identified with a single final cost objective but identified with two or more final cost objectives or with at least one intermediate cost objective. The indirect cost rate is the percentage or dollar factor that expresses the ratio of allowable indirect expense incurred in a given period to direct labor cost, manufacturing cost, or another appropriate allocation base for the same period.

Indirect costs are costs that support the main business of the company but cannot be directly assigned to individual projects or contracts. These costs should be accumulated by logical cost groupings or pools with due consideration of the reasons for incurring the costs. Manufacturing overhead, engineering overhead, and general and administrative costs, including B&P costs, commonly are grouped separately. It also is common to find separate overhead pools for material, tooling, selling, and offsite labor. Overhead pools may be set up on a companywide basis or may be accumulated by division, plant, department, or cost center. Practical considerations should govern the number and composition of the groupings.

OTHER DIRECT COSTS

List all other costs not otherwise included in the categories described above (e.g., special tooling, travel, computer and consultant services, preservation, packaging and packing, spoilage and rework, and federal excise tax on finished articles) and provide your bases for pricing.

DIRECT COST OF ROYALTIES

Contractors generally pay royalties by virtue of license agreements. If royalties exceed fifteen hundred dollars, you must provide all the associated information (identification of licensor, date of license agreement, patent serial numbers, brief description, percentage or dollar rate of royalty per unit, unit price of contract item, number of units, and total dollar amount of royalties). Many license agreements are not clear on their applicability to the items on the contract being negotiated. Unless the license agreement explicitly describes the item or items it covers, it is not adequate cost or pricing data.

FACILITIES CAPITAL COST OF MONEY

The purpose of the facilities capital cost of money element is to encourage contractor investment in new facilities and thereby reduce dependence on government-furnished facilities. "Facilities capital cost of money" means cost of money as an element of the cost of facilities capital. When you elect to claim facilities capital cost of money as an allowable cost, you must submit Form CASB-CMF and show the calculation of the proposed amount. The base for this element is net book value of facilities capital as determined on DD Form 1861, Contract Facilities Capital and Cost of Money. Several factors influence the weight you assign for facilities capital. New, productivity-enhancing facilities would be assigned a weight at the top of the sixteen-to-twenty range, and older, slower, more general purpose facilities would be assigned at the lower part of the range (between sixteen and eighteen).

Step 3 (Including Overhead)

The third step of cost estimating is to add to the bare costs determined in step 2 your firm's allocable indirect or overhead costs (calculated using Equations E-3 and E-4). This step should allow you to have the costs fully covered. You now have calculated the proposed total costs (Equation E-2). Remember that in government contracting we do not add any contingency costs for possible material price increases or new increased wage rates since the government maintains a number of clauses (suspension, termination, stop work, changes in specifications, value engineering) allowing cost in the contract to be adjusted up or down, more commonly known as "equitable adjustments" to the contract price.

Step 4 (Adding Profit)

In this final step one needs to assess the amount of profit to be added to the sum of steps 1 to 3. Without including profit a firm will eventually go out of business because there is no other way to reward investors for their investment. Except for sealed bids and government awards made only on initial proposals without any communications, contractors generally will have the opportunity to negotiate profit with the contracting officer. Profit is determined on a percentage of total costs:

EQUATION E-5:
$$\text{profit} \quad = \quad \text{percentage} \ x \ \text{total costs}$$

Contracting officers typically use the unstructured profit-analysis factors or a structured approach (weighted guidelines) for establishing a profit objective. The weighted guidelines method focuses on four profit factors: performance risk, contract type, facilities capital employed, and cost efficiency. The contracting officer then assigns values within a designated range to each of the mentioned profit factors. Then the value multiplied by the cost base results in the profit objective.

Keep in mind as a trader with the government that contracting officers have their hands tied because an officer cannot negotiate a price or fee that exceeds the following statutory limits on selected types of work or services and type of contracts imposed by Congress as shown in figure 8-6.

For experimental, developmental, or research work performed under a Cost-Plus-Fixed-Fee Contract, the fee should not exceed 15 percent of the contract's estimated cost, excluding fee. For architect-engineer services for public works or utilities, on the other hand, the contract price or the estimated cost and fee for production and delivery of designs, plans, drawings, and specifications must not exceed 6 percent of the estimated cost of construction of the public work or utility, excluding fees. For other Cost-Plus-Fixed-Fee Contracts the fee must not exceed 10 percent of the contract's estimated cost, excluding fee.

There are no statutory limitations on the profit submitted in a sealed bid since by definition no negotiations take place. When a sealed bid is submitted the amount of the profit in comparison to the direct and indirect costs of performance are not able to be dissected since such costs are buried inside the overall contract price itself. There is no requirement to reveal what the markup to cost is owing to overhead or profit.

The burden of performance and all the cost risk rests on the shoulders of the trader rather than the government. On the other side of the coin, a trader stands to reap significant profits if he can complete the project efficiently and

FIGURE 8-6. Statutory Limits for Profit and/or Fees	
PROFIT AND/OR FEES	STATUTORY LIMIT (PERCENT OF ESTIMATED COST)
Experimental, Research, or Development Work with cost-plus-fixed-fee contracts	15%
All other cost-plus-fixed-fee contracts	10%
Architect-Engineering Services for Public Works types of contracts	6%

well before the time agreed on. The trick for a trader in sealed bidding is to bid high enough to win the project, covering your full costs and still making a respectable profit.

When the price negotiation is not based on cost analysis, contracting officers are not required to analyze profit. However, when the price negotiation is based on cost analysis, and especially for sole source contracts, contracting officers in agencies that have a structured approach must use it to analyze profit. When not using a structured approach contracting officers should consider the series of profit-analysis factors shown in figure 8-7 in addition to any additional factors which foster achievement of program objectives.

PRACTICING BUSINESS TIPS

The federal cost-accounting and estimating relationships shown in figure 8-8 should be applied in a disciplined and ethical manner supported by books of accounts on each cost element.

I have seen traders leaving the bid room, the negotiation room, the debriefing room, or the phone the apparent winner but unhappy. Too much money was left on the table. The bid or cost proposal could have been substantially higher and still have been the lowest offered. When the bidder's estimating is off, the winning trader will have to work hard, with little or no reward, to meet costs on the project and shield his or her reputation. Do not let that happen to your firm.

Use both the unstructured and structured approaches to establish profit objectives. Cost estimating and profit setting goes to the core of government contracting. You will use it to win contracts and thereafter use it time and again during contract performance and administration to price modifica-

---

FIGURE 8-7. Profit–Analysis Factors (Unstructured Method)

- Contractor effort based upon complexity of the work and resources required
- Contract cost risk as a result of the contract type contemplated
- Extent of support to federal socioeconomic programs
- Contribution to capital investments for efficient and economical performance on prospective contract end item and follow-on contracts
- Cost control and other past accomplishments
- Recognition of independent development on contract item without government assistance

FIGURE 8-8. Summary of Accounting Equations

EQUATION E-1:

proposed total price or = total costs + profit/fee +
submitted bid   facilities cost of capital

EQUATION E-2:

total costs = allowable direct costs +
       allocable indirect costs

EQUATION E-3:

indirect rate = net allowable expenses ÷
       allocation base

EQUATION E-4:

allocable indirect costs = allowable direct costs x
       indirect rate

EQUATION E-5:

profit = percentage x total costs

---

tions for changes and delays to the contract work (equitable adjustments) regardless of the type of contract. Remember that an estimated or incurred cost must be found allowable, especially in Cost-Reimbursement Contracts. Apply the factors discussed above. You need your engineers to work with the cost estimators hand in glove. Do not forget your subcontractors and suppliers; they too have a stake in your success. You need the software tools to support them. Keep them all sharp.

As a prime contractor, subcontractor, or supplier your business development folks will bring you plenty of contracting opportunities to dissect. But it will be your diligent efforts in cost estimating in support of your B&P efforts that will pay off and grow your firm without having to jeopardize its economic health. It is better to have bid high and not won the contract but be able to sleep well. Uncle Sam will give you the opportunity again tomorrow.

At the risk of being redundant in closing this chapter, remember that even after you have won the government contract, cost estimating will still be used in responding to requests for a proposal owing to changes to the scheduled contract work. Cost analysis will be exercised by the government finance office to assess whether each of your payment requests present cost elements that meet the test of allowability on all Cost-Reimbursement Contracts.

Study and refer frequently to the cost principles and procedures for the pricing of contracts, subcontracts, and modifications to contracts and subcontracts contained in FAR Part 31 whenever cost analysis is performed and the determination, negotiation, or allowance of any costs is on the table when required by contract clause for an equitable adjustment to the contract.

Do not allow cost estimating, cost analysis, and incurred-cost invoicing to be your Achilles' heel.

CHAPTER 9

Protecting the Business Jewels
Intellectual Property

J ust as you may own real property and personal property, you own personal or corporate intellectual property—your "business jewels." The term "intellectual property" describes the ownership of the product of creative ideas or creative means of expression. It includes rights that are formally recognized and created by patents or copyrights, as well as rights that are recognized or created less formally, as by asserting and maintaining ownership of unregistered trade secret information.

Firms attempt to leverage their intellectual property in order to create an income stream—royalties—from those who use this property. The vaults are being opened and corporate managers realize that just keeping the technology as a trade secret does not create full value. The users of intellectual property are called licensees, and its owners are the licensors. The royalties flowing from the licenses generate a valuable but depreciable income stream. This trend has been accelerating because as globalization intensifies, it behooves U.S. firms to reap the income from the patents and copyrighted works that is not being maximized.

Hence we see the creation in many firms (for profit and nonprofit) of separate departments or the hiring of third parties to manage a firm's technology and its legal transfer within the United States and outside its borders. Firms are tapping into their dormant proprietary information by proactively marketing the technology underpinning their intellectual property products or processes or creativity, which they developed either privately or with public funds.

For a small business or start-up, an ideal, positive atmosphere currently exists because of Uncle Sam's policy, regardless of whether the business is small or large, of allowing a firm to keep ownership of the technology, processes, and procedures it developed while performing a government contract.

The U.S. Treasury is paying the contractor first and foremost to meet a bona fide government requirement, but it also provides the environment for the firm to commercialize the product developed or to sell the product developed for the government to another country. In return all the U.S. government asks is that it be granted a worldwide, irrevocable, nonexclusive, and fully paid-up license to be able to use the technology for its own purposes.

The problem one always faces when dealing with intellectual property is identifying vital company technologies, discoveries, processes, product applications, and business methods that are not in the public domain and have not been developed by any third party as work for hire or paid for development by the federal government. In essence such intellectual property possesses the characteristics of a product being developed exclusively at private or internal expense. In many instances, the researcher or systems analyst, including management, fails to appreciate the significance of an employee's work in the overall field until that work is released, purposely or unintentionally, to the public. In such a case, it becomes part of the public domain and no longer warrants any protection. Coupled with this issue is the matter of placing a price tag on the value of the intellectual property itself. Valuation of a firm's technology is an important discipline, requiring a firm to seek out professional assistance.

Moreover, a company's database of past engineering and production drawings, including manufacturing, shop line drawings, jig drawings, and testing modules on paper, mylar, CDs, or stored on tape or disk, are a treasure trove, reflecting the configuration management control effort over the years for various product lines. Firms that "track" all changes to their product designs, to include parts, processes, text fixtures, software, and/or assembly drawings, are said to exercise configuration management. These drawings reflect numerous hours of effort and represent the good will of the firm in the form of proprietary technical data, also known as trade secrets.

Deciding how to protect these "jewels" leads to a multiple set of protection processes (see fig. 9-1) that have, as the technology matures and the protection process fits the creative property, coexisted in the United States for many years. These processes can be applied independently or concurrently, depending on the technology or art, with legal effectiveness. Foreign countries have similar processes that vary in terms and enforceability.

For example, a process for making synthetic rubber may initially start off as a trade secret under state law. The resultant chemical composition and process leading to a commercial product eventually matures, along with associated software, to a U.S. awarded utility patent with a fanciful marketing mark or name protected by a U.S. registered trademark, both issued by the U.S. Patent and Trademark Office (USPTO). One should not forget that the USPTO registers many types of trademarks—sound, configuration, color, motion, and scent. The related computer object code itself, controlling the curing process for synthetic rubber, in addition to having a fanciful mark and being patentable, may carry a copyright notice confirming that it has been registered with the U.S. Copyright Office of the Library of Congress. The federal copyrighting of computer software is particularly a recent and

FIGURE 9-1. U.S. Intellectual Property Protection Systems

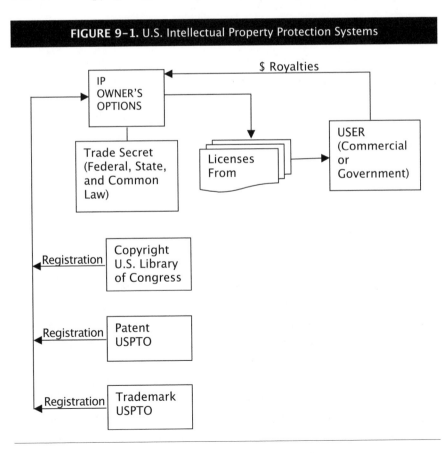

important trend to such firms as Microsoft, Yahoo, Apple, Boeing, and others large and small.

What intellectual property should or can be disclosed and to whom requires compliance with the export control laws and those related to security, especially in the current era of international terrorism, multinational business competition, and industrial espionage. Therefore, both the prime defense contractor and its subcontractors have to be sensitive to not only the protection of one's intellectual property but also to complying with the export licensing requirements for the disclosure of the intellectual property outside the United States. Software, technical data and various equipment, defense or commercial items, representing U.S. technology advances or in some cases capable of being used for weaponry, may not be transferred to designated third parties.

Export control is executed under the Arms Export Control Act, which enforces the International Traffic in Arms Regulations, with its related Munitions List issued by the Department of State (go to www.pmddtc.state.gov and click on "Elements of Defense Trade Control, Laws and Regulations").

Export licenses also may be required under the Export Administration Act and its related Export Administration Regulations (EAR) from the Department of Commerce (go to www.export.gov and click on "Regulations and Licenses"). The EAR may require a license to a country if your item is listed on the Commerce Control List (CCL), and the Country Chart in Part 738 of the EAR lets you know if a license is required to that country. Virtually all Export Control Classification Numbers (ECCN) on the CCL are covered by the Country Chart in Part 738 of the EAR. These ECCNs state the specific countries that require a license or refer you to a self-contained section. A license requirement may be based on the end use or end user in a transaction, primarily for proliferation reasons.

A license is required for exports to embargoed destinations, such as Cuba. Part 746 of the EAR describes all the licensing requirements, license review policies, and license exceptions that apply to such destinations. If your transaction involves one of these countries, you should first look at this part. This part also describes controls that may be maintained under the EAR to implement UN sanctions.

In addition to the export control regulations for intellectual property, the security and disclosure requirements required by contract with the DoD or another federal agency are applied under the umbrella of the Defense Security Agency and verified by the Defense Logistics Agency.

The intellectual property protection and disclosure issues lead one into business decisions of important consequences and a variety of costs depending on the combination of protection methods—all of which require trade-offs. Before the freight forwarder drives up to your ramp and picks up the documents and any equipment for overseas shipment, ensure that your firm has the requisite issued export license and that your firm is compliant with all security requirements. Violations can carry both civil and criminal penalties.

PATENTS

Patent Basics

Federal statutes permitting patenting and copyrighting have been enacted under the authority of Article 1, Section 8 of the U.S. Constitution, which states, "The Congress shall have power . . . to promote the Progress of Science and useful Arts, securing for limited Times to Authors and Inventors the exclusive Right to their respective Writing and Discoveries." Thus the Constitution provides an incentive to inventors and in turn to industry because it grants to an inventor the privilege of preventing others from making, using, or selling his or her creation without permission—in essence a legal monopoly for a limited, nonrenewable time. USPTO under the Department of Commerce is the federal agency that administers the U.S. patent and trademark systems.

This exclusive right held by a patentee extends throughout the United States and its territories and possessions. To obtain protection in foreign countries the inventor must make application in each country in which one seeks protection unless an international application is filed under the International Patent Cooperation Union, of which the United States is a member. The length of the grant varies from country to country.

This statutory monopoly granted by the U.S. government also provides the opportunity to enforce that control by court action against infringers. All U.S. utility patents based on applications filed on June 8, 1995, and thereafter have a term of twenty years from the filing date of the patent application or its earliest parent application if such an application is a continuation, divisional, or continuation-in-part application. Design-type patents grant a term of fourteen years (go to www.uspto.gov).

Patents are granted on new and useful processes, machines, manufacture or composition of matter, business methods, computer hardware/software systems fulfilling a practical application, or an improvement to one of the above. Patents are granted for distinct and new varieties of plants, bacteria, and animals, such as a genetically engineered mouse designed to be susceptible to breast cancer for use in cancer research. Micro-organisms produced by genetic engineering are not excluded from patent protection. As long as the discovery is the product of human ingenuity, intervention, and research, the patentability of the subject matter is feasible in as much as the patent laws are given wide scope. The intent is to grant human ingenuity liberal encouragement.

A useless device, printed matter, or an improvement to an existing device that is obvious to a person skilled in the art will not warrant issue of a patent. Applications for patents on devices that provide action and amusement but add little to the world's storehouse of knowledge are consistently rejected. The laws of nature, physical phenomena, and abstract ideas have been held to be not patentable. Einstein could not have patented his celebrated law that energy is proportional to the mass of an object multiplied by the square of its acceleration, nor could Newton have patented the law of gravity. To be patented an invention must be more than an idea. The formula definition of an invention is:

$$\text{Invention} = \text{Conception} + \text{Reduction to Practice}$$

Patents are applied for by humans, not nonprofit entities such as universities or for-profit business organizations, whether or not they are self-employed. The hope of the individual or group of inventors is to become a patentee, to be issued a legal monopoly of their invention—a product, chemical composition, medical instrument, biological composition, software-controlled process, design, or business method.

Conception is the mental part of the inventive act, but it must be capable of proof through drawings and complete disclosure to another person. Conception is more than a vague idea of how to solve a problem. The means themselves and their interaction also must be comprehended. The inventor must form a definite and permanent idea of the complete and operable invention to establish conception. A conception of an invention, though evidenced by disclosure, drawings, and even a model, is not a complete invention under patent laws, confers no rights on an inventor, and has no effect on a subsequently granted patent to another, unless the inventor follows it with reasonable diligence by some other act, such as actual reduction to practice or filing an application for patent.

An inventor may consider and adopt ideas, suggestions, and materials derived from many sources—a suggestion from an employee, a hired consultant, or a friend—even if the adopted material proves to be the key that unlocks the problem, as long as the inventor maintains intellectual domination of the work of making the invention, down to the small details, including successful testing.

Lastly, there must be a contemporaneous recognition and appreciation of the invention for there to be conception. An accidental and unappreciated duplication of an invention does not defeat the patent right of someone who, though later in time, was the first to recognize that which constitutes the inventive subject matter. An inventor does not need to know that the invention will work for there to be complete conception.

The reduction to practice of the concept may be an actual reduction or a constructive reduction to practice via the filing of a patent application. Proof of constructive reduction to practice requires sufficient disclosure under the "how to use" and "how to make" requirements of current law. Proof of actual reduction to practice requires showing that the apparatus actually existed and worked for its intended purpose. However, there are some devices so simple that a mere construction of them is all that is necessary to constitute reduction to practice. The invention must be recognized and appreciated for a reduction to practice to occur. The same evidence sufficient for a constructive reduction of practice may be insufficient to establish an actual reduction to practice, which requires a showing of the invention in a physical or tangible form that show every element of the count. Every element of the invention is numbered (counted) sequentially and explained in the specification of a patent application. For an actual reduction to practice, the invention must have been sufficiently tested to demonstrate that it will work for its intended purpose in its contemplated applications, but it need not be in a commercially satisfactory stage of development. Tests must be conducted under circumstances sufficient to demonstrate workability of each element by use of a prototype, model, simulation, or other demonstrative means. Proof of the invention's utility for its intended purpose does not require proof of its flawlessness; it is only necessary to show that the invention is able to perform its intended purpose beyond a probability of failure.

If an inventor is working for a business entity or a nonprofit entity, it is common practice that the inventor, concurrently with the filed patent application, assigns the patent to be issued to the employer. Once the patent has been issued and is assigned by the inventor, the successor title holder (generally the employer) becomes known as the patentee.

Since in most cases the invention is made on company time and the employee has signed an assignment agreement of intellectual property upon his employment, it is common to read the names of several inventors who worked as a team on an issued patent and then to see that it was assigned to a firm such as IBM, Apple, DuPont, General Dynamics, Google, or Boeing, their employer and assignee.

Real Case in Point

The well-dressed, nervous lady was sitting in the waiting room of my law firm clutching a shopping bag. She had an appointment with me to discuss her invention. Like most people she considered her invention "top secret" and was scared that someone would steal it from her, even the lawyer from whom she was seeking counsel. (Names, locations, and other identifying facts have been altered in light of the attorney-client privilege; the only facts revealed are those that are public.)

By the end of our office conference I had her described invention written in rough draft form, conventionally witnessed and notarized in our law offices as evidence of the conception. In essence I had prepared the disclosure document for her invention ready for filing with the USPTO. (For some reason many people have been told to mail a disclosure to oneself or another person by certified mail and that this action protects them. I believe this popular practice is not credible.)

The filing of a disclosure document under the USPTO rules was the more credible form of evidence, costing nothing more than a short preparation time and some minimal filing fee. At the USPTO it is date-stamped and numbered. The office maintains disclosure documents for two years as evidence of the dates of conception of inventions. Such a paper disclosing an invention and signed by the inventor or inventors may be forwarded to the USPTO by the inventor, by the owner of the inventions, or by the attorney or agent of the inventors or owner.

The disclosure document will be retained for two years and then be destroyed unless it is referred to in a separate letter in a related application filed within those two years. The document is available to the public when a patent application that refers to it issues as a patent. The document is not a patent application, and the date of receipt in the USPTO will not become the effective filing date of any patent application subsequently filed. Like patent applications, however, these documents will be kept in confidence by the USPTO. You will receive a stamped dated copy of the disclosure document showing its serial number and confirming that your invention description has been filed and that you have some two years to file your patent, after which time your recorded disclosure document will be discarded. Keep in mind that this filing does not give you a first-to-file patent right but is an indication of your diligence and can be helpful to resolve disputes between filed patent applications as to dates of original conceptions.

An even better but more expensive approach would be to have the inventor file a provisional application. This permits an inventor to file a specification and drawings without preparing any claims or providing an oath. The filing date of a provisional application is the date on which the specification and any required drawings were received in the USPTO. The applicant has one year to file a completed application; otherwise it shall be considered abandoned, and such an application cannot be revived. The provisional application does not receive a right of priority over any other application or the benefit of an earlier filing date in the United States. Our client decided it was more cost effective to file the disclosure document previously discussed.

After I had taken the time (some thirty minutes) to dissuade my client from the notion of attorney theft, she confided in me that she was a school nurse. She then proceeded to pull two dolls that she had designed and constructed out of her shopping bag, plus a teacher's manual she had written and illustrated. The statutory utility the invention was to fulfill was that of teaching health education in kindergarten through eighth grade.

First I had to decide in my own mind whether or not the doll items were patentable subject matter that would meet the criteria of the law. The dolls were made by a human. Their designs were unique in terms of their dress, shape, sex, color, and cloth. After fifteen minutes of discussion I told the client that she had met the "usefulness" hurdle. (The Patent Act of 1793 was authored by Thomas Jefferson, who defined statutory subject matter as "any new and useful art, machine, manufacture, or composition of matter, or any new useful improvement thereof." The act embodied Jefferson's philosophy that "ingenuity should receive a liberal encouragement.")

The nurse's conception involved patentable subject matter (an article of manufacture by a human) fulfilling an important use. She had met in my opinion the useful invention or utility requirements of our laws. Now the dolls had to meet the remaining novelty and non-obviousness statutorily mandated conditions for patentability.

The requisite novelty was associated with the two separately shaped dolls used to teach students health as related to the differences in body parts, family reproduction, and other human health subjects at appropriate grade levels. To be found novel an invention must not have been known or used by others in this country or patented or described in a printed publication in this or a foreign country before the invention by the applicant. Loss of right to patent would also occur if the invention was patented or described in a printed publication in this or a foreign country or in public use or on sale in his country more than one year prior to the date of the application for patent in the United States.

In determining novelty with respect to design patents, the standard recognized by the courts is whether the prior art shows an article of "substantially the same appearance" to an ordinary observer. Absolute identity of design is not required to support a rejection for lack of novelty.

According to my client dolls like hers were nowhere to be found in the current art (trade magazines, existing patent, teachers manuals, health/nurse teaching guides, or magazines). I advised her to take more time and conduct a more thorough search of the printed art with emphasis on the USPTO patent database (which includes national and international patents), which can be accessed at www.uspto.gov or by visiting the nearest public library that offers computerized searching of patents and trademarks or the USPTO Public Search Facility in Alexandria, Virginia. The Public Search Facility provides access to patent and trademark information from 1790 to the present in a variety of formats, including online, microfilm, and print. If her concept was encompassed in any texts on health and hygiene, in a school supply catalogue, or in an existing patent, in the United States or worldwide, then it would not be able to jump the novelty hurdle.

The last statutory requirement for patentability of the nurse's invention is the finding of non-obvious subject matter (see fig. 9-2). Finding non-obviousness is always the most difficult hurdle to jump. The non-obviousness test requires four factual inquiries as the background for determining obviousness.

FIGURE 9-2. The Factual Inquiries to Non-Obviousness

- Determining the scope and contents of the prior art
- Ascertaining the differences between the prior art and the claims at issue
- Resolving the level of ordinary skill in the pertinent art
- Evaluating evidence of secondary considerations such as unexpected results, commercial success, long-felt but unsolved needs, failure of others, copying of others, licensing, and skepticism of experts

The inquiries illustrated in figure 9-2 provide information that can serve only as indications of obviousness or non-obviousness. The standards on the issue of non-obviousness were tightened by the U.S. Supreme Court in 2007. The Court made it clear that patents were being issued on obvious inventions and it tightened the reins. The Court stated that if a person of ordinary skill, in the relevant subject area, would be able to fit the teaching of multiple patents together like pieces of a puzzle, then the patent is obvious.

Subsequently other court rulings have found that patents made of combinations of elements publicly available were obvious and have discarded a claimant's (patent owner's) demands of infringement. An idea centered on integrating different components was not novel. Thus the courts have tightened up the statutory requirements not only for non-obviousness but also for novelty.

With respect to the nurse's dolls this latter condition could not be fully assessed by the undersigned because of lack of facts and time. Moreover, I was not skilled in the art of making teaching dolls. However, I was amazed that no one had worked on such a concept or had commercialized such an inexpensive "doll design or apparatus" since it is well-known that a need for continuous, age-appropriate health education exists in the schools to fill the sensitive void caused by busy parents.

One must keep in mind that the USPTO confines its review of patentability to the statutory requirements of patent law discussed above and is guided by key Supreme Court decisions. Other executive agencies of the government, such as the Food and Drug Administration (FDA) and Federal Communications Commission, have the responsibility of ensuring conformance to standards established for the advertisement, use, safety, sale, or distribution of such products as drugs, SUVs, baby chairs, and devices that use portions of the frequency spectrum.

My client and I then came to the issue of whether or not she was blocked from filing a patent application, meaning that some statutory bar to the filing of an application had been triggered. When an invention has actually been reduced to practice and sold, offered for sale, or even publically published or made known to others (technical conference presentation, etc.) more than one year before filing of the application, a patent will be barred.

In her case I felt that the invention had been pretty well definitized but not advertised or offered for sale. So I recommended that she promptly proceed to prepare and file a patent application. The design was not complex. In essence reduction to practice had been achieved of a working set of dolls that would trigger the one-year clock for an "on sale" bar the instant she offered for sale or sold a set of these dolls at the next annual New Jersey state teacher's convention in Atlantic City.

By they time my client departed we had discussed which type of patent application she needed. The choices were a utility patent, design patent, or both. A utility patent protects the way the article is used and works, while a design patent protects the way an article looks.

The ornamental appearance of an article includes its shape/configuration or surface ornamentation. It is not uncommon to find design patents for pistols, toys, phones, autos, pots, irons, and chairs. Recently even computer-generated icons, such as full-screen displays and individual icons, two-dimensional images that alone are surface ornamentation, have been considered statutory subject matter eligible for design patent protection.

Both design and utility patents may be obtained on an article if invention resides in both its utility and ornamental appearance. While utility and design patents afford legally separate protection, the utility and ornamentality of an article is not easily separable. Invention is a blend of function and ornamental design. Articles of manufacture typically possess both functional and ornamental characteristics. The other remaining type of patent, the plant patent, did not fit the subject matter of my client's invention. I recommended that she concurrently file both utility and design patent applications for the dolls.

My client and I discussed that the specification, along with its drawings of the utility patent application, must include a written description of the invention or discovery and of the manner and process of making and using the same. Such a description is required to be in full, clear, concise, and exact terms so as to enable any person skilled in the art or science to which the invention or discovery pertains, or which it is most nearly connected, to make and use it.

The specification must also set forth the precise invention for which a patent is solicited, in such a manner as to distinguish it from other inventions and from what is old. It must describe completely a specific embodiment of the process, machine, manufacture, composition of matter, or improvement invented, and it must explain the mode of operation or principle whenever applicable. The best mode contemplated by the inventor of carrying out his or her invention must be set forth. The utility patent application comprises generally the sequenced elements in figure 9-3.

Although it is not the case in this instance, as the nurse was a private inventor, when federal-sponsored research or development has been the basis of an invention, the specification would include a statement similar to the one that follows, revised appropriately: "The U.S. Government has a paid-up license in this invention and the right in limited circumstances to require the patent owner to license others on reasonable terms as provided by the terms of [Contract No. xxx or Grant No. xxx] awarded by [agency]."

Lastly my client and I had a discussion related to claims. The specification of a patent concludes with one or more claims (independent or dependent) numbered consecutively in arabic numbers, particularly and distinctly claiming the subject matter that the applicant considers the invention or discovery.

FIGURE 9-3. Elements of a U.S. Patent Application

1. Specification
   a. Title of invention
   b. Cross-reference to any related applications
   c. Statement regarding federally sponsored research or development
   d. Background of invention
      i. Field of the invention (see patent classification definitions)
      ii. Description of related art, including references
      iii. Problems previously existent in the prior art
2. Summary of invention
   a. Directed toward the nature and gist of the invention
   b. Advantages of the invention
   c. How it solves the prior art problems
      i. Brief description of several views of the drawings
      ii. Detailed description of the preferred embodiment
      iii. Claims
3. Abstract of the disclosure
4. Drawings
5. Oath and fee

The claims are derived and crafted from the contents in the detailed description of the preferred embodiment found in the specification. More than one claim may be presented provided they differ substantially from one another and are not unduly multiplied. The least restrictive claim would be presented as the first claim, and all dependent claims should be grouped together with the claim or claims to which they refer to the extent practicable.

The dolls were unique in their body part movements and material, but they also reflected new, original, and ornamental designs for articles of manufacture. The design application would be easier because such an application comprises only one claim and a drawing that depicts the ornamental design of the product. Even black-and-white photographs are accepted under certain conditions in lieu of drawings. I cautioned my client that the design application, however, would receive the same scrutiny under the same criteria as a utility patent by the patent examiner, as the same rules apply.

Once granted a design application requires no maintenance fees to be paid periodically during the life of the patent to the USPTO as compared to a utility patent. The term of a design patent is only fourteen years from the date of grant in comparison to some twenty years for a utility patent from the date of filing.

My client left with a notarized, witnessed disclosure as proof of her date of conception and a pile of assigned homework to undertake if she wanted to attempt to file a patent with our coaching. Being an inventor is not easy. Numerous individuals come to my office for consultations on their inventions. They come happy and excited with ideas and little or no financial backing. Most do not follow through with our recommendations because they are unwilling to perform the detailed research and study required to perfect their specifications, much less draft the requisite sketches of working drawings, from which a competent lawyer licensed before the USPTO can draft a set of claims and a professional draftsman can create compliant drawings.

I also recommended that in addition to the draft patent applications, one seek protection by filing a copyright application through the U.S. Library of Congress Copyright Office with its registrar. There is an area of overlap between copyright and design patent statutes where the author/inventor can secure both a copyright and a design patent. In the above instance a copyright notice could be placed in both the design and utility patent application adjacent to copyright material contained therein. For example, "© 2007 Jane Doe" would be the legally sufficient notice. In addition I recommended that the teacher's handbook be filed concurrently with the registrar of copyrights when the patent was filed with the USPTO. My client understood that a patent protects one's conception and ideas, whereas copyrights serve the purpose of controlling the reproduction of a literary work such as, in this case, the computer software code, and in other cases such works as books, music, sculpture, comic characters, architectural and engineering drawings, dress designs, and dolls, whose unauthorized reproduction would create an irreparable loss to their authors.

I was glad that the nurse had walked into my office because to have kept the dolls as a trade secret would have prevented their use in the schools. We were not dealing with the secret formula for Coca-Cola, which can be kept in a vault while at the same time be distributed in a controlled manner to make the composition of the drink worldwide. Needless to say, my client's dolls were not high-tech products, but they were just as important to her as high-tech inventions are to the clients who invent them. Similar issues typically exist.

We first have the utility, novelty, and non-obviousness conditions to meet for patentability. Then we have reporting and ownership issues, particularly in government contracts as a function of funding (discussed below). What if the design and prototype were built or developed at private expense, wholly using private company overhead funds before a contract was awarded by the government? What about an improvement to a design with "mixed" money, public and private? What if the government wholly funds the project? Who owns the patents that arise from the contract work?

Privately Funded Inventions and Patents

If your firm (profit or nonprofit) has conducted its own funded research, then the technology to be offered is that described in your technical proposal to the government. It should be adequately identified in your proposal via your patent filings with their associated registration numbers. In such event your cost proposal or bid will include the one-time costs or overhead incurred that one hopes to recover in developed technology. Since the technology that is to be embedded in the product or system is necessary to meet the government's specifications, its cost, if reasonable, would be accepted for the obvious benefits it grants the government in terms of just delivery times. The government would have no rights to these patents, except for their one-time use in the performance of the contract unless the terms of the contract included such rights.

Frequently a trader identifies certain patents that the offeror deems essential to the performance of the technical proposal and to compliance with the government's specifications. These patents may be held by third parties who are unwilling to grant your firm licenses despite your willingness to pay fair royalties for their use. It could be that the royalties being requested are unreasonable. In such an event, if the government considers the use of these patents essential to the timely and efficient performance of your technical proposal, it will incorporate into your contract the Authorization and Consent clause, which will allow your firm to use the identified patents and not be held responsible as an infringer. Ask for such a clause to be inserted before bidding or before completing negotiations on a submitted initial proposal.

With such a clause in your contract, which of course can be passed down to your subcontractors, the government assumes liability for all infringement in the performance of the contract, provided the patent's invention

1. is embedded in the structure and composition of any article delivered and accepted by the government; or
2. is used in the machinery, tools, and methods, the use of which necessarily results from compliance by the contractor or subcontractor with government specifications or instructions given by the contracting officer directing the manner of performance.

Discoveries as By-products of Government-Funded Contract Work

As a general rule, the federal government has the right on a nonexclusive basis to use royalty-free those ideas, improvements, discoveries, and subject inventions crystallized during the performance of the federal contract that have a "close and umbilical relationship" to the work and research funded by the United States without further charge.

The contract and regulations define a subject invention as any invention or discovery, whether or not patentable, conceived or first actually reduced to practice in the course of or under the federal contract. Otherwise, the government, as any infringer, must pay the patent holder a reasonable royalty fee.

In essence, the government is granted a royalty-free, irrevocable, worldwide license. Having borne the expense of that effort the public is entitled to enjoy the fruits without further charge. Therefore one will look critically to examine the scope of the federal contract and as to when conception of the subject matter of the invention occurred. It had to occur during the performance period of the contract.

The license clause precludes the blanketing of a non-obvious "invention, improvement and discovery" conceived after the termination of the inventor's federal connection, even though that separate invention may have a close connection with the preceding government work. Keep in mind that the government pays for the exploration of a field and the acquisition of new knowledge. It is entitled to the crystallized ideas, improvements, and inventions emerging from the process of ongoing study, inquiry, and creation.

Figure 9-4 summarizes the patent license rights that may arise out of work during a federally funded project as a function of which entity—government or contractor—holds title (ownership) of the patent.

Patent Rights Retention Clauses

Through the years the government has accumulated numerous patents arising out of its own research laboratories, industry, nonprofit grants for medical research, space program, and contracts for weapons systems (see fig.

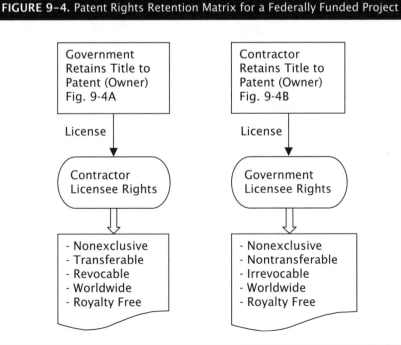

FIGURE 9-4. Patent Rights Retention Matrix for a Federally Funded Project

Government Retains Title to Patent (Owner) Fig. 9-4A

License

Contractor Licensee Rights

- Nonexclusive
- Transferable
- Revocable
- Worldwide
- Royalty Free

Contractor Retains Title to Patent (Owner) Fig. 9-4B

License

Government Licensee Rights

- Nonexclusive
- Nontransferable
- Irrevocable
- Worldwide
- Royalty Free

9-4). However, its agencies have moved away from being the titleholder, depository, and licensor to industry or individuals. Its policy is to transfer its archived technology from the laboratories to industry for commercialization by assignment or licensing agreement to include participating in cooperative research efforts. The government does not want to serve as the depository titleholder of those patents that evolve out of its funded R&D, engineering development programs, or grant programs (SBIR, STTR). It prefers to hold irrevocable, paid-up licenses.

To avoid conflicts and define each parties' intellectual property rights arising from the public contract or grant, the government places into its solicitations clauses for sealed bidding or acquisitions by negotiation that define what patent rights will flow to the government. This is even more important in the case where a mix of private and public funds will be used in the project. In this regard one needs to scrutinize the IFB and RFP, especially if your firm will be performing any type of research or development, product- or software-wise, for the inclusion of the proper patent rights clauses. The common threads in these clauses are the following:

1. The contractor may retain the entire right, title, and interest throughout the world to each invention.
2. The government shall have a nonexclusive, irrevocable, paid-up license to practice or have practiced for or on behalf of the United States the subject invention throughout the world.
3. The contractor discloses each subject invention to the federal agency within two months after the inventor discloses it to contractor personnel responsible for patents.
4. The contractor must file its initial patent application to which it elects to keep title within one year (or earlier) prior to the end of the statutory period wherein valid patent protection can be obtained in the United States after a publication, sale, or public use. International applications are to follow in a timely manner.
5. The contractor will convey to the federal agency, upon request, title to any invention the contractor does not elect title or fails to disclose or fails to file in other pertinent countries.
6. The government retains "march-in" rights in the event the titleholder does not exercise reasonable business activity to practice the invention, allowing the government with adequate notice to the titleholder

of the invention to regain title over the invention and award it to another firm that has a plan to develop the invention described in the patent.

7. In those cases in which title and ownership return to the United States, the contractor retains the minimum rights, which include a nonexclusive, royalty-paid-up license to the invention.

The above policies adopted by the federal government to promote commercialization are to allow a business to keep the patents as owners even if the inventions arise from a government-funded project. In return the government is granted a nonexclusive, worldwide license to use the patent for its own purposes. This leaves the private firm with the ownership rights, thus allowing the firm to license others worldwide. One may argue that this policy allows the government to subsidize U.S. industry to keep U.S. technology at the forefront. Why not?

TECHNICAL DATA AND COMPUTER SOFTWARE

The government has the need to procure warfighting and support systems such as ammunition, cannon, ships, planes, trucks, tanks, communication systems, and related spare parts. Uncle Sam needs their relevant data. Warfighting systems require developmental and engineering drawings as well as production-type drawings, including detail drawings for the jigs and fixtures required for manufacturing and testing. Written procedures are required to explain the what and how of tests along an assembly line necessary to ensure that the item being manufactured meets quality specifications. All such information is technical data, whereas financial, accounting, and cost or pricing information, including computer software, are excluded and considered to be just "data" or other categories of "data."

When the government pays for all of the above technical information, it expects to own the technical data package from the original developer. Hence it expects to receive "unlimited" data rights to all the drawings and written procedures so that the item can be reproduced by a new party under competitive bidding. Without this data the government would be dependent on a sole source, which could prevent the government from surging production concurrently with multiple sources to meet urgent war needs and would cause the government to pay higher prices for the products than would be paid under bidding procedures.

Where a contractor has at its own expense developed design specifications or manufacturing data pertaining to items, components, or processes that enable its competitors to produce a competitive item, the government need not be granted the unrestricted rights to use or disclose the data unless it elected to do so. One reason a contractor might elect to do so would be if it could receive compensation, such as by selling unrestricted rights to the government.

It is difficult to discuss this subject without establishing some definitions. "Technical data" means recorded information, regardless of form or character, of a scientific or technical nature, such as research and engineering writings and drawings, technical specifications, technical reports, and the documentation, instructions, or explanation for using computer software. The term "computer software" encompasses computer programs, source codes, source code listings, object codes listings, design details, algorithms, processes, flow charts, formulas, and related material that enable the software to be reproduced, recreated, or recompiled. The computer software itself (the code) is not considered technical data but falls in a separate category of data. Computer software does not include computer databases or computer software documentation, such as owner's manuals, user's manuals, installation instructions, and operating instructions.

Business plans, financial and management information, and customer lists, while considered proprietary, are not covered by the regulations as technical data. Moreover, data incidental to contract administration, such as financial and management information, is not technical data to which the trader is free to place restrictive markings before its submission to the contracting officer.

Today the rights in technical data between various contracting parties are associated with the definitions applied to five types of data rights licenses (see fig. 9-5). The regulations behind these types of licenses favor the interests of traders who develop new technologies or under performance specifications over the interests of traders who make items according to government-furnished design specifications. The regulations are also intended to provide favorable treatment to manufacturers of commercial items and software. For industry the regulations mean that developers can keep their proprietary technical data and computer software out of the reach of competitors who previously relied on free access to this information for the purpose of bidding on government contracts.

FIGURE 9–5. Types of License Rights in Technical Data

- Unlimited rights
- Limited rights
- Government-purpose rights
- Restricted rights
- Special rights

Federal agencies buy numerous commercial items and acquire the same commercial licenses for them as granted to the public. If for some reason such standard licenses are inconsistent with federal regulations or agency needs, then a special license can be negotiated. Modifications made with DoD funds to commercial software will not prevent an item from qualifying as commercial computer software as long as the modifications are of the kind offered on the commercial market.

The allocation of rights between the government and its contractors turns on whether the development of an item or process took place exclusively with federal funds, exclusively at private expense, or with mixed funds. The focus is on the development of an item or process, not on the development of the data describing the process. However, if the contract calls only for conceptual design, the government's rights would depend on the source of the funds used for creation of the data.

The Unlimited Rights License

The term "unlimited rights" means the right to use, release or disclose technical data in any manner and for any purpose, including the right to permit others to do so. When the government has "unlimited rights" in technical data, it may make the data freely available to anyone who wants it. Such rights accrue to the government when the government fully funds the development of the technical data. In such a case the government will ensure that the correct clause is incorporated in the contract.

The Limited Rights License

The term "limited rights" means the right to use, duplicate, or disclose technical data by or for the government with the express limitation that unless the contractor grants permission, the data will not be (1) disclosed outside the government, (2) used by the government for manufacture (or, if computer software is involved, for preparing similar software), or (3) used by anyone other than the government except in narrowly stated circumstances. Technical data developed with costs charged to the trader's indirect cost pools, costs not allocated to a government contract, or any combinations thereof are classified with the limited rights license.

Such technical data may be used by someone outside the government to perform emergency repair or overhaul, but the government must prohibit that person from further use or disclosure of the data. Concurrently, subject to compliance with U.S. export laws, the data (other than detailed manufacturing or process data) may be disclosed to a foreign government for information or evaluation purposes, subject to the same prohibition against further use or disclosure.

If the technical data to be delivered applies to a commercial item or if part of the proposal is that the trader will use its own previously developed and privately financed technical data to meet the government's requirements, then we are talking of not only the cost of this effort but also the need of the government to be granted a license to receive at least form, fit, and use data. This translates itself into the trader granting the government a limited rights license.

Since the government should have limited rights in technical data pertaining to items, components, processes, or computer software developed exclusively at private expense, a trader to protect his intellectual property must be able to apply three tests to establish its position to grant only limited rights to the technical data delivered to the government. These are:

1. Identify some item, component, or process set forth in the technical data delivered to the government that meets the private expense test as further described below.

2. Demonstrate that nongovernment funds were used to finance the development process where "to be developed" means that an item, component, or process exists and is workable. Thus the item or component must have been constructed or the process practiced. Workability is generally established when the item, component, or process has been analyzed or tested sufficiently to demonstrate to reasonable people skilled in the applicable art that there is a high probability that it will operate as intended. Whether, how much, and what type of analysis or testing is required to establish workability depends on the nature of the item, component, or process and the state of the

art. To be considered "developed," the item, component, or process need not be at the stage where it could be offered for sale or sold on the commercial market, nor must the item, component, or process actually be reduced to practice within the meaning of Title 35 of the U.S. Code.

3. There must be no direct government funding of the development work. "Developed exclusively at private expense," as used in connection with an item, component, or process, means that no part of the cost of development was paid for by the government and that the development was not required for the performance of a government contract or subcontract. One hundred percent of the development work must be at private expense to meet this test. Independent research and development (IR&D) and B&P costs, whether or not included in a formal independent research and development program, are considered to be at private expense. All other indirect costs of development are considered government-funded when development was required for the performance of a government contract or subcontract. Indirect costs are considered funded at private expense when development was not required for the performance of a government contract or subcontract.

Government Purpose Rights License

"Government purpose rights license" as a term is relatively new in origin. It was created as an intermediate class of rights that the government may acquire in technical data. In the event of "mixed" funding (government and trader have both invested funds in the development of the product or software), the government will generally accept a "government purpose rights" license for five years, after which its license converts to unlimited rights. Specifically this license fits when development was accomplished partially with costs charged to indirect cost pools and/or costs not allocated to a government contract and partially with costs charged directly to a government contract.

Such rights allow the government the right to use, duplicate, or disclose technical data in any manner, for government purposes only, and to permit others to do so for government purposes only. The term "government purposes" is defined to permit disclosure for "purposes of competitive procurement," but it specifically does not permit the government to allow others to use the data for commercial purposes.

Thus "government purpose rights license" gives the government greater rights in the data than when it obtains "limited rights" but fewer rights than when it obtains "unlimited rights." The government may disclose the data and software to a third party, provided the recipients sign nondisclosure agreements. Government purpose rights are normally limited to five years, although the time period is negotiable. At the end of the time period the government purpose rights revert to unlimited rights.

Restricted Rights License

Restricted rights are similar to limited rights except that these rights apply to computer software. For computer software developed fully at its own expense by a vendor, the government is generally granted restricted rights or, if it is commercial software, the same license rights granted to the vendor's commercial and retail customers.

Restricted rights software may be used by the government on only one computer at a time. The software may be copied for backup purposes and it may be transferred to another government agency as long as the transferring agency does not retain copies and notifies the software manufacturer of the transfer. The government may modify the software.

Finally, the government may allow its service contractors to use the software to perform analytical services on the software and to perform emergency repairs on related equipment. In such events the government has the obligation of notifying the licensor that a release or disclosure has occurred and for obtaining use and nondisclosure agreements from such third parties.

The Special License

If none of the above standard licensing forms fit, one should proceed to negotiate a "special" license with the contracting officer, regardless whether the item(s) is commercial, noncommercial, or noncommercial computer software. Noncommercial means an item(s) or process developed specifically by a trader for the government customer to meet military or agency needs.

Now that we have described the various possible licenses available to the government, our attention turns to the class of item(s) being acquired under the government contract as a function of which entity is responsible for its funding. Items or processes are divided into three categories: noncommercial items, noncommercial computer software, and commercial items. Figures 9-6, 9-7, and 9-8 summarize the license received by the government in sequence of categories.

Figure 9-6. Government License Rights in Technical Data (Noncommercial Items)

Funding Source	Government License
Developed exclusively with government funds	Unlimited rights
Developed exclusively at private expense	Limited rights (form, fit, use data); term as negotiated, normally no more than seven years)
Developed with mixed funding. License to government for five years, thereafter government has unlimited rights	Government-purpose rights

Figure 9-7. Government License Rights in Noncommercial Computer Software and Noncommercial Computer Software Documentation

Funding Source	Government License
Developed exclusively with government funds	Unlimited rights
Developed exclusively at private expense	Restricted rights
Developed with mixed funding. License to government for five years, thereafter government has unlimited rights	Government-purpose rights

Figure 9-8. Government License Rights in Technical Data (Commercial Items)

Funding Source	Government License
Commercial item developed exclusively at private expense	Same commercial license rights as granted to public
Modifications made with government funds to commercial software are of kind offered on commercial market, permits modified software to qualify as commercial computer software	Same commercial license rights as granted to public

ORDERING TECHNICAL DATA

The contract may specify a date when the technical data are to be delivered, or it may provide for the contracting officer to later designate a date for delivery. This flexibility allows the government to reduce storage requirements and save space, time, and money. Deferred ordering reduces the possibility that the government will receive and use data that are obsolete because of changes in the system.

When the contract does not specify a time for delivery of the data, the contracting officer may require the deferred delivery of data until two years after acceptance by the government of all items under the contract. However, the contract must specify which data are deferred delivery data. The contracting officer must give ample notice of the post-award delivery date to permit timely delivery.

Unlike deferred delivery, in which the contract specifies the data to be delivered but determination of the time of delivery is deferred, in "deferred ordering" the government defers the decision whether to actually order delivery of the data. The data may be ordered up to three years after acceptance of all items under the contract. When the data is ordered the parties negotiate the terms for compensation for converting the data into the prescribed form. Compensation would not include payment for the cost of generating the data because that cost was included.

COPYRIGHTS

A copyright is similar to a patent in that it is a statutory grant of a monopoly. In case of a copyright, it gives the author or the creator of an artistic work exclusive right to print, reprint, publish, copy, and sell the copyrighted work (see fig. 9-9). Copyright in a work created on or after January 1, 1978, subsists from its creation and endures with few exceptions for the life of the author or creator and seventy years after the author's death. As with patents the author may assign the work to an employer or may have created the work "for hire." In the case of works made for hire the copyright endures for a term of 95 years from the year of its first publication or a term of 120 years from the year of its first creation, whichever expires first (www.copyright. gov). An item must be the product of original creative authorship and it must be in the form of a "writing" to be eligible to be registered as a U.S. copyright. The latter means that it must be recorded in some tangible form. Copyright protection is also available for computer software.

FIGURE 9-9. What Matter Is Covered by Copyright?

Products of original, creative authorship
Product must be in written form
- Books
- Periodicals
- Lectures
- Dramatic and Musical Compositions
- Works of Art and their Reproductions
- Scientific (e.g., engineering, production) or plastic works
- Photographs, Prints
- Motion Pictures
- Computer Software
    Source Code and Object Codes
    Program's Structure, Logic, Sequence, Organization

Computer Software Works

The preferred form of protection for computer software has generally been by copyright in as much as the courts have held that a copyright protects not only the literal elements of a work, but also the organization of those elements. The structure and logic software are considered to be part of the expression of an idea and therefore eligible for copyright protection.

If the software's logic is found to be the underlying idea, it can not be protected by copyright; only the expression of an idea, not the idea itself, can be copyrighted. Hence copyright protection provides the incentive for programmers by protecting their most important product the structure and logic of the program.

The protection given by copyright laws emphasizes encouragement of continued production of literary and artistic works by enabling an author to protect his or her work from unauthorized reproduction. It should be noted that the protection afforded by a copyright does not give a monopoly to idea, but only to the expression of ideas. It is the words or the way in which the words are put together, or the way an idea is embodied, that is the copyright.

Government Policy on Copyrights

The government copyright policy has three objectives. First, it seeks to avoid copyright infringement and the liability it entails. Second, the rights of private creators or owners of copyrighted material are to be respected. Third, when the government pays for the development of copyrighted material it should be entitled to at least a royalty-free license for future use of that material.

Although a contractor may copyright data originated under a federal contract, the government retains a royalty-free, nonexclusive, and irrevocable license to reproduce, translate, publish, and use the data. When data are copyrighted by a third party the contractor must obtain permission from the owner before the data may be delivered to the government. The contractor should report to the government any notice or claim of copyright infringement.

Scientists and educators often wish to publish reports of research work performed under government contracts in books and journals. At times publishers will not accept such works because they want the exclusive publishing right for at least a limited time. Since the government recognizes that publication is vital to scientific advancement, it may wish to facilitate such publication and therefore may relinquish its own publication rights if it is asked and the proper clauses in the federal contract are included.

In such a case the contractor will be required to publish within a certain number of months specified in the contract schedule. This period may not exceed twenty-four months after the final settlement of the contract. The limitation on the contractor's rights to publish the data for sale lasts only as long as they are protected by copyright and are reasonably available to the public for purchase.

PROPOSAL PROTECTION

Before submitting an initial proposal to the government the trader needs to think through its intellectual property strategy as it pertains to technical data and computer software. Such data should be delivered with protective markings as described in chapter 4, and it should be noted that it is being disclosed on a "limited rights" versus "unlimited rights" basis. As warranted, copyright notices also must be placed. The government is thus placed on notice that it is dealing with sensitive corporate information, the loss of which or the unauthorized release of which could cause irreparable damage to the trader. The intentional release to interested outside parties by a government insider would be a violation of the U.S. Trade Secrets Act, which provides for criminal penalties and other sanctions. This act precludes the unauthorized disclosure of confidential information relating to processes, operations, styles of work, statistical data, and trade secrets.

Sometimes a trader attempts to exercise the Freedom of Information Act to obtain a copy of a competitor's submitted proposal. In anticipation of such activity that act provides an exemption to competitive proposals, prohibiting the government from releasing them. This prohibition does not apply if the competitive proposal that was submitted for evaluation with revisions resulting from negotiations is set forth or incorporated by references into a winning contract.

It is important in discussions to negotiate a fair allocation of both the technical data and software rights at the pre-award stage using the proper technical data license. If the government wants technical data or software to be delivered based on the statement of work in the proposed contract, the solicitation should have attached a series of DD Forms 1423-1, Contract Data Requirements Lists (which describe the data to be delivered, to whom it is to go, in what medium, and in how many copies). Individual DD Forms 1664, Data Item Descriptions, also should be attached to describe the format and content preparation instructions for the data product generated by the specific and discrete task requirement for data included in the contract.

Depending on the data rights licenses to be received by the government, one must take the necessary procedural steps to preserve a firm's technical data and software rights during contract performance. One of the key steps is to properly mark data being delivered for acceptance and payment, showing the retention of data rights and thus providing notice to the government. A vendor must methodically institutionalize the critical processes for marking technical data within a firm and delivering such data to the government with the requisite markings.

PRACTICING BUSINESS TIPS

One cannot overemphasize the importance of a company's brainpower. It is vital to cultivate, grow, and protect it. Clients who employ engineers are advised to tie their salaries and bonuses to the quality of the technical data they generate and number of patents and copyrights they have filed and assigned to the company. After all, what good are professional engineers if they are not creative? It is management's job to protect that intellectual property and to have it generate royalty income streams.

Once one realizes that the government contract provides your firm the vehicle for funding creativity and future growth, you are on your way. Not only do you get paid to perform satisfactorily for Uncle Sam, but generally you are allowed to keep title to that creativity in hopes that you can commercialize the product or data and to sell it to international customers, of course abiding within the disclosure rules for national security.

Your firm can design and manufacture for Uncle Sam a combat helmet global positioning system for soldiers and Marines. Later, with some value engineering, the system can be commercialized to a version under a royalty license providing the production drawings and know-how to a Canadian firm to build such a commercial product in South Korea and to market it worldwide.

Rights in technical data are extremely important to both the government and the trader. The government desires the use of data to obtain competition among the suppliers, ensure logistic support, and document the results of research and development. The contractor has property rights in data resulting from private investment. The data may have to be protected from unauthorized use and disclosure by the government to avoid jeopardizing the contractor's commercial position. With the development of the DoD technical data licensing classifications and contract clauses, the opportunity exists to balance the government's need for data against the contractor's economic interest in maintaining its control and secrecy.

What better way is there to create and use your business jewels— whether they are patents, copyrights, technical data represented by engineering/ production drawings, or computer software—to increase sales and income?

CHAPTER 10

Avoid Being Blacklisted
Procurement Integrity and Ethics

The preservation of the integrity of the U.S. procurement system and fair dealing with all competitors go to the heart of the acquisition process. The recent exposed greed of certain sectors of corporate America as reflected in runaway corporate governance and backdated incentive stock option grants, the excesses of the financial markets (stocks, brokerage houses, mortgage backed securities, the mutual funds industry, the insurance industry, commodities speculation, and subprime mortgages), and the accommodating accounting industry have had an impact on Americans' trust in their financial, business, and investment institutions.

The procurement system also has not been spared reports of fraud, waste, and abuse. The Global War on Terror (GWOT), the wars in Iraq and Afghanistan, the related rebuilding efforts in those countries, and, on our doorstep, the recovery from Hurricane Katrina in New Orleans—all have been affected by overcharging, defective pricing, quality deficiencies, product substitution, false claims, misuse of classified and procurement sensitive information, labor mischarging, foreign military sales, bribery, and the corruption of U.S. public officials.

This chapter is intended to alert the reader, whether in government or in industry, to those practices that should not be tolerated or allowed to occur whether one is in or out of government service or a prime contractor, subcontractor, supplier, consultant, or claim recipient.

Moreover recent FAR regulations emphasize the critical need for contractors to establish and practice a strict code of business ethics and conduct coupled with an active employee ethics and compliance training program.

This effort must be supported by an internal control system with prompt reporting and disciplinary elements to ensure timely disclosure of improper conduct and the implementation of corrective measures. (Fig.10-5 depicts the elements of such a program regardless of business size).

VIOLATIONS OF STANDARDS OF CONDUCT

A former Air Force acquisitions official who joined Boeing's missile defense unit . . . was negotiating on behalf of the government (Pentagon) . . . as the architect of the Tanker Lease Plan . . . at the Pentagon . . . while allegedly discussing employment . . . with Boeing's chief financial officer. . . . It is expected to delay a government contract to lease Boeing jetliners as airborne refueling tankers. (*Wall Street Journal*, November 2003)

This acquisitions official did not request a written determination from the designated agency ethics official saying the conflict of interest was not substantial enough to affect the integrity of the officer's performance of government duties. He thus failed to comply with the Procurement Integrity Act. He could have done this by contacting the DoD's Standards of Conduct Office at www.dod.mil/dodgc/defense_ethics/ or by e-mail at soco@aosdgc.mil to arrange for an appointment to discuss his particular situation.

A government procurement official in such a high position is required to notify a supervisor or superior upon his or her first contact with another official regarding future employment. The acquisitions official should have taken timely action to become self-disqualified from all participation in any procurement function involving Boeing Company in order to remove any cloud of impropriety. This official had a duty to immediately terminate any discussion of future employment; otherwise, the employee had a duty to report the contact to a supervisor. Even if the official had immediately terminated the initial discussion with Boeing, a subsequent offer within ninety days would obligate the official to report both the initial as well as the subsequent offer, even if the official terminated the second offer.

This former Air Force employee, after being employed by Boeing, was precluded from participating in any matter for a period of two years involving the Tanker Lease deal, including offering negotiation advice to that deal. As a general rule after former government employees resign they cannot try to influence the government on a particular matter in which they were personally and substantially involved. In addition, federal law establishes a one-year cooling-off period during which former senior officials are not supposed to lobby at all before the executive branch where they worked. They often, however, give their employers or clients informal advice about the federal bureaucracy, who to see, and how to handle a particular matter.

Government agents (contracting officers, support staff, lawyers) who perform or support procurement functions are subject to high standards of conduct. Violations of such standards can lead to their prosecution as well as fines and removal from office. There are a number of statutes and regulations that govern the conduct of federal employees in their dealings with each other and, in particular, with government contractors. One complex but important piece of federal legislation is the Procurement Integrity Act, which deals with a series of activities.

In part the act requires any former or present agency employee who is personally and substantially involved in a competitive agency procurement for noncommercial items that is expected to exceed the simplified acquisition threshold and who has contact with a bidder/offeror regarding future non-federal employment or business opportunities to report the contact and either reject the employment or disqualify him or herself from further participation in the procurement. Employment discussions during such transactions at any dollar level are a violation. "Personal and substantial participation" means you are directly participating in procurement or have a subordinate whom you are actively and directly supervising directly participating. In particular it means active and significant involvement in any of the activities shown in figure 10-1. If any of the these activities apply to your situation, you may not seek employment unless you disqualify yourself. "Seeking employment" is defined as contacting or being contacted by a bidder or offeror regarding possible nonfederal employment. For DoD purposes there is an "employment contact" when you are seeking employment from a trader.

FIGURE 10-1. Personal and Substantial Participation Activities

- Drafting, reviewing, or approving the specification or performance work statement
- Preparing or developing the solicitation
- Evaluating bids or proposals
- Negotiating price or terms and conditions
- Reviewing or approving the award

Disqualification is simple: Do not do any work on the task. To consummate the disqualification one is required to submit a written notice with the details of the contact (date, identity of the offeror, and interest) to the head of contracting activity of one's agency and send copies to the contracting officer, source selection authority, your immediate supervisor, and the ethics counselor. This head of contracting activity will decide whether or not to authorize your resumption of participation based on when the potential employer is no longer a bidder or offeror or all employment discussions have terminated without an agreement.

The Procurement Integrity Act also prohibits the acceptance of any compensation from a contractor as an employee, officer, director, or consultant of the contractor within a period of one year after the official

1. served at the time of selection as a procuring contracting officer, the source selection authority, a member of the source selection evaluation board, or the chief of a financial or technical evaluation team in a procurement that exceeded ten million dollars;
2. served as the program manager or deputy, or administrative contracting officer for a contract that exceeded ten million dollars; or
3. Personally made the agency decision to award a contract, subcontract, modification, task order, or pay or settle a claim; approve insurance; or establish overhead rates for a contract that exceeded ten million dollars.

The act prohibits present or former government officials or individuals advising or acting for the government from disclosing any contractor bid or proposal information before the award of a federal agency procurement contract to which the information relates. In addition it prohibits any person from knowingly obtaining source selection information or contractor bid or proposal information regarding a competitive procurement prior to award. The prohibition does not apply to soliciting information, only to obtaining it.

Aside from discussing future employment during the conduct of any ongoing federal agency procurement, some of the classic violations of standards of conduct by public officials while in government service are shown in figure 10-2.

Remember that the above restrictions are not the only ones that apply to a government employee, one seeking employment outside of government,

FIGURE 10-2. Other Classic Violations of Standards of Conduct

- Acceptance of bribes or gratuities (transportation, meals, ski trips, sexual favors, Broadway-type theater and sport-event tickets, liquor, or hotel accommodations)
- Improperly disclosing acquisition information
- Preferential treatment to a potential bidder
- Use of insider information for personal benefit
- Ownership of stock in a corporation with which one is negotiating a contract

and one leaving government service. Individual mores and one's conscious are not sufficient tools to avoid violation of the complex and often conflicting rules of government procurement. Cross this area with the caution you would exercise in crossing a minefield.

Call your ethics counselor or the Standards of Conduct Office to discuss your particular situation before accepting any compensation. The ethics official should issue a written opinion within thirty days after receiving facts as to whether compensation would be proper or a violation. Your new employer would welcome such a written opinion. It is certainly a better route for all to take than finding oneself reading adverse reports in the media or from the Defense Criminal Investigative Service or inspector general.

THE REVOLVING DOOR

Revolving door is a concept used to describe the phenomena where employees cycle between roles in industry and roles in government that influence that industry. Often these roles overlap with politicians, civil servants, and soldiers simultaneously being employed in the private sector. This concept invariably creates at least the appearance of serious conflict of interest.

The "revolving door" label applies to the actions of a civil servant or soldier who exits the halls of government and becomes employed as a consultant, strategist, or registered lobbyist to a third party that has an interest in influencing the former government official's office. One must not forget that such an employee is personally responsible for leaving the service in an ethical manner and complying with the standards of conduct. In most cases your new employer, which generally is a small business or public corporate office, is unfamiliar with such standards and has its own rationale for hiring you.

Former soldiers, airmen, and sailors, not to mention Marines, make excellent corporate managers at all levels of a firm. Many have learned by experience how to be leaders. They are disciplined, in good health, family-based, well educated by the services, and mission-oriented. They understand orders, they are trainable, and above all, they are dependable. Their word is their honor. All these attributes are sought not only by firms in the so-called military-industrial complex but also by many private, nonprofit, and public organizations (such as GM, IBM, CitiCorp, Wal-Mart, and GE). Many former military officers can be found in positions such as corporate executive, plant manager, city manager, or even mayor or councilman of a small town or city such as Columbus, Georgia. Former military police, regardless of military service, make excellent municipal police and security consultants. The negative Blackwater incidents in Iraq, which allegedly occurred while the company was providing contractual security services on behalf of the State Department, should not be allowed to blemish the services and sacrifices of many other former government employees to that war effort.

After some twenty years of Army service I joined a midsized law firm in the New Jersey shore town of Red Bank in Monmouth County. From Red Bank it takes only thirty minutes by boat to travel from the Atlantic Highlands to Wall Street. I was forty-three years old when I walked down the aisle for my juris doctorate degree in the East Orange campus of Seton Hall University after four grueling years of both night school and Army project management work. My service in Lai Kai, Vietnam, in 1969 was rewarded by the GI bill, which defrayed the primary cost of my graduate study in the law and which today is funding in part the education of some Iraq veterans.

Most of my 1982 classmates in law school were younger. I traded my khaki uniform for a pin-striped suit and was excited to start a new career. I had just turned down a project management job—and the chance to live on the edge of an Arnold Palmer golf course by a lake—with what was then Martin Marietta involving laser-guided munitions in the Orlando and the Ocala, Florida, areas. Such a position, despite its compensation, would have had me performing work similar to what I had been doing in uniform. I wanted a change. Hence my focus was on seeking employment with a law firm in lieu of competitive high-tech firms actively bidding on DoD programs.

Evans, Koelzer and Kreizman, P.C., as it was known then, maintained an office at World Trade Tower I. This office was only a "show" stop where we rented a conference room, had our phones answered, and retained shared receptionists to escort our clients to our time-shared conference room. I used these offices several times, and even today I wonder "what if." What if it had been my luck to be in those offices on that fateful morning of September 11, 2001? It is standard for law firms to maintain a shared Manhattan office space in support of business operations in the metropolitan New York area. My new firm marketed to and handled maritime and financial business clients, necessitating such a New York City presence.

Red Bank also is just some ten minutes from Fort Monmouth, the location of the Communications Electronics Command of the U.S. Army, with its large engineering and information technology procurement staff for Army command, control, communications, intelligence, surveillance and reconnaissance systems. Though it was left unspoken I am sure I was hired because of the law firm's desire to increase its client base. I would handle the anticipated specialized government acquisition business, which would spill over traditional legal services (new start-up corporations, estate planning, real estate, litigation, etc.) to the partners. That I had just passed the Patent Bar was also a favorable qualification for employment with the firm, as the growth in computer use and the need for software protection generated the potential for a plethora of intellectual property issues. Less than ten minutes away, Bell Laboratories, owned by AT&T at that time, was located in Holmdel. Lucent had not as yet been christened.

From Fort Monmouth one need not look far to see the Earle Naval Weapons Station to the north, the Lakehurst Naval Air Engineering Center at Lakehurst to the south, the Army Munitions Center at Picatinny Arsenal to the northwest outside of Dover, New Jersey, and the Fort Dix Army Training Center and McGuire Air Force Base complexes to the west, all within two hours' travel of each other. To this day it is a critical mass of potential defense-wide government and consumer buyers. Despite the projected base closures looming on the horizon, many of these bases (except Fort Monmouth recently) continue to survive the DoD budget ax because of their importance.

The large defense contractors (Lockheed Martin, Boeing, United Technologies, General Dynamics, L-3 Communications) have satellite marketing offices in Washington, D.C., to cultivate business opportunities. The Fort Monmouth area is not the only hub for such traders. In addition to the District of Columbia, which also encompasses the Maryland and Virginia suburbs, one can find such hubs in or near San Antonio and Fort Hood; Orlando, with the Navy Training Center; Jacksonville; Fort Belvoir; Quantico; and, not least of all, the Navy's supply and ship complexes at Charleston, South Carolina, and San Diego—to mention a few.

My ability to speak Greek was not lost on my employers since Monmouth County, with its Rumson, Fair Haven, Red Bank, and other Shore areas, was not only affluent but also populated with a substantial Greek business presence (largely in construction). Such operations were being conducted all along the East Coast in government (federal, state, and local) installations from Hanscom Air Force Base in Massachusetts to the Brooklyn Naval Shipyard and Fort Belvoir, Virginia. Monmouth County was the home of numerous small construction companies that owed their growth and profitability to the renovation and maintenance of military housing and office facilities as well as new construction.

Before my retirement ceremony, since I had been a senior procurement official (colonel) involved in the selection of traders and the purchase of Army electronic systems, I visited the Ethics Office of the command. Each government agency has an assigned ethics officer. This official is usually an attorney. My purpose was to discuss and be debriefed on questions of my civilian job search, future civilian employment, and standards of conduct.

Advice from ethics counselors with respect to such matters is advisory only. In this instance my counselor was acting on behalf of the United States, not as my personal representative. There was no attorney-client relationship created by the consultation. One may, however, rely in good faith on written opinions given under the Procurement Integrity Act by such counselors. My meeting with the counselor was standard and complemented the earlier debriefing to close out my classified security clearances.

Since my new employer was a law firm that had no government contracts and did not provide advice to clients on any federal contracts, there were no problems in accepting the employment. I also acknowledged that I could not give advice and counsel to anyone (individual or firm) related to the government work I had been involved in previously.

In my case I was lucky because I soon became embroiled in numerous construction issues. New projects along the East Coast from Niagara Falls, New York, to the Naval Submarine Base at Groton, Connecticut, with claims filed with various government administrative boards of contract appeal, provided me an intense first salvo into the prosecution of procurement claims. However, none of these claims or controversies involved missiles, electronics, or the procurement of radio or computer systems, the areas I had contracting experience in while serving at Fort Monmouth and the Pentagon. The government had trained me well. Now I had the chance to correct procedural errors committed by the government and to reel in my sometimes over-reaching clients. The practice of law does require the exercise of restraint, a professional demeanor, humility, courtesy, and honesty. Most of my cases were able to be resolved because there existed a basis to provide an equitable adjustment to the contract price and both sides found they were being treated fairly with a reasonable manner and not being jerked around or threatened with litigation.

Coming from government one always feels that you will be used by your new employer. This energizes your consciousness and prepares you to draw a line if need be. My test occurred sooner than I expected.

I was called into an unscheduled meeting with a group of private equity joint venturers in which the topic was the building of an "automated coal port" using the old existing train tracks in Weehawken near the Hudson River Tunnel. The object was to transport to Weehawken, New Jersey, by rail coal from the mines of Pennsylvania and transship it in special barges to electric generation plants up the Hudson and around Long Island to New England using an efficient automated coal port facility. The competing site was to be Philadelphia.

The main issue was whether or not the permits for the deep-water dredging, required to accommodate the new custom-built barges for this purpose, would be approved by the Army Corp of Engineers. In addition the environmental issues, especially because of the nearby location of the New Jersey wetlands, were to become just as challenging. Needless to say I was assigned the task of approaching the New York office of the Corps of Engineers because of my former service in the Army. I was familiar with this office and its counselors, having worked at arm's length with them in settling various construction cases.

The project carried a sense of excitement because it was bold. This excitement was accentuated because in 1982 crude oil prices were increasing. I met meet with the Corp of Engineers for the dredging permits as well as the environmental impact statements. I must admit that my prior service did open the necessary discussion doors. But with all the cards on the table I found that the civil service employees were pleased that I was a former professional officer who brought with him openness about my mission in their offices.

Eventually, this coal energy project was ruled environmentally unacceptable and cost prohibitive. This same project may be resurrected one day soon, as NYMEX crude oil futures continue their march well past $100 dollars per barrel. On NYMEX light, sweet crude oil for August 2008 delivery closed up $0.57 at $140.21 per barrel at the end of trading June 27, 2008. As this text went to publication such oil hovered around $100 per barrel.

FRAUD IN GOVERNMENT CONTRACTS

Sir, the wife admits that she was the preparer of the submitted overall invoice as the company treasurer; but she had no intent to cheat the government to be paid for supplies never received and installed. It was the fault of the subcontractor who compiled the false invoice using the letterhead-stationery of the supplier upon which the prime contractor relied in the preparation of its invoice. (Private counsel, October 2002)

Responsibility and Debarment

In addition to the real possibility of civil and criminal enforcement against individuals and corporations for procurement fraud, independently the prohibition, through the statutory or administrative processes of debarment, of individuals and their company to obtaining new government business from any federal agency, is triggered.

Poor past contract performance and unethical conduct by a prospective trader could lead to the refusal of the government to do further business with that trader. This refusal can arise under two different but related prongs—"lack of responsibility" or "debarment"—the latter a dreaded word in the security/defense industry. A trader has no inherent "right" to do business with Uncle Sam. This does not mean that the government can act arbitrarily. Persons or entities are entitled to challenge the processes and evidence before being declared ineligible for government contracts owing to debarment. Doing business with Uncle Sam, however, depends on a prospective contractor being found to be responsible at the time of contract award.

The concept of statutory debarment originates primarily in the labor statutes, including the Davis-Bacon Act, the Walsh-Healey Act, the Service Contract Act, and a number of other statutes related to labor conditions (see chapter 7). Administrative debarment is found for violations of the equal employment standard; on the basis of criminal convictions and other serious misconduct, such as fraud; and willful violations of contract provisions, such as the Buy American Act, by supply contractors. Debarments are for reasonable periods of time but generally do not exceed three years.

However, a debarred trader or one proposed to be debarred, unless that proposed debarment is lifted prior to the date and time for award, cannot be awarded the new contract even if it is the lowest bidder. The lifting or removal of a proposed debarment must be done by the department's designated debarment official. Contracting officers can access the list of debarred parties excluded from procurement programs by querying the Excluded Parties Listing System (including the Departments of Treasury and State) at www.epls. arnet.gov.

Despite the fact that anyone may submit a bid or proposal under the full and open competition rule, to be awarded a contract—no matter how favorable in price to the government—the trader still must be found to be responsible by the contracting officer at the time of award. If the trader is a small business, an adverse responsibility determination by the contracting officer may be submitted to the Small Business Administration for a Certificate of Competency and Determination of Responsibility.

To be determined responsible as a general standard among several, a prospective trader must have a satisfactory record of integrity and business ethics. It is not enough to have adequate financial resources or possess the necessary production, construction, and technical equipment and facilities. A responsible prospective trader has a satisfactory performance record. A trader that is or recently has been seriously deficient in contract performance will be presumed to be nonresponsible unless determined otherwise by the contracting officer.

For responsibility determinations contracting officers have access into the Past Performance Information Retrieval System to examine the past performance of a vendor who is being considered for the award of a contract (fig. 10-3). It behooves vendors to check this database to see their report cards from each project that has had an evaluation. To do so a vendor needs its MPIN, which is obtained from the CCR once a vendor registers in that database.

Fraud

Fraud in government contracts occurs before and after contract awards. One of the forbidden actions before or during the bidding period is collusive bidding using the public wire services, including the Internet. Such bidding could be in violation of the Sherman Anti-Trust Act since it generally involves a conspiracy to defraud the government. It includes bid limiting or suppression, which are antitrust violations.

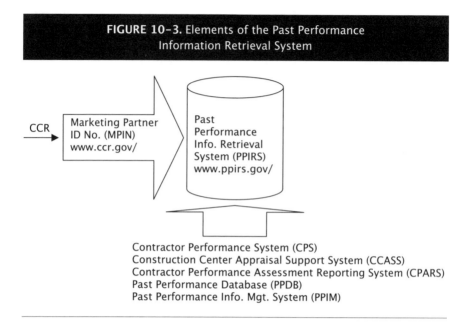

FIGURE 10-3. Elements of the Past Performance Information Retrieval System

Contractor Performance System (CPS)
Construction Center Appraisal Support System (CCASS)
Contractor Performance Assessment Reporting System (CPARS)
Past Performance Database (PPDB)
Past Performance Info. Mgt. System (PPIM)

After winning the contract the trader must be alert to the submission of false claims related to payment requests in which the invoices are false. Such false claims are not new and existed even during the Civil War, when traders invoiced defective products such as cannon and munitions as well as bogus services. Product substitution and deliberate mislabeling are examples of invoice false claims. A trader that deliberately substitutes a cheaper low-carbon shell backing for the harder high-carbon one during the manufacture of quality ball bearings could cause a propeller to collapse under stress while in flight, leading to serious injury and death. Such unethical and fraudulent conduct with other weapons systems and supplies, from rifles to missiles to medical items, could result in deviations from the prescribed specifications that cause malfunctions or defects to occur and lead to loss of life, not to mention increased operating costs.

Profile of a Fraud Case

The elegantly dressed lady in a pin-striped business suit was weeping in her chair. Her husband, the president of a small company, was standing next to her, trying to console her. (Names, locations, and other identifying details have been altered in light of the attorney-client privilege; the only facts revealed are those that are public.)

We were in the Pentagon in the Army's JAG office. The officer sitting behind the government-issued mahogany desk was a brigadier general. He had the responsibility of determining whether or not individuals and their associated firms should be debarred from doing business with the Army. I was explaining to the general that the wife was unaware that included with her company's invoice was a mason subcontractor's invoice with false invoices and letterheads from its supplier attached. The masonry supplies had not been installed, purchased, or delivered to the work site, yet payment requests for thousands of dollars had been submitted by the prime contractor, my client, for payment by the Army without verification. My immediate concern was the loss of new government business that had been won by sealed bid.

This was the perfect fact pattern containing the legal elements for a finding of fraud activating a host of federal laws (civil and criminal). Figure 10-4 provides a list of various federal statutes and common laws that one may be accused of breaching by a U.S. attorney based only on a single fraudulent event. The Department of Justice has made the prosecution of procurement fraud, including fraud related to the wars in Iraq and Afghanistan and the rebuilding of those countries, a priority.

Several weeks earlier a proposed debarment had been issued by the Army. My client's only prompt relief was to appear before the Army in an informal hearing and to explain why the small husband-wife construction business should not be blacklisted for three years. This was not a criminal or civil hearing. Such further legal actions could follow independent of this proposed debarment hearing by the U.S. attorney general. I also had to remind my client that a firm has no right (legal or otherwise) to do business with Uncle

---

FIGURE 10-4. Fraud Laws Applicable to Procurement

- False Claims Act
- Product substitution
- Deliberate mislabeling
- Labor mischarging
- Wire fraud
- Illegal collusive bidding using public wire services
- Conspiracy to defraud
- Bid suppression or limiting
- False Statements Act
- Defective pricing

Sam. That business is a privilege, not a right. The government can choose with whom it wants to do business. Just being proposed for debarment by one federal agency, even without proof, aside from any conviction in a trial court, is a clear signal that Uncle Sam (including all executive agencies) does not want to do business with you.

We had flown in from LaGuardia to Reagan National Airport early that day and taken the shuttle over to the Pentagon in Arlington. Needless to say my three-year tour in the Pentagon helped us navigate from the concourse of the Pentagon with its familiar barbershop to the E-ring of that building and to the Army JAG main offices.

The president of the small business testified that his firm had never had any invoicing issues and was an honest firm with a good track record on numerous DoD construction projects in Pennsylvania, New Jersey, New York, and Connecticut. He stated that his firm had never been proposed for debarment before, nor had his corporation been the subject of any indictment or criminal prosecution. From an economic standpoint debarment was a serious matter. It would have an impact on the carpenters, plumbers, electricians, laborers, and other craftsmen on the company's payroll, not to mention its subcontractors. Since the firm and its officers had been "proposed" for debarment by the Army, the firm could no longer be awarded any new contracts or modifications on existing contracts by any federal agency throughout the government until a final ruling on the debarment was issued. If debarred, the blacklisting generally lasted three years from the date that the debarment official rendered the ruling. Forming a new corporate entity would be of no help, since the officers by name had also been proposed for debarment.

No doubt the reader may recall reading about allegations of overbilling, hours padding, and defective invoicing which in the past have caused the debarment firms—in portion or in whole.

Debarment Remedies

Boeing has been plagued by other controversies in recent months. Earlier this year, the company lost $1 billion in Air Force business after the government learned that Boeing employees possessed more than 25,000 pages of proprietary documents from rival Lockheed Martin Corp. That matter [related to the competition as to who builds the next generation rocket] continues to be investigated by the Justice Department which has brought criminal indictments against two former Boeing managers.

The scandal also led to the rocket division [Boeing's] being suspended by the Air Force from competing for new contracts. (*Wall Street Journal*, November 25, 2003)

[In] 2006, Boeing agreed to pay . . . $565 million relating to a conflict of interest involving [a] high . . . Air Force procurement official and . . . use of competitor's proprietary info . . . with rocket launch contracts. (B. M. Sabin, Department of Justice, U.S. House of Representatives, June 2007)

How can such a large firm as Boeing, which has numerous subsidiaries and divisions that were not involved in the illegal activities and are engaged in ongoing defense work (aircraft, missiles, communications, etc.), be debarred?

One could argue that even to debar an entire firm, such as Haliburton, which supports the U.S. military worldwide by operating dining facilities, trucking supplies, repairing oil pipelines, and so on, could entail a serious blow to the coalition's mission in Iraq. What about the financial hardships to innocent employees and their families?

The Justice Department, using the threat of prosecution, imposes severe financial penalties as a minimum on large firms. On June 30, 2006, Boeing, in addition to losing a significant amount of defense business, agreed to pay $565 million to settle claims relating to a conflict of interest involving a high-level Air Force procurement official and its improper procurement and use of a competitor's proprietary information in connection with the Air Force and NASA rocket launch contracts. The same year PeopleSoft settled a case involving allegations by the Justice Department that it made pricing disclosures to GSA that were not current, accurate, and complete concerning the sale of software licenses and related maintenance services. Oracle, which had purchased PeopleSoft, agreed to pay the United States $98.5 million as part of the settlement.

My client had recently been notified by the Air Force that his company was the lowest apparent bidder for a housing renovation project at Dover Air Force Base in Delaware with a bid of six million dollars. But the Air Force could not by law award the contract because of the proposed debarment issued by the Army. The proposed debarment had to be lifted before the date of contract award. If not the award would be shifted to the second lowest responsive, responsible bidder. The Air Force did not want to lose the benefit of the cost savings provided by my client's low bid; on the other hand, the seriousness of the allegations made my client's firm not responsible. The Small Business Administration could not help this small business in these circumstances.

The brigadier general heard our pleas and decided that he would order the lifting of the proposed debarment order and allow the firm to accept the award of the Air Force contract on certain conditions. First, the wife would have to resign from the position of treasurer and finance officer of the small business since she had erred in her responsibility to verify the validity of all invoices submitted for payment for incurred costs. She could not be employed by the firm in any capacity. The firm itself and the husband (also the chairman of the board and president, plus majority shareholder) were spared and allowed to continue to manage the firm.

Second, the wife's shares in the stock of the firm would have to be placed in a voting trust over which she would not have any voting power. Third, the overpayment owing to the fraudulent invoicing would be an immediate debit from the existing earned retainages on other completed work being withheld by various contracting officers. And fourth, both the employment bar and stock voting trust conditions were to last for three years.

Overall the conditions were reasonable from a corporate standpoint. The Army allowed the firm to return to a "responsible" status so that the Air Force contracting officer could proceed to award the Wherry Family Housing Rehabilitation Project at Dover Air Force Base. The general did not want to penalize the company's craftsmen and their families and wanted to allow the Air Force to receive the benefit of the low bid. The past performance record of the firm had been satisfactory up until this incident.

As we lifted off from Reagan National Airport for the flight back to LaGuardia, we all breathed a sigh of relief. The firm was awarded the Air Force project. The wife would go home on a three-year sabbatical leave and would tend to her children. Business would now have to be conducted, if at all, in the matrimonial bedroom, away from the eyes of any government investigator or auditor.

A cloud of risk remained over the wife because the attorney general could, if he wished, proceed, independent of the Army debarment proceeding, to obtain a criminal indictment against both her and the small business with possible civil and criminal penalties. The stress level, though lessened, was still present.

I now had some more legal services to bill and the continued gratitude of a corporate client. The client had learned an important lesson. There would be no second chances in this incident since the proposed debarment, despite the fact it had been lifted, went into the company's performance database (www.ppirs.gov.), which future contracting officers may access.

My client would have to certify in its company's Online Representations and Certifications Application that it had been proposed for debarment as it submitted bid after bid—for three years. The firm's president had to toe the line from now on. The next performance report card had to show stellar performance in all contract execution categories.

The Army had helped the Air Force obtain the benefit of the low bid while at the same time providing a stern warning to a small business: "We may not be doing business with you in the future." There is no citizen's right to do business with the government. Uncle Sam can choose with whom it wants to do business, just as you can when you decide what firm will install the family swimming pool.

PRACTICING BUSINESS TIPS

Standards of conduct for government employees (civilian or uniformed) in the professional field of procurement require individual discipline, foresight, and every effort to avoid even the appearance of any impropriety. Supervisors must be constantly alert to ensure compliance and ethics training.

A trader (except a small business) selling to the government must establish an effective compliance and ethics program that includes providing training in the standards of conduct to its own employees (fig. 10-5). A baseline standard for a contractor's code of business ethics and conduct may be found in the federal sentencing guidelines. Such a code must be provided to each employee within thirty days of the date of award of a federal contract in excess of five million dollars and with a performance period of 120 days.

Corporate management must set the example by providing an atmosphere of strict compliance with the regulations and due diligence to prevent and detect criminal conduct and by promoting an organizational culture that encourages ethical conduct and a commitment to compliance with the law in dealing with the government and its acquisition officials. Business ethics are crucial to the successful performance of a firm, whether it is classified as a small or large business. Personal and corporate reputations are at stake, not to mention the loss in revenue caused by imposed monetary civil penalties.

A contractor must establish and maintain an internal control system to detect and prevent fraud in its contracts, and it must notify the contracting

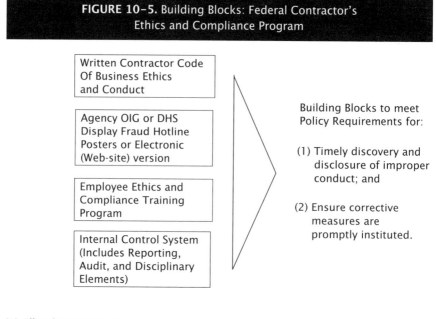

FIGURE 10-5. Building Blocks: Federal Contractor's Ethics and Compliance Program

OIG: Office of Inspector General
DHS: Department of Homeland Security

officers without delay whenever it becomes aware of a contract overpayment or fraud. In addition Office of the Inspector General Fraud Hotline posters, for confidential reporting by employees, should be visibly posted by a large business engaged in substantial government business.

A proposed debarment, if not lifted, or a finding of debarment for both the individual and the firm, are serious matters. Its impacts are detrimental to a firm's financial well-being and performance record. The government will consider such a company a performance risk and not responsible. The award of new contracts or new delivery/tasking orders to an existing IDIQ Contract, or the exercise of options even to existing contracts, will be curtailed, if not stopped, cancelled, or terminated.

CHAPTER 11

The Governance Game
Tools for Contracts Administration

Once the euphoria over winning a government contract has passed, the serious business of performance starts. Although the signatories to the contract who are in privity remain the same, their authorized agents could well change. With the government's permission the contractor could change its project manager.

For the government the contracting officer has several choices. He or she can delegate the contract's administration functions by specific written instructions to the nearest in-plant government contract management office (CMO) (formerly known as a contact administration office, or CAO) listed in the Federal Directory of Contract Administration Services Components, which is maintained by the Defense Contract Management Agency (DCMA) (see fig. 3-2).

The in-plant or field office government agent to whom responsibility has been delegated is not authorized to interfere with contract performance but is supposed to

1. conduct reviews for compliance with the terms of the contract;
2. observe quality control procedures;
3. perform the final acceptance function of the contracting officer; and
4. verify cost data by performing cost analysis before the payment of submitted invoices.

There may be a series of post-award meetings between the vendor and government agents to discuss performance just before any work commences and during the progress of the work.

In other cases the contracting officer assigns an administrative contracting officer (ACO) from his or her own agency to administer the contract and a contracting officer technical representative, called the contracting officer's representative (COR) or contracting officer's technical representative (COTR). Sometimes one see their abbreviation as COR/COTR. The COR/COTR serves as the contracting officer's representative to answer technical questions and be the liaison between the contracting officer and the vendor during the performance of the project. When no in-plant contract administration official is assigned, the COR/COTR's function becomes even more important in monitoring contract progress.

The COR/COTR is the "eyes" of the contracting officer for progress under the contract. This agent performs an oversight function. The government's objective is to receive products or services that meet or exceed the performance-based or design specifications within the contract price by the contract's completion date with no surprises and no cost overrun. The contractor's objective is to perform the contract within budget and on time with receipt of both prompt payment and a satisfactory performance evaluation report. Both parties want to avoid disputes.

Just as a rural doctor has a tool bag containing his thermometer, stethoscope, and other medical instruments, a federal contract has a number of standard contract clauses (see fig. 11-1), the tools for the contracts manager. The specific contract clauses and their effective dates are listed in Part II, Section 1 of the Uniform Contract Format (fig. 3-3).

Both the contractor and contracting officer need to exercise skillfully these clauses during the performance of a contract, each to promote its self-interest. To promote team partnering in the performance of an awarded contract, each party needs to remember that along with these clauses certain principles apply.

First, the contractor is responsible for ensuring that the labor, materials, and equipment necessary for timely delivery are available, without excuses, for the prosecution of the work. If it fails to so ensure, it must suffer any consequences arising from that failure. Second, contract interpretation begins

FIGURE 11-1. Clauses and Tools for Contract Administration

1. Quality Assurance
   a. Inspection and acceptance
   b. Warranty, if applicable
2. Contract payments and financing
   a. Invoice payments
   b. Contract finance payments (government)
      i. Advance payments
      ii. Interim payments (cost contracts)
      iii. Progress payments (fixed-price contracts)
      iv. Performance-based payments
   c. Assignment of claims (private financing)
3. Contract modifications via equitable adjustments
   a. Changes
   b. Delays
      i. Stop work order
      ii. Government delay of work
      iii. Suspension of work
      iv. Differing site conditions
   c. Terminations
      i. Deletion of selected contract work
      ii. Convenience
      iii. Default
4. Disputes
   a. Disputes
5. Reports and records
   a. Progress reports, accounting systems
   b. Records retention
   c. Contractor's performance evaluation
   d. Limitation of cost or funds clauses

with the plain language of the written agreement. In contract interpretation the plain and unambiguous meaning of a written agreement controls. A contract construction that gives a reasonable meaning to all parts of a contract is preferred to one that leaves a portion of the contract useless, inexplicable, inoperative, insignificant, void, meaningless, or superfluous. And third, it is an implied provision of every government contract that neither party will do anything to prevent, interfere with, or hinder performance (e.g., providing misinformation) by the other, thus avoiding accusations of a breach of contract based upon this implied duty.

QUALITY ASSURANCE

Inspection and Acceptance

When acquiring commercial items the government is required to rely on the vendor's existing quality assurance systems as a substitute for government inspection and testing before tender for acceptance. Upon acceptance the government assumes ownership of the supplies or equipment being purchased. Any in-process inspection by the government is conducted in a manner consistent with commercial practice.

Moreover, the government will rely on the vendor to accomplish all inspection and testing needed to ensure that supplies or services acquired at or below the simplified acquisition threshold conform to the contract quality requirements before they are tendered to the government. However, the government need not rely on inspection by the vendor if the contracting officer determines that the government has a need to test the supplies or services in advance of their tender for acceptance or to pass judgment upon the adequacy of the contractor's internal work processes.

As a normal practice for purchases, at least above the simplified acquisition threshold, the government requires the standard inspection requirements be included in its solicitations and contracts. The standard clauses (such as FAR 52.246-2 to 12)

1. require the contractor to provide and maintain an inspection system that is acceptable to the government;
2. give the government the right to make inspections and test while the work is in process; and
3. require the contractor to keep complete, and make available to the government, records of its inspection work. Higher-level quality standards (e.g., International Organization for Standardization 9001(3) and ANSI/ISO/ASQ Q9001-2000) may be found in the specifications for complex or critical items.

When the government chooses to inspect it has broad latitude in selecting the type of inspection and the number to be conducted. Such inspection may not impose a higher standard of quality than that required by the specifications. Also, when conducting an inspection the government may delay the performance of a contract for a reasonable time for that purpose. In the absence of a suspension of work clause, however, unreasonable delay constitutes a breach of contract by the government. The government's inspection is generally documented on a material inspection and receiving report and/or commercial shipping document/packing list to evidence government inspection and acceptance. The quality assurance process is depicted in figure 11-2.

When the government inspects and discovers defects it may reject or refuse to accept the contractor's tendered performance or the contracting officer may direct correction of the defects. The latter action permits the contractor to replace or correct the defective material, and if that is not done promptly, the government may do so by contract or otherwise at the cost of the contractor. This avenue allows the government through supervision to obtain timely performance in accordance with the specifications. If time for delivery has already passed, the government at its discretion may accept defective performance with a corresponding reduction in contract price. This does not constitute a waiver of those defects for any subsequent performance.

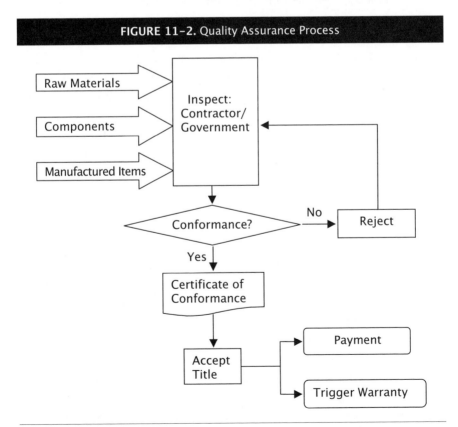

FIGURE 11-2. Quality Assurance Process

The government is entitled to strict compliance with the specifications, and the alternate relief through correction of defects, or price reduction for defects, has been viewed as discretionary and does not affect the determination to reject performance.

In construction contracts the strict compliance with specifications rule has been diminished somewhat by the doctrine of substantial performance. The courts have used this doctrine to deny rejection for minor defects where the work has been substantially completed in good faith and the cost of correcting the defects would be greatly disproportionate to the damage to the government in accepting the work. This doctrine is not applicable in supply contracts. In any case the contractor must be notified of rejection and the reasons for the rejection within a reasonable time. If the government fails to give notice of rejection within a reasonable time, the government's acts may be construed as a waiver of defects and acceptance of the otherwise nonconforming performance. Payment creates the presumption that the transaction is closed. However, payment must be authorized by the same person who is authorized to accept or reject the performance.

Acceptance, under the standard inspection articles in supply and construction contracts, is conclusive on the government except for latent (hidden) defects, fraud, or such gross mistakes as amount to fraud. The government's rights under the inspection clause are largely extinguished. Where any remedies remain available after acceptance under both the Inspection and Guaranty clauses, the government may proceed under either clause. The government has the burden of proving the existence of latent defects. Latent defects are those defects that exist at the time of acceptance but are not discoverable by a reasonable inspection.

Warranty

When the government purchases commercial items or services the price generally includes the same customer warranties offered by the supplier to the public at large. It is not uncommon but good business practice for the government in purchasing noncommercial items, supplies, or services to consider including a government warranty clause (FAR 52.246-17 to 21) in the contract price. Such a warranty is triggered once the government accepts title (see fig. 11-2). The use of warranties is not mandatory.

The contracting officer will need to weigh the nature and use of the supplies or services (e.g., complexity, end use, difficulty in detecting defects before acceptance, etc.), warranty costs, its administration and enforcement, trade practices, and reduced requirements for the government's quality assurance where the warranty provides adequate assurance of a satisfactory product. When the decision is made to include a warranty in the procurement action, the contracting officer should ensure that the warranty clearly states

1. the exact nature of the item and its components and the characteristics that the contractor warrants;
2. the extent of the contractor's warranty, including all obligations to the government for breach of warranty;
3. the specific remedies available to the government, which also should allow the government to obtain an equitable adjustment to the contract price; and
4. the scope and duration of the warranty.

CONTRACT PAYMENTS AND FINANCING

After acceptance the government incurs the obligation to make payment (see fig. 11-2). This is normally the primary obligation of the government in contracts and is set out in the payments clause of the contract, which contains certain requirements, including the submission of invoices.

Invoice Payments

Invoice payments are disbursements of monies to a contractor under a contract for supplies or services accepted by the government. Such payments include payment for completed or partial deliveries accepted by the government and final cost or fee payments where amounts owed have been settled by the government and contractor.

The vendor must submit a correct public payment voucher for satisfactory, completed performance consistent with the contract's specifications, terms, and conditions. The smart vendor will work closely with its ACO or COR to ensure the proper payment voucher is submitted and a paper chase is avoided. A by-product of such communication is that you have a heads-up as to whether or not your ACO is going to approve your invoice for payment request. If you need assistance in preparing a voucher you may refer to the Defense Contract Audit Agency's Web-accessible booklet (www.dcaa.mil, click on "Information for Contractors" under "Publications" in the menu), which contains samples, among other pricing and cost matters, on how to prepare the public payment voucher.

The Department of Defense's primary system for electronic processing of invoices and receiving reports is the Wide Area Workflow system, on which a contractor should register its contract (www.dfas.mil/contractorpay/electronic commerce/wideareaworkflow.html).

Government Contract Financing

Contract financing involves contract arrangements for infusing money, interest free, to a contractor as work progresses and in advance of payment for delivered end products or services. In most commercial settings it is customary for the work to be completed in a satisfactory manner prior to invoicing the customer. In federal contracting the work to be performed may take six months to several years of effort before the service (R&D, security) has been rendered or items (carrier aircraft, combat vehicles, hurricane levees, vaccines, government housing) delivered. The government, therefore, uses various contracting financing methods to help offset costs incurred by the vendor in the performance of the contract.

Such financing varies with the type of contract. In some cases advance payments for Fixed-Price Contracts may be appropriate even when no work has as yet been performed. Such a clause would provide for the payment of supplies for a construction project delivered, stored, and secured at a construction site even before the work crews arrive to install them. In cost-reimbursement contracts, provision is made for interim payments for some costs incurred to be submitted on SF 1034, Public Voucher for Purchases and Services Other than Personal. Fixed-Price Contracts provide financing through cost-based or percentage of completion progress payments requested on SF 1443, Contractor's Request for Progress Payment. The contract will designate an address to which these forms are to be submitted and the distribution and number of copies. These forms can be found at www.arnet.gov/far/ (click on "GSA Standard Forms").

Increasingly for Fixed-Price Contracts the Department of Defense is supporting the use of performance-based payments. Such payments are not based on costs incurred but on the successful completion of events or other quantifiable measures of results. Such requests for payments are submitted in a form and manner acceptable to the contracting officer.

When contract performance is funded by cost-based means, such as interim cost-reimbursement or by the cost-based progress payments discussed above, the billing system and the contract costs are subject to periodic audits by the DCAA. The purpose of such audits are to verify that the costs billed have been incurred in performance of the contract; that they are in agreement with the accounting records; and that they are in accordance with the contract terms.

Billed indirect cost expenses are based on the application of estimated allowable expense rates for the fiscal year adjusted at the end of the fiscal year to represent allowable recorded year end rates. The estimated allowable rates should be based on the current operating budgets for the fiscal year.

Private Contractor Financing

Aside from the government's financing as discussed above, a contractor with a federal contract, especially a Fixed-Price Contract, may seek its own private financing from a commercial bank or finance center. A contractor may assign its rights to be paid amounts due or to become due because of the performance of its federal contract to a bank, trust company, or other financing institution, including any federal lending agency. For this assignment to be implemented, the Assignment of Claims clause must be included, at least by reference, in the awarded contract at Part II, Section I of the Uniform Contract Format. Even if one does not foresee the need for private financing, a smart practice is to bid only on pending solicitations that contain this clause.

The alternative would be to take the initiative to have the contracting office to amend the solicitation prior to submission of offers to include the clause therein. One never knows what unforeseen event may occur which will require a firm to use its income stream from its federal contract as collateral for a line of credit.

CONTRACT MODIFICATIONS VIA EQUITABLE ADJUSTMENTS

The trader has a need to work closely with the various government players (contract administrators and on-site inspectors) to be able to efficiently and economically complete contract performance. Regardless of the type of contract one can expect changes to the work statement, especially if the contract involves a build-to drawing set, a design specification, or even a performance-based specification.

These changes lead to written modifications that need to be handled in a timely, nonconfrontational manner. The equitable adjustment route, using the applicable contract clause normally found in Section I of the awarded federal contract, promotes such administrative settlements. Figure 11-3 outlines the clauses that are generally included in most federal contracts that call for equitable adjustments to a contract that are necessary to affect its modification. The term "equitable adjustment" is construed as a fair, reasonable, just or right arrangement or administrative settlement. In federal contracts this involves a determination regarding adjustment of the contract price, the period of performance, or both.

Changes Clause

The trader should bring changes to the solicitation that involve work unknown or not contemplated when the bid was prepared promptly to the attention of the contracting officer. It is possible that this work arose out of necessity as the work progressed. A proposed change must be within the scope of the original

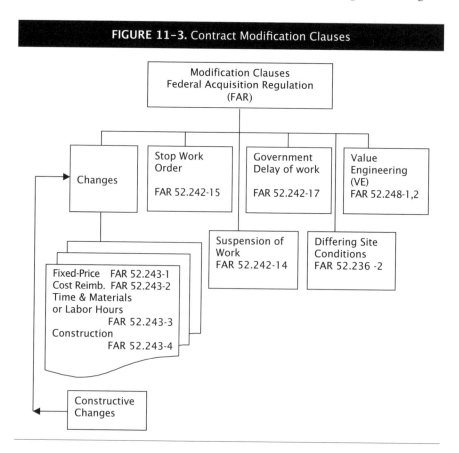

FIGURE 11-3. Contract Modification Clauses

contract work and not a cardinal change. A cardinal change is an alteration beyond the scope of the contract that is inconsistent with the changes clause, being out of the permissible limits. This determination involves the totality of the change, considering both its magnitude and quantity. Neither the number of changes nor the characteristics of the work to be performed are by the determinative factor themselves. The written change order could involve adding or deleting work related to the services, drawings, designs, or specifications; method of shipment or packing; and place of delivery.

As long as such added work is within the scope of work of the original contract, it should be able to be accommodated within the same contract instrument. Such changes require additional resources and time and may even have an impact on the completed work aside from extending the time allocated for performance under the contract. Changes for that matter can be proposed by the contracting officer on behalf of the government and are not the sole domain of the trader. Regardless of who initiates the request for a change order, a responsive change proposal, delivered by a contractor for consideration by a contracting officer, should contain the estimated cost of the new work. Figure 11-4 depicts some of the key elements in such a proposal. One should also refer to the discussion on cost estimating in chapter 8.

The equitable adjustment to the contract price for extra work caused by a change, generally in addition to the direct costs, includes indirect costs, possible unabsorbed overhead, and a reasonable profit on such work as part of the price of the work, less any credits. The formula for an equitable adjustment is the difference between the reasonable cost of performing the work without the change or deletion and the reasonable cost of performing with the change or deletion. A practical model may be found in the equation:

FIGURE 11-4. Elements of Estimated Cost (Change Order Proposal)

- Labor and requisite additional materials or supplies costs for the performance of the work to be changed or deleted
- Impact or ripple effect on the costs of incompleted work or completed work that has to be redone
- Share of indirect costs and any unabsorbed overhead
- Share of profit/fee
- Less any credits to buyer owing to the cost of the contract work being changed or deleted that was included in the original contract price
- Additional performance time needed to complete the changes

$$\text{Equitable adjustment} = \text{cost of performing the changed work or}$$
$$\text{deletion} - \text{cost of the work under the existing}$$
$$\text{contract without any changes or deletions}$$

What contractors and even the government at times forget is that to receive an equitable adjustment for changed work, a contractor must show that it incurred costs because of the change. Unless there is an increase in the contractor's cost of performing the contract work, the contractor is not entitled to receive an equitable adjustment.

One of the most troublesome areas of contract changes has been the measure of the equitable adjustment to the contract. The standard used is the reasonable cost to the contractor, not a hypothetical third party. The actual cost is presumed to be reasonable unless shown to be otherwise. Costs are estimated since the clause provides for adjustment at the time of change, not after performance. The courts and administrative boards of contact appeals have used, in addition to other methods, a jury verdict method of weighing the separate cost items in preference to a total approach whereby the cost is reviewed as a whole to determine reasonableness. The total cost method has been used especially where precise costs cannot be determined or isolated.

Impact Costs owing to Ripple Effects and Acceleration under the Umbrella of Changes Clause

Such impact factors as the interruption to the work sequence, lack of a steady flow of work, and the unavailable use of skilled labor may seriously affect a contractor's efficiency. The government has awarded equitable adjustments to the contract price for such "ripple effects." In recent times we have also seen equitable adjustments to existing contracts for the need for the "acceleration" of deliveries or completion dates on selected supplies and equipment (e.g., armored plates for military vehicles and improved warrior body armor kits) for the war efforts in Iraq and Afghanistan and public-works reconstruction projects in war-torn or natural disaster areas.

In the event an acceleration is required and no provision is present in the changes clause found in the existing contract, the best course of action is to negotiate a bilateral supplemental agreement adjusting the schedule. In any event the contractor will be entitled to an equitable adjustment if the acceleration causes an increase in costs.

The changes clause for construction, FAR 52.243-4, explicitly provides for changes in time of completion and delivery, which creates the right of a contracting officer to order an acceleration. That clause requires compensation for any increased cost in the performance of any part of the contract in the contractor's costs by an equitable adjustment through a written modification to the contract.

Government contracts do not require a posting of a cash reserve for such changes or allow for the inflation of a bid to cover unforeseen changes. The reason for these exclusions is that the government wants bidders to provide their lowest responsible bids absent of contingency reserves. In return the government includes the changes clause in its contracts to compensate bidders for in-scope changed, new, or added unforeseen work that arises during the performance of the contract.

Under the changes clause the contracting officer may unilaterally make specified changes in contract terms. Then, whenever one of those changes causes an increase or decrease in the cost of, or time for, performance of contract work, the contracting officer is required to make an equitable adjustment to the contract price. Compressing the time for delivery or completion of a project because of an acceleration requirement creates a loss of efficiency. An acceleration of deliverables is such a major change that it has a ripple effect on the remainder of the contract work.

A failure to agree to an adjustment becomes a dispute under the disputes clause of a contract, which requires a contractor to proceed with contract work pending a final resolution of any dispute arising under the contract.

The purpose underlying an equitable adjustment is to safeguard both contractors and the government against increased costs triggered by modifications. Hence an equitable adjustment must be closely related to and contingent on the altered position in which the contractor finds itself by reason of the modification. An adjustment should not increase or reduce a contractor's profit or loss, or convert any loss to a profit or vice versa, for reasons unrelated to a change. Simply put, equitable adjustments are administrative corrective measures used to keep a contractor whole when the government modifies a contract. Such adjustments are similar to the recovery of damages (pecuniary compensation), except no breach of contract is involved, nor is there any judicial involvement.

The changes clause allows the contract to be modified for extra or changed work the government orders. The trader should ensure that it does not perform any changed work until such time as the contracting officer agrees in writing by the issuance of a modification to the original contract. These contract modifications are sequentially numbered, and each will describe the amended work to be performed, the extra time allowed for overall contract performance, and the adjusted price of the overall contract.

Keep in mind that the adjusted contract price need not always increase because of a negotiated change order, especially if because of the change work is deleted or credits are negotiated to the benefit of the government. On a large contract it is not unreasonable to have over fifty or more contract modifications owing to negotiated change orders, significantly adjusting upward the overall contract price and duration of contract performance.

Such changes may be caused by numerous engineering design changes to a product specification or to production line drawings, causing numerous engineering change proposals for changes to specifications, changes to processes, and changes to test procedures or qualification procedures. Such upward adjustment could be characterized as a project "overrun," which on major military or construction projects such as aircraft or ships has been the cause of significant adverse publicity and independent auditor scrutiny.

Each modification is numbered sequentially and includes a description of the added/changed work and invariably a release of all further claims by the trader against the buyer related to the change order. The language of the release from any further government liability should be closely scrutinized by the contractor. Once the contract modification is signed "without any reservations," the contractor generally forfeits any further rights, including monetary compensation, owing to the changes bilaterally agreed. The trader must keep in mind that each modification is a "minicontract" within itself, requiring all the elements of an enforceable agreement (see fig. 3-1).

Hint: As a contractor, be vigilant about what you sign so you do not waive claims that are either unrelated to the change or related to the change but not able to be resolved under that particular equitable adjustment. Reserve in writing in the negotiated modification your firm's right to unresolved claims requiring further negotiations at a later date.

If the contract modification does not include a waiver or release of claim and circumstances do not indicate the parties' intention to include delay costs, failure of a contractor to reserve a claim for delay costs is not fatal to its presentation of such a claim later. Even an agreement to a new performance schedule does not eliminate causes of delay prior to the extension of performance time.

Traders who "jump the gun" and undertake the changed work without any written documentation from the buyer perform such work at their risk of not being paid for it. This is especially true in a Cost-Reimbursement Contract in which an estimated ceiling price, exclusive of fee, has been set by the contracting officer in the schedule and the limitation of cost clause has been included in the contract. The object is to not exceed the estimated cost without the contracting officer being informed and an agreement being reached to increase the cost ceiling.

If the buyer and the vendor cannot agree on the terms of the change, which in essence is a minicontract itself, it should be noted that the buyer unilaterally may order the changed work to be performed. In such event the trader must initiate prompt performance even under protest or face a default termination with all of its deleterious consequences of possibly not being awarded any future contracts.

Never forget that it is the contracting officer or his designated agent that must issue the change order modification (whether mutually or unilaterally agreed) increasing or decreasing the original contract price, changing substantive work requirement, or extending or accelerating the baseline schedule for performance under the standard changes clauses in federal contracting.

Constructive Changes under the Changes Clause

Where the contracting officer, through his actions or through the directions of his agents, has changed the work to be performed but failed to issue a change order, the scenario is set up for a constructive change. There are three elements to a viable constructive change (fig. 11-5). If all of these elements are found to exist and be meritorious on the facts of a submitted request for a change order, the contracting officer has the authority to include such a constructive change under the standard changes clause. Such action would resolve the issue by the issuance of a contract modification incorporating the change and amending the contract price and schedule. The concept of constructive changes is well recognized in the Federal Acquisition Regulation (43.104) and in FAR's Notification of Changes clause (52.243-7). If no resolution occurs the request submitted by the trader becomes a disputed claim.

In summary, a constructive change occurs where the contractor performs work beyond contract requirements, without a formal order under the changes clause, either because of an informal order from or through the fault of the government. The constructive change theory has been used often to allow for the administrative settlement of cases involving defective or impossible specifications and in acceleration of performance situations where the

FIGURE 11-5. Elements of Constructive Change

- A change occurred;
- Change resulted from a government directive rather than a voluntary undertaking; and
- Contrator relied on the government directive thereby increasing costs

---

contractor encountered intervening excusable delays known to the government but for which the government refused to extend performance time. If the contractor is not given credit (i.e., a time extension) for the excusable delays, the contracting officer may be held to have constructively shortened the delivery schedule, which has the same effect as ordering the contractor to perform faster.

When a contract contains the standard change provisions and the contracting officer, without issuing a formal change order, requires the contractor to perform the work or to use materials the contractor regards as being beyond the requirements of the pertinent specifications or drawings, the contractor may elect to treat the contracting officer's directive as a constructive change order. This allows the contractor to prosecute a claim for an equitable adjustment under the changes provision of the contract. Hopefully the equitable adjustment claim will be resolved by the two immediate parties, the buyer and the vendor, without its rise to becoming a dispute under the disputes clause.

I urge traders in such a dilemma to perform the changed work (either as unilaterally directed or constructive) and thereafter to submit a written claim for consideration (see fig. 11-6). A good practice would be to certify the claim if it exceeds the simplified acquisition threshold of one hundred thousand dollars in the event it became disputed, so that it is prepared to be appealed to the federal agency's administrative Board of Contracts Appeals, such as the DoD Armed Services Board of Contract Appeals, in the event of an adverse decision.

The contracting officer has ninety days to review the claim and to issue a final decision. If the decision is adverse, a dispute has occurred. The trader, now having the adverse final decision, can elect to appeal the decision either to the designated procuring agency's administrative Board of Contracts Appeals (within sixty days) or file a suit in the U.S. Court of Federal Claims (within one year).

Value Engineering Clause

The value engineering clause is inserted in supply contracts or service contracts when the government anticipates a contract of one hundred thousand dollars or more. The clause is not used in contracts involving R&D prior to full-scale development, not-for-profit and nonprofit engineering services, personal services contracts, product or component improvement except in areas not covered by the contract for improvement, commercial products with no special specifications, or any area exempted from value engineering application by the federal agency head.

A Value Engineering Change Proposal (VECP) is submitted before or within a reasonable time after contract completion by the contractor pursuant to the provisions of the value engineering incentive clause. The VECP is a proposal to reduce overall costs to the government through the incorporation of the contractor's ideas into the item or services being purchased by the government. It includes acquisition and collateral savings based upon an appropriate sharing rate.

The incentive approach is used to encourage the contractors to voluntarily suggest methods for more economic performance, following which they share in the resulting savings. Negotiations are conducted and a final payment based upon projected savings within the sharing period is agreed upon. When a VECP is accepted not only are the savings shared, but the contractor's allowable development and implementation costs are paid by the government.

Delays

A contractor is entitled to receive equitable adjustments in its contract price owing to changes to contract work made by an agency and delays in contract work caused by the agency. To receive an equitable adjustment owing to delay a contractor must be able to show three elements—liability, causation (the fact of being the cause of something produced by or of happening or true act by which a true effect is produced), and resultant injury. The contractor bears the burden of proving its affirmative claims against the government and establishing its entitlement to an equitable adjustment by a preponderance of the evidence using one of the following clauses.

Stop Work Clause (Supply Contracts)

Under the Stop Work clause the contracting officer may at any time, by written order to the contractor, require the contractor to stop all or any part of the work under the contract for ninety days. An adjustment under the Stop Work clause is used on supply contracts. The clause gives the government increased flexibility and control over the performance of a contract without incurring a claim of breach of contract. The adjustment under the Stop Work clause includes profit of the cost incurred. The clause restricts the time period (ninety days) for which the government may unilaterally delay performance. If that period is exceeded a termination for the convenience of the government is triggered. This clause also includes a time period within which the contractor must assert its claim for delay, and this time has been strictly enforced. The boards of contract appeals have increased the coverage of the Stop Work clause by invoking the doctrine of constructive suspension of work, as in the changes clause discussed previously, where the government should have issued an order but failed to do so.

Government Delay of Work Clause (Supply Contracts)
This Delay of Work clause is used in Fixed-Price Contracts for supplies other than commercial or modified-commercial items. It is optional for Fixed-Price Contracts for services or for commercial or modified-commercial items. The clause provides for an equitable adjustment for delays and interruptions caused by acts (or failure to act) of the contracting officer in the administration of the contract that are not in the contract, expressly or implied, or by a failure to act within the time specified in the contract or within a reasonable time if not specified. The contractor must give prompt notice (twenty days) to the contracting officer of the pending exercise of this clause.

In such cases an adjustment is allowed for any increase in the cost of performance of the contract caused by the delay or interruption, and the contract shall be modified in writing accordingly. No profit is allowed, however, in the equitable adjustment.

Mention should be made of concurrent delays, which are delays that have multiple (concurrent) causes. No adjustment is allowed under this type of clause for any suspension, delay, or interruption to the extent that performance would have been suspended, delayed, or interrupted by any other cause, including the fault or negligence of the contractor. The determination of whether an adjustment is required may be complex. The use of program evaluation review techniques, including earned value management systems and critical path charts, could be needed. This similar issue would have to be dealt with in the use of the Suspension of Work clause.

Suspension of Work Clause (Construction)

The Suspension of Work clause is similar (e.g., concurrent delays and no fault) to the government Delay in Work clause, but it is exercised in construction contracts. And unlike the government Delay in Work clause, the Suspension of Work clause expressly provides for suspension, delay, or interruption of the work at the government's convenience.

Rather than the use of judicial precedent to expand its reach, the Suspension of Work clause in construction cases expressly covers constructive suspensions of work in those cases where the government failed to issue an order when it should have done so.

Differing Site Conditions Clause (Construction)

The Differing Site Conditions clause is required in fixed-price construction, demolition, dismantling, and removal of improvement contracts exceeding the small purchase limitations, and at the contracting officer's discretion it is permissive within the small purchase limitations.

One of the purposes of this clause is to eliminate the tendency of contractors to submit inflated bid prices based on the worst physical conditions that might be encountered by providing simple, quick relief for such a situation. The clause requires the contractor to give prompt notice to the contracting officer of subsurface or latent physical conditions at the site that differ materially from those indicated in the contract or unknown physical conditions at the site of an unusual nature that differ materially from those ordinarily encountered and generally recognized as inhering in work of the character provided for in the contact. Under this clause the contractor receives an equitable adjustment similar to that under the changes clause, either for the delay in performance or increase in costs caused. Claim relief under this clause falls under two categories. Under Category I claims relief is contingent upon the presence of a misrepresented condition that differs materially from that indicated in the contract or that could not be reasonably expected from the contract documents. Under Category II claims recovery is not dependent on the contract documents but on the discovery of unexpected conditions not normal and usual in the character of the work required by the contract.

Unabsorbed Overhead

During the performance of a contract there are often delays emanating from a government-issued written or constructive stop work order, untimely delivery of government-furnished equipment or material, unforeseeable work site conditions, or natural causes (weather) or terrorist catastrophic events. When such events occur the contractor may be entitled to receive an equitable adjustment in its contract price for unabsorbed supported overhead. Government contractors incur indirect costs that are not attributable to any one contract but arise from their general operations. These costs, such as general insurance, accounting payroll services, senior management salaries, heat, electricity, taxes, and depreciation, generally are incurred even when there is no activity on a government contract.

A contractor recovers these costs by allocating the expenses on a proportionate basis among all it contracts. If the government suspends work on a contract the contractor's indirect costs often accrue beyond the amount originally allocated to that contract. The additional costs thus may be "unabsorbed."

The government has adopted a formula, commonly called the "Eichleay" formula, for estimating proportionate home office overhead unabsorbed because of a suspension. It is now well established that if the government suspends or delays work on a contract for an indefinite period, this formula will be used to calculate the amount of unabsorbed or extended home office overhead the contractor may recover:

$$\$ \text{ Net extended overhead claimed} = \$ \text{ daily overhead rate x number of} \\ \text{delay days} - \text{direct overhead already} \\ \text{paid by modifications}$$

To recover under the Eichleay formula a contractor must first show that there was a government-caused delay to its planned contract performance that was not concurrent with a delay caused by the contractor or some other reason. The contractor must also show its original contract performance time was thus extended or, alternatively, that it completed performance on time or early but incurred additional, unabsorbed overhead cost because it planned to finish even earlier.

Finally, after proving the above elements, the contractor must show it was required to remain on "standby" during the delay. Where the contractor proves these elements it has made a "prima facie case" of entitlement. The burden of production then shifts to the government to show that it was not impractical for the contractor to take on replacement work and thereby mitigate its damages.

In summary one has to prove the extent of the delay, that the delay was proximately caused by the government action, and that the delay harmed the contractor. The contractor has the burden to show that it could have finished the contract work earlier and would have done so but for the government's delay. The contractor, to recover, must establish that completion of the entire project was delayed by reason of the delay to the segment.

As a final note it is well established that overlapping delays that are caused by the government and its contractor do not afford either party a basis for an award of delay costs against the other.

TERMINATIONS

The termination of a federal contract is always a significant business event to both contracting parties with a variety of impacts. In many instances, rather than a termination of the entire contract, there may be a partial termination. Such a termination uses some of the standard clauses in the contract to delete selected work no longer required by the buyer. In other instances the termination could be abrupt and encompass the entire contract.

Deletion of Selected Work

Under the government Property, Changes, or Termination for Convenience clauses, a contracting officer may alter the contract to delete work originally specified to be performed. Such partial deletion of work by the contracting officer is not a breach of contract.

If a contracting officer deletes contract work under the government Property or Changes clause, any resulting equitable adjustment may allow for profit on work actually performed but cannot encompass anticipated (but unearned) profits upon unperformed deleted work.

Termination of Entire Contract

Terminations of a government contract generally fall within two major groupings: (1) by default of the trader in the performance of the contract, including abandonment of the project, or (2) by termination of the contract (total or partial) for the convenience of the government.

The Termination for Convenience clause gives the government the right to cancel a contract when to do so is in the best interest of the government, notwithstanding the contractor's ability and readiness to perform. Currently procurement regulations make the inclusion of a termination for convenience clause mandatory in federal contracts. Contracting officers are granted broad discretion by this clause, a discretion with which the courts have been reluctant to interfere.

The real effect of this clause is to establish the measure of compensation the contractor may recover for the government's termination of the contract. In the absence of this contract right, the unilateral repudiation of a contract would be a breach of contract on the part of the government. In a breach of contract the aggrieved party may recover its expected or anticipated profits as damages. Under the clause, however, the contractor recovers only its costs and the profit earned on work actually accomplished—and the latter only if it is in a profit position at the time of termination. The contractor's recovery has been limited to this measure even when the government failed to invoke the termination article.

Normally the contractor will have one year after the termination for convenience order is received to file a settlement proposal. It is critical to confirm the last due date because if that date passes without a submitted settlement proposal, the contractor can be deemed to have lost its rights to recover its termination costs. The format and contents of such a proposal are found in the clause itself.

The right to terminate a contract for default is discretionary with the procurement activity, and the appropriate contract officials should exercise judgment in reaching a decision to terminate. The default clauses provide two bases for terminations. One is for failure to perform within the time required, and the second is for failure to make progress with the work or to perform any other contract requirements within the period provided by a "cure notice" from the government.

When the government terminates a contract for default the contractor should expect to be liable for the reasonable excess costs of reprocurement of items substantially the same as required under the original contract and liquidated damages accrued. Even in the absence of liquidated damages or excess costs of reprocurement, the actual damages suffered by the government, despite its efforts to mitigate the damages, are recoverable.

Failure to Perform within Time

In the event of the failure to perform within the time required the government may show that it reasonably exercised its right to terminate simply through evidence that the time for performance has passed. But where a project is

substantially complete by the time required or supplies in substantial conformance with the specifications are delivered by the due date, default termination may not be effected unless time is of the essence.

Failure to Make Progress

In a termination for failure to make progress the burden of proof becomes
more difficult and the government must show the contractor would not have
performed timely had the contract not been terminated. The government may
lose the right to terminate for default through waiver if it allows a contractor
to continue to perform and incur expenses for an unreasonable time.

Once a delivery schedule is waived the government must reinstate a schedule for time to be of the essence so as to invoke later default action. Where the
work is divisible the government may terminate for failure to make progress
only on that part of the work on which the contractor fails to make progress,
not the whole contract.

DISPUTES

The disputes clause, FAR 52.233–1, incorporated by reference in federal contracts, derives its authority from the Contract Disputes Act (CDA) of 1978
(41 U.S.C. 609h), which provides that all disputed claims by a prime contractor against the government "relating to the Contract" shall be submitted to
the contracting officer for a decision. The contracting officer's decision is final
unless the contractor appeals or files a suit provided in the act. Such claims
must be in writing and be submitted within six years after accrual of the claim
to the contracting officer for a written decision. If entitlement is found simple
interest is paid to the claimant from the date that the claim was submitted to
the contracting officer.

A claim is a written demand by one of the contracting parties seeking
as a matter of right the payment of money in a sum certain, the adjustment
or interpretation of contract terms, or other relief. Thus both disputes under
the contract and breach-type claims are handled under the same procedure.
Claims from subcontractors or suppliers are processed through the prime
contractor.

A payment voucher, invoice, or other routine request for payment that
is not in dispute when submitted is not a claim under the Contract Disputes
Act of 1978. Such a submission may be converted to a claim, however, by
complying with the submission and certification requirements of the disputes

clause, if it is disputed either as to liability or amount or is not acted upon in a reasonable time. Figure 11-6 depicts the current disputes process.

The Contract Disputes Act (P.L. 95-563) allows federal government contractors to sue the U.S. government for monetary damages related to their contractual dealings. This act is important to the numerous contractors that provide the federal government with billions of dollars of services, supplies, and construction each year. The act waives the government's sovereign immunity, permitting contractors to sue the government in either an administrative tribunal (a board that hears appeals such as the Armed Services Board of Contract Appeals) or in a federal court. The act establishes the procedures to be used by contractors and contracting officers (those authorized to bind the government in contract) in resolving disputes involving contracts with the federal government, specifically the executive branch.

The act allows contractors to appeal a contracting officer's "final" decision to the cognizant procurement agency's administrative Board of Contract Appeals (BCA) within ninety days of the receipt of a final adverse decision on a claim. The act also allows contractors direct access to the federal courts by filing a suit as an alternative to appealing to a Board of Contract Appeals. The U.S. Court of Federal Claims (COFC), which has jurisdiction in such cases, must receive the appeal within one year of the contracting officer's final decision.

A contractor's claim exceeding one hundred thousand dollars, or any claim regardless of amount when using alternative dispute resolution procedures, is required to be accompanied by a certification that

1. the claim is made in good faith;
2. the supporting data are accurate and complete to the best of the contractor's knowledge and belief;
3. the amount requested accurately reflects the contract adjustment for which the contractor believes that the government is liable; and
4. the person signing the certification is duly authorized to certify the claim on behalf of the contractor.

This certification may be executed by any person duly authorized to bind the contractor with respect to the claim. Defective certifications, moreover, can be "cured" if any appeal has been initiated on the claim.

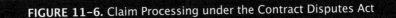

FIGURE 11–6. Claim Processing under the Contract Disputes Act

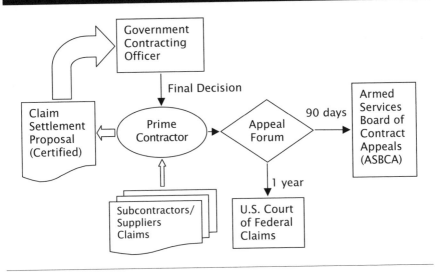

For contractor claims of one hundred thousand dollars or less the contracting officer must, if requested in writing by the contractor, render a decision within sixty days of the request. For contractor's claims over one hundred thousand dollars the contracting officer must, within sixty days, render a decision or notify the contractor of the date by which a decision will be made.

Large firms may request use of the CDA's small claims procedures for claims less than $50,000. These procedures (such as shorter discovery periods, less paperwork submission, etc.) were included as part of the CDA to expedite the resolution of minor government contractor disputes. The procedures provide an efficient and cost effective resolution of small claims. Small businesses may use the small claims procedures for appealing a contracting officer's final decision if the claim is under the ceiling of $150,000.

What does not fall under the jurisdiction of the disputes clause, however, is just as important. The boards do not have jurisdiction over value engineering or award-fee determinations, which are the responsibility and discretion of the contracting officer, nor torts or fraud cases. Contract award controversies are not heard but are referred primarily to the Government Accountability Office. Controversies on labor standards are referred to the Department of Labor.

REPORTS AND RECORDS

Progress Reports and Accounting Systems

The need for a trader to submit periodic reports on an awarded contract is on many occasions built into the contract itself by the inclusion of Contract Data Requirements Lists (CDRL), DD Form 1423s, with their associated data item descriptions, for example, DI-MGMT-8004, Management Plan. In many cases each CDRL carries a separate Contract Line Item Number (CLIN) since reports take time to prepare and each has a cost associated with it. Without a CLIN for the data item requiring the submission of a report or some other type of technical data, none should be submitted until the contract is modified to include the requisite requirement and its cost of generation, reproduction, and submission to the government.

If you had used a work breakdown structure to prepare your cost proposal as discussed in chapter 8, you would find that you have a highly useable tool from which to not only allocate and expend resources during performance but generate technical, schedule, and cost data for reporting purposes. CDRL reports such as Cost Performance Reports, Cost/Schedule Status Reports, and others may be generated from your work breakdown structure. In essence by using a comprehensive work breakdown structure for your cost estimating, you also have the framework for a trader's management/cost control system.

On major defense programs or as required by the contracting officer on a particular procurement (services, warfighting equipments or supplies), the solicitation may require the use of an earned value management system (EVMS), a program management tool that effectively integrates the project scope of work with cost, schedules, and performance elements for optimum project planning and control. An EVMS allows the government to maintain insight into the contractor's performance through the evaluation of cost and schedule performances.

In most cases an EVMS must be certified as complying with the American National Standards Institute and Electronics Industries Alliance (ANSI/EIA) Standard 748 at the time a proposal is submitted. In the event an offeror does not have such a certified system in existence, the offeror may still submit its proposal, but an EVMS implementation plan must be submitted with its proposal.

In addition to mandating the use of a certified EVMS on a project the government will require a pre-award or post-award Integrated Baseline

Review (IBR) of the EVMS. In such event clarification should be sought as to the amount of and how the cost to the offeror of the IBR will be defrayed by the government. The purpose of the IBR is to verify the technical content and realism of the related performance budgets, resources, and schedules. The risks in the contractor's plans and the underlying management control system are evaluated, and a plan is formulated to handle such risks. The administrative contracting officer from the Defense Contract Management Agency approves a contractor's EVMS.

It is expected that an experienced contractor will have an established, certified computer system with reliable software to allow for contract management being integrated with the firm's supply, labor/payroll, production, and payment subsystems. Such system(s) are commercially available. An operable accounting system that is under general ledger control is of paramount importance when performing government contracts. Refer to the DCAA at www.dcaa.mil for more detailed requirements regarding accounting systems for federal contracts. A vendor's existing accounting system may have to be upgraded when awarded a government contract. Better still, such upgrades should take place in anticipation of the contract to be operable and validated by contract award time.

Tracking Contract Funding and Expenditure

Of particular importance is the need for both the government and especially the contractor to monitor their Cost-Reimbursement Contracts to ensure compliance with the applicable reporting requirements of the limitation of cost or funds clauses to prevent surprises owing to cost overruns over estimated costs specified in the contract schedule.

Policy states that no government official may create or authorize an obligation in excess of the funds available or in advance of appropriations unless authorized by law. Hence before executing any contract, including tasking and delivery orders, the contracting officer must confirm that adequate funds are available or expressly condition the contract upon the availability of funds. The government cannot accept any supplies or services until the contracting officer has given the contractor notice, confirming in writing that funds are available.

If the contract is fully funded, funds are obligated to cover the price or target price of a Fixed-Price Contract or the estimated cost and any fee of a Cost-Reimbursement Contract. On the other hand, if a contract is incrementally funded, funds are obligated to cover the amount allotted and any corresponding increment of fee.

Limitation of Cost

The Limitation of Cost clause is inserted in solicitations and contracts if a fully funded Cost-Reimbursement Contract is contemplated. By executing the contract the parties to the contract agree that the performance of the contract will not cost more than the estimated cost specified in the schedule. The contractor agrees to use its best efforts to perform the work specified in the schedule and all obligations under the contract within the estimated cost.

In addition the contractor is required to report to the contracting officer in writing whenever it has reason to believe that the costs the contractor expects to incur under the contract in the next sixty days (can vary from thirty to ninety days), when added to the all costs previously incurred, will exceed 75 percent (can vary from 75 to 85 percent) of the estimated cost specified in the schedule, or that the total cost for the performance of the contract, exclusive of fee, will be either greater or substantially less than had been previously estimated.

Limitation of Funds

The Limitation of Funds clause is inserted in solicitations and contracts if an incrementally funded Cost-Reimbursement Contract is contemplated. By executing the contract the parties to the contract estimate that the performance of the contract will not cost more than the estimated cost specified in the schedule.

The contractor agrees to use its best efforts to perform the work specified in the schedule and all obligations under the contract within the estimated cost. The schedule specifies that amount presently available for payment by the government and allotted to the contract, the items covered, and the period of performance it is estimated the allotted amount will cover. The parties to the contract contemplate that the government will allot additional funds incrementally to the contract up to the full estimated cost the government specified in the schedule, exclusive of any fee. The contractor agrees to perform or have work performed on the contract up to the point at which the total amount paid and payable by the government under the contract approximates but does not exceed the total amount actually allotted by the government to the contract.

In addition the contractor is required to report to the contracting officer in writing whenever it has reason to believe that the costs the contractor expects to incur under the contract in the next sixty days (can vary between thirty and ninety days), when added to the all costs previously incurred, will exceed 75 percent (can vary between 75 and 85 percent) of the total amount so far allotted to the contract by the government. The notice must state the estimated amount of additional funds required to continue performance for the period specified in the schedule.

Contract Records Retention

An essential function of contract administration is records retention. Both the government and contractor have independent responsibilities for this function established by procurement law and regulations. The vendor has this requirement embedded by contract clause (Audit and Records) in its firm's contract.

As a general rule the retention period for a contractor is three years after final payment for available records. Such records include books, documents, accounting procedures and practices, and other data (regardless of type and regardless of whether such items are in written form, in the form of computer data, or in any other form), as well as other supporting evidence to satisfy contract negotiation, administration, and audit requirements of the contracting agencies and comptroller general.

On the other hand, the government is required to keep the "contract file." The official "contract file" comprises three groups of file documents (see fig. 11-7). The contracting office file documents the basis for the acquisition, the award, and the assignment of contract administration responsibilities. The contract administration office file documents actions reflecting the basis for and the performance of contract administration responsibilities. The paying office contract file documents the actions prerequisite to substantiating and reflecting contract payments.

A central control and a locator system ensures the ability to locate promptly the contract file so that it is readily accessible to principal users, so that it can be protected from disclosure to unauthorized persons, and to safeguard classified documents.

The normal period for retention for contracts with their successful proposals exceeding the simplified acquisition threshold, as well as for construction contracts in excess of two thousand dollars, is six years and three months

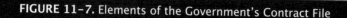

FIGURE 11-7. Elements of the Government's Contract File

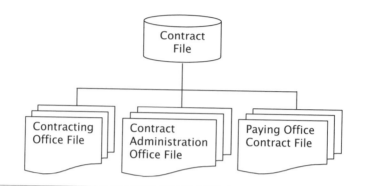

after final payment. For contracts at or below the SAT and construction contracts at or below two thousand dollars, the retention period is three years after final payment.

PRACTICING BUSINESS TIPS

Effective contract management by both the contractor and the government should not be driven for just minimal compliance. Rather, it requires teamwork between the two parties despite differences that may arise to the level of a dispute. It becomes a matter of mutual civility, ethics, and courtesy.

Such a management environment will allow the project to come first and be completed while financially the contractor remains "whole" and prospers, if not on the first project then on many more to come. It becomes a matter of professional reputation. A contractor has to be able to elicit teamwork from its subcontractors, which in many instances have some of the same contract management clauses flowed down from the prime to them in their subcontracts. The successful federal contractor practices sound contract administration diligently on a daily basis.

The cumulative effect of the Changes, Payments, Stop Work, Government Delay of Work, Suspension of Work, Disputes, and Termination for Convenience clauses is to give the government extraordinary control over the performance of its contracts and to establish the measure of reimbursement to be given to contractors when the government exercises these rights.

The Limitation of Cost or Funds clause used in Cost-Reimbursement Contracts presents not only a critical compliance effort for proper fund expenditure tracking and reporting but also a wise fiscal management requirement to prevent cost overruns. How well a contractor handles such tracking and reporting will certainly show up on a firm's past performance reports. A good job in this contract administrative area will avoid payment issues between the parties, late payments, and the need to resort to claims under the Disputes Act.

The power of the contracting officer to issue unilateral change orders provided under the Change clause becomes even more remarkable when coupled with the Contract Disputes clause of the contract, which establishes the contracting officer as the final arbiter of any disputes arising under the contract. His or her decisions on questions of fact are final, subject to an appeal to an administrative Board of Contract Appeals. More important, a contractor is required to perform in accordance with the contracting officer's final decision pending final resolution of the disputes.

Do not allow all of the procurement rules to discourage you from participating in U.S. procurement. Imagine that you are playing a football game in which the rules are well established. The Federal Acquisition System is intended to keep the football field level so that you can compete on an equal footing and successfully complete the game. Winning a federal contract in an ethical manner comes first and foremost. Thereafter, sound, compliant contract management is the key attribute in completing an awarded contract. It takes leadership, integrity, teamwork, and perseverance.

Uncle Sam needs responsible, innovative, and ethical contractors. In return Uncle Sam will pay you a fair, reasonable price. Without your participation the United States would not be the free and dynamic country it is today. Competent, honest traders are the best hope for the future. Good luck!

Source Notes

The notes below include citations for the academic papers in which the material was based. Materials not listed in these notes were drawn from readily accessible databases, news reports, and reference works. Web sites have been referenced alongside relevant text. Texts referenced include relevant Federal Acquisition Regulation revisions through Federal Acquisition Circular 2005-26, June 12, 2008.

In addition to the references below a key source was the development of improved concepts and materials derived from the contents and notes of *The Government Contracts Reference Book for Engineers, Program Managers, and Contract Administrators (2000–2005)*, by Bill C. Giallourakis, which was tested on government and industry student attendees over a number of years at the Professional Development Center, Armed Forces Communications Electronics Center (AFCEA) in Fairfax, Virginia. That reference book was part of the teaching packet a student received when he or she attended the AFCEA course on government contracts I taught over a period of years.

Chapter 1. Winning the First Job

1. Edgar H. Schein, Peter S. DeLisi, Paul J. Kampas, and Michael M. Sonduck, *DEC Is Dead, Long Live DEC: The Lasting Legacy of Digital Equipment Corporation* (San Francisco: Barrett-Koehler, 2003).
2. Bill C. Giallourakis, "Cost Analysis Software for Contract Administration," Abstracts of Phase I Awards in the Department of Defense, Defense Small Business Innovation Research Program, 1993, 30.
3. United Technologies (Alternate Fighter Engine) under contract F33657-84-C2014, Armed Services Board of Contract Appeals (ASBCA) 51410, et al. (January 19, 2005), 1–6.
4. *The Small Business Innovation Development Act of 1982*, U.S. Public Law 97-219; SBIR program reauthorized through 2008, U.S. Public Law 106-554, October 1, 1982.
5. *Small Business Technology Transfer (STTR) Program*, U.S. Public Law 107-50.
6. Martin H. Weik, *A Third Survey of Domestic Electronic Digital Computing Systems*, Report No. 1115, Ballistic Research Laboratory, Aberdeen, Md., 1961, p. 0254. (Note: The FADAC system starts on this page.)

7. Robert Block, "Shielding the Shield Makers," *Wall Street Journal*, November 26, 2003, B1–B2.
8. Definitions, Information Technology, FAR 2.101. "Information Technology" includes computers, ancillary equipment (including imaging peripherals, input, output, and storage devices necessary for security and surveillance), peripheral equipment designed to be controlled by the central processing unit of a computer, software, firmware and similar processes, services (including support services), and related services. "Principal functions of information technology" are the automatic acquisition, storage, analysis, evaluation, manipulation, management, movement, control, display, switching, interchange, transmission, or reception of data or information. "Information technology" means any equipment or inter-connected system(s) or subsystem(s) of equipment used in the aforementioned functions.
9. Acquisition of Information Technology, FAR Part 39.
10. Web pages accessed April 20, 2008.

Chapter 2. Market Research and Acquisition

1. Market Research, Policy, FAR 10.001(a)(2), (3).
2. Definitions, FAR Subpart 2.1; Micro-purchase Threshold, Simplified Acquisition Threshold, FAR 2.101.
3. Test Programs for Certain Commercial Items, FAR 13.500; 41 U.S.C. 428a; FAR 13.500(e).
4. Other Full and Open Competition, FAR Subpart 6.3.
5. Disaster or Emergency Assistance Relief, FAR Subpart 26.2.
6. Federal Supply Schedule Program, General, FAR 38.101; 41 U.S.C. 259(b), (3) (A)(A).
7. Use of Federal Supply Schedules, FAR 8.404.
8. EEO Clearance Prior to Contract Award from OFCCP, 41 C.F.R. 60-1.29.
9. David Wessel, "There Is No Denying the Math: Taxes Will Rise," *Wall Street Journal*, November 20, 2003, A2.
10. Source list (Central Contractor Registration Database), FAR 13.102.
11. Central Contractor Registration, FAR Subpart 4.11; Policy, FAR 4.1102.
12. Annual Representations and Certifications, FAR Subpart 4.12; Policy, FAR 4.1201.
13. Emergency Acquisitions, FAR Part 18; Available Acquisition Flexibilities, FAR Subpart 18.1; Incident of national significance, emergency declaration or major disaster declaration, FAR 18.203.
14. *Robert T. Stafford Disaster Relief and Emergency Assistance Act*, 42 U.S.C. 5121, amended October 30, 2000, U.S. Public Law 106-390; *Local Community Recovery Act of 2006*, Amendment 42, U.S.C. 5150, Public Law 109-218.
15. "Alpha contracting," Department of the Navy, Acquisition One Source, http://acquisition.navy.mil/acquisition_one_source/. Click on "Program Assistance and Tools," click on "Tools: Best Practices and Lessons Learned," then click on "Alpha Contracting to the JSOW LRIP Program."
16. U.S. Public Law 109–62 contains emergency supplemental legislation.
17. "Contingency Operational Contracting Support Program," Air Force FAR Supplement, Appendix CC, September 2005.

18. Department of Transportation, "DOT Emergency Contracting Kit," Washington, D.C., April 2005.
19. Department of Homeland Security, "National Response Plan," December 2004.
20. James Roloff, *Contingency Contracting: A Handbook for the Air Force* (Maxwell AFB, Ala.: Air Force Logistics Management Agency, February 2003).
21. Office of Management and Budget, Office of Federal Procurement Policy, "Emergency Acquisition Guide," Washington, D.C., May 31, 2007. Online at http://www.whitehouse.gov/omb/procurement/index_contracting.html.
22. Emergency Response and Recovery Contracting Community of Practice Web site (best practices from Hurricane Katrina and other emergency situations), http://acc.dau.mil/emergency_response.
23. GAO bid protest decision: Ash Britt, Inc., Comp. Gen. Dec. B-279889, B-297889.2, March 20, 2006.
24. Block, "Shielding the Shield Makers," *Wall Street Journal*, November 26, 2003: B1–B2.
25. Extraordinary Contractual Action, PL 85-804, FAR Part 50; 50 U.S.C. 1431-1435, Executive Order 10789, November 14, 1958.
26. Rapid Validation and Resourcing of Joint Urgent Operational Needs, Chairman of the Joint Chiefs of Staff Instruction 3480.01, July 15, 2005.
27. Statement of Guiding Principles for the Federal Acquisition Team, FAR 1.102.
28. Role of the Acquisition Team, FAR 1.102-4(e).
29. GAO bid protest decision: Specialty Marine, Inc., Comp. Gen. Dec. B-2769888 (11 October 2005); FAR 5.101.
30. Methods of Disseminating Information, FAR 5.101, Part 5, Publicizing Contract Actions; FAR 5.101(a)(2) apply unless an exception in FAR 5.202 applies. Time periods in FAR 5.203 do not apply to simplified acquisition procedures; they are much less stringent for SAP. No J&A is required for unusual and compelling urgency. FAR 6.302-2(c)(1).
31. Web pages accessed April 21, 2008.

Chapter 3. The Federal Contract
1. Joseph R. Nolan and Jacqueline M. Nolan-Haley, *Black's Law Dictionary, with Pronunciations*, 6th ed. (St. Paul, Minn.: West Publishing, 1990), 322.
2. "Chapter 7-000 Contract Types," Information for Contractors, DCAAP 7641.90, DCAA, January 2004, pp. 7-1–7-6.
3. Negotiating Contract Type, FAR 16.103.
4. Uniform contract format, FAR 14.201–1.
5. Fixed-Price Contracts, FAR Subpart 16.2.
6. Cost-Reimbursement Contracts, FAR Subpart 16.3; Limitation of Cost and Funds, FAR 32.704.
7. Indefinite-Requirements Contracts, FAR 15.503, DFARs 16.503.
8. Indefinite-quantity contracts, FAR 16.504; Ordering, FAR 16.505; Advisory and assistance services, FAR 37.201; GAO bid protest decision: Palmetto GBA, L.L.C., Comp. Gen. Dec. B-299154, December 19, 2006.
9. Variation in estimated quantities, FAR 52.211-18.
10. Performance-based acquisition (PBA), definitions, FAR 2.101; Modular contracting, FAR 39.103(a).
11. Development of acquisition plans, bundling, FAR 2.101; Rules on Use of Funds, 31 U.S.C. 1501(a)(1).

12. Orders under Multiple Award Contracts–Fair Opportunity, FAR 16.505(b)(1).
13. *National Defense Authorization Act for Fiscal Year 2008*, S. 1547 PCS, amending Sections 2304 a(d), 2304c, 10 U.S.C.A. Section 821, Enhanced Competition Requirements for Task and Delivery Order Contracts, passed by the Senate October 1, 2007. The House version, known as H.R. 1585, passed on May 17, 2007. The act (H.R. 4986) was finally signed into law by the president on January 28, 2008.
14. The National Defense Authorization Act (NDAA) of 2008 amended the Federal Acquisition Streamlining Act (FASA) of 1994 to authorize for the first time the GAO to consider protests in connection with the issuance of tasking orders in excess of ten million dollars. GAO's exclusive jurisdiction of such protests took effect on May 27, 2008.
15. Time-and-Materials Contracts, FAR 16.601; Payments under Time-and-Materials and Labor-Hour Contracts, FAR 52.232-7; Labor-Hour Contracts, FAR 16.602.
16. Letter contract–application, FAR 16.603-2.
17. Basic ordering agreements, FAR 16.701-703.
18. Blanket purchase agreements, FAR 13.303-3.
19. "Special Report, the Future of Technology," *Business Week*, June 20, 2005, n.p.
20. Web pages accessed April 22, 2008.

Chapter 4. Writing a Winning Proposal

1. Acquisitions subject to qualification requirements, FAR 9.206.
2. QPLs, QMLs, and QBLs, FAR 9.203; Opportunity for qualification before award, FAR 9.205.
3. Department of Commerce, Defense Priorities and Allocation System, 15 C.F.R. 700; Priorities and Allocations, Solicitation Provision and Contract Clause, FAR Subpart 11.6, FAR 11.604(b), FAR 52.211-15; Department of Defense, *Defense Priorities and Allocation Manual*, Washington, D.C., DoD 4400.1-M, February 21, 2002.
4. Contractor Personnel in a Designated Operational Area or Supporting a Diplomatic or Consular Mission Outside the United States, FAR 52.225-19.
5. Best Value Continuum, FAR 15.101; Trade-off process, 15.101-1; lowest price technically acceptable source selection process, FAR 15.101–2.
6. Seven Steps to Performance-Based Acquisition, http://acquisition.gov/sevensteps. This Web page specifically contains the most current information, training, and assistance for federal buyers and sellers.
7. Performance-Based Contracting: General, FAR 37.601; elements of performance-based service contracting, FAR 37.602-1- 5.
8. Exchanges with offerors after receipt of proposals, FAR 15.306; clarifications and award without discussions, FAR 15.306(a); communications with offerors before establishment of the competitive range, FAR 15.306(b).
9. Unsolicited proposals, FAR 15.603(c); Receipt and Initial Review, FAR 15.606-1; Evaluation, FAR 15.606-2.
10. Limited use of data (unsolicited proposal), FAR 15.609.
11. Competition Advocates, FAR Subpart 6.5.
12. *Freedom of Information Act*, 5 U.S.C. 552, FAR 24.202; FAR 24.202(a); FAR 15.403-3(b); 10 U.S.C. 2306a(d)(2)(C) and 41 U.S.C. 254b(d)(2)(C).

13. Web pages accessed April 22, 2008.

Chapter 5. Simplified Acquisitions, Sealed Bidding, and Acquisition of Commercial Items

1. Statement of Guiding Principles for the Federal Acquisition System, FAR 1.10.
2. Simplified Acquisition Procedures, FAR Part 13.
3. Legal effect of quotations, FAR 13.004.
4. *Federal Acquisition Streamlining Act of 1994*, list of inapplicable laws, FAR 13.005.
5. Soliciting competition, evaluation of quotations or offers, award and documentations, FAR 13.106.
6. Actions At or Below the Micro-Purchase Threshold, FAR Subpart 13.2.
7. Sealed Bidding, FAR Part 14.
8. Elements of sealed bidding, FAR 14.101.
9. Preparation of invitations for bids, FAR 14.201.
10. Bidding time, FAR 14.202-1.
11. Methods of soliciting bids, FAR 14.203.
12. Pre-solicitation Notices, FAR 14.205.
13. Two-step Sealed Bidding, FAR 14.5.
14. Submission, modification, and withdrawal of bids, FAR 14.304.
15. Opening of bids, FAR 14.402.
16. Special Aspects of Contracting for Construction, FAR 36.2.
17. Bonds and Other Financial Protections, FAR 28.1.
18. Price-related factors, FAR 14.201-8.
19. Unbalanced pricing, FAR 15.404-1(g).
20. Responsible bidder—reasonableness of price, FAR 14.408-2; Standards, FAR 9.104; Causes for debarment, FAR 9.406-2(b)(1)(v).
21. Conditions for pre-award surveys, FAR 9.106-1; Affiliated concerns, FAR 9.104-3(c).
22. SBA Certificate of Competency, FAR 19.6; 15 U.S.C. 637(b)(7) as amended by U.S. Public Law 95-89, August 4, 1977, 13 C.F.R. 125.5.
23. Award (bids), FAR 14.408.
24. Rejection of bids, FAR 14.404-1.
25. Two-Step Sealed Bidding, FAR Subpart 14.5.
26. Reverse auctions. There is no specific designated Web site for reverse auctions. Each agency has its own procedures that are provided in the solicitation for a particular procurement. The Army, GSA, and Navy have conducted some of the earliest auctions. For a summary look at www.ustreas.gov/offices/management/dcfo/procurement/training/primer.pdf.
27 Existence of a mistake and the bid actually intended, FAR 14.407-3(a).
28. Definitions (Commercial Item), FAR 2.101.
29. Acquisition of Commercial Items, FAR Part 12; Applicability, FAR 12.102 (41 U.S.C. 437).
30. Procedures for solicitation, evaluation and award, FAR 12.203; Special Requirements for the Acquisition of Commercial Items, FAR Subpart 12.2.
31. Test Program for Certain Commercial Items, FAR 13.5, 41 U.S.C. 428a.
32. Contract type, FAR 12.207.
33. Web pages accessed April 22, 2008.

Chapter 6. Contracting by Negotiation

1. *Competition in Contracting Act of 1984*, 10 U.S.C. 2304(a)(2).
2. Best value continuum, FAR 15.101.
3. Trade-off process, FAR 15.101-1.
4. Lowest price technically acceptable source selection process, FAR 15.101-2.
5. Oral presentations, FAR 15.102.
6. Request for proposals, FAR 15.203.
7. Uniform contract format, FAR 15.204-1.
8. Evaluation factors and significant subfactors, FAR 15.304.
9. Source selection—responsibilities, FAR 15.303.
10. Proposal evaluation, FAR 15.305.
11. Department of Defense, Deputy Undersecretary of Defense (Science and Technology), *Technology Readiness Assessment (TRA) Deskbook*, Washington, D.C., May 2005, to ascertain Technology Readiness Level for evaluation (http://acc. dau.mil).
12. Contract pricing, FAR 15.4.
13. Obtaining cost and pricing data, FAR 15.403; information other than cost and pricing data, FAR 14.403–3.
14. Proposal analysis, FAR 15.404.
15. Contractor Performance Information, FAR Subpart 42.15; General, FAR 42.1501.
16. Profit, FAR 15.404–4.
17. Price negotiation, FAR 15.405.
18. Trulogic, Inc., Comp. Gen. B–29725.3, January 30, 2006.
19. Pre-award debriefing of offerors, FAR 15.505.
20. Post-award debriefing of offerors, FAR 15.506.
21. U.S. Government Accountability Office, Office of the General Council, *Bid Protests at GAO: A Descriptive Guide*, 8th ed., GAO-06-797SP (Washington, D.C.: GPO, 2006).
22. Bid Protests Regulations, 4 C.F. R. Part 21.
23. The Boeing Company, Comp. Gen. B-311344, et al., June 18, 2008, pp. 1–67.
24. *The Consolidated Appropriations Act of 2008* (CAA), P.L. 10-161, 121 Stat. 1844 (12.26.2007) granted jurisdiction to the GAO to hear Transportation Security Administration (TSA) protests in lieu of the FAA, effective June 28, 2008.
25. Web pages accessed April 22, 2008.

Chapter 7. My Small Business Is Special

1. Size Standards, 13 C.F.R.121; FAR 19.102; Representations and re-representations, FAR 19–301, Federal Acquisition Circular 2005–18, July 5, 2007.
2. Issuing or denying a Certificate of Competency, FAR 19.602–2.
3. Determination fair market price, FAR 19.202–6(a); Subsection 2332(e) of Title 10, U.S.C., amended by Section 801 of the Strom Thurmond National Defense Authorization Act for fiscal year 1999 and Section 816 of the Bob Stump National Defense Authorization Act for fiscal year 2003 requires the DoD to suspend the regulation implementing the authority to enter into a contract for a price exceeding fair market cost if the secretary determines at the beginning of the fiscal year that the DoD achieved the 5 percent goal established in 10 U.S.C. 2323(a) in the most recent fiscal year for which data are available.

4. Size Standards, 13 C.F.R., Part 121; FAR 19.102.
5. Set-Asides for Small Business, FAR Subpart 19.5; Historically Underutilized Business Zone, FAR 19.13, 45 U.S.C. 632 et seq.; Service-Disabled Veteran-Owned Small Business Procurement Program, FAR 19.14.
6. Contractor Team Arrangements, FAR Subpart 19.6; Policy, FAR 9.603; Joint Ventures (small disadvantaged business), 13 C.F.R. 124.1002(f).
7. The Small Business Subcontracting Program, FAR Subpart 19.7.
8. Statutory requirements, FAR 19.702; Representations and Re-representations, FAR 19.301; Federal Acquisition Circular 2005–18; Post-Award Small Business Program Representation, FAR 52.219–28.
9. Section 8(a) Contractor, 15 U.S.C. 637(a); Contracting with SBA, FAR Subpart 19.8.
10. Price Evaluation Adjustment for SDBs, FAR Subpart 19.11 and DFARS 219.11.
11. *Contract Work Hours and Safety Standards Act*, FAR 22.403–3.
12. Equal Employment Opportunity, 41 C.F.R., Chapter 60; FAR 22.800; Exemptions, FAR 22.807.
13. *Walsh-Healey Public Contracts Act*, 41 U.S.C. 35.
14. *Service Contract Act of 1965*, FAR 37.301; 41 U.S.C. 351; Exemptions, FAR 22.10.
15. *Davis-Bacon Act*, FAR 22.403–1, 40 U.S.C. 276a.
16. *Buy American Act–Supplies*, FAR Subpart 25.1; General, FAR 25.101; Exceptions, FAR 25.103; *Buy American Act–Construction Materials*, FAR Subpart 25.2
17. Free Trade Agreements, FAR Subpart 25.4; *Trade Agreements Act* (19 U.S.C. 2501 et seq.; Evaluating Foreign Offers–Supply Contract, FAR Subpart 25.5.
18. Wyse Technology, Inc., Comp. Gen. Dec. B-297454, January 24, 2006.
19. Environment, Energy and Water Efficiency, Renewable Energy Technologies, Occupational Safety, and Drug-Free Workplace, FAR Part 23.
20. Federal Procurement of Bio-based Products, 7 U.S.C. 8102.
21. Web pages accessed April 22, 2008.

Chapter 8. Show Me the Estimate

1. *Truth in Negotiations Act*, par. 3-701, 10 U.S.C. 2306a and 41 U.S.C. 254b.
2. Prohibition on obtaining cost or pricing data, FAR 15.403-1.
3. Requiring cost or pricing data, 10 U.S.C. 2306a and 41 U.S.C. 254b, FAR 15.403–4(a)(1).
4. Defective cost or pricing data, FAR 15.407–1(b)(1).
5. Appeal of United Technologies Corporation, ASBCA Nos. 51410, 53089, 53349, January 19, 2005.
6. Solicitation provisions and current clauses, FAR 15.408; Instruction for Submitting Cost/Price Proposals When Cost or Pricing Data are Required, FAR Table 15–2.
7. Requiring information other than cost or pricing data, FAR 15.403–5(b)(2).
8. Proposal analysis techniques (Price Analysis), FAR 15.404–1(b).
9. Proposal analysis techniques (Cost Analysis), FAR 14.404–1(c).
10. Procedures for requesting wage determinations, FAR 22.404–3.
11. Cost Accounting Standards (Appendix to FAR Loose Leaf), 48 C.F.R., Chapter 99.

12. Make-or-buy programs, FAR 15.407–2.
13. Military Handbook 881A, July 30, 2005.
14. Contract Cost Principles and Procedures, FAR Part 31.
15. Reporting of royalties, anticipated or paid, FAR 27.204.
16. Royalties and other costs for use of patents, FAR 31.205–37.
17. Cost of money, FAR 31.205–10.
18. Weighted Guidelines, DFARS 215.404–4; Record of Weighted Guidelines Application, DD Form 1547, prescribed at DFARS 215.404–70 (July 30, 2002).
19. Profit, FAR 15.404–4; 10 U.S.C. 2306(d); 41 U.S.C. 254(b).
20. Department of Defense, *Armed Services Pricing Manual* (Washington, D.C.: GPO, 1986).
21. Department of Defense, Defense Contract Audit Agency, *Information for Contractors*, DCAAP 7641.90 (Fort Belvoir, Va.: Defense Contract Audit Agency, January 2005) (http://www.dcaa.mil/dcaap7641.pdf).
22. Penalties for Failure to Exclude Certain Projected Unallowable Costs, FAR 31.201–6.
23. Use of Recovered Materials, FAR Subpart 23.4; Estimate of Percentage of Recovered Material Content for EPA-Designated Items, FAR 52.223-9; www.epa.gov/cpg/products.htm.
24. Defense Procurement, Acquisition Policy, and Strategic Sourcing, Contractor Pricing Reference Guides, http://www.acq.osd.mil/dpap/cpf/contract_pricing_reference_guides.html.
25. Web pages accessed April 22, 2008.

Chapter 9. Protecting the Business Jewels

1. *Diamond v. Diehr*, 450 U.S. 175, 209 U.S.P.Q. 1(1981).
2. U.S. Constitution, art. 1, sec. 8.
3. *Arms Export Control Act of 1976*, 22 U.S.C. 2751 et seq., FMS acquisitions under the act. The act is implemented by the International Traffic in Arms Regulations, 22 C.F.R., Subchapter M, Part 120, Munitions List, Chapter 1, Section 121.1. This act is administered by the Directorate of Defense Trade Control, Department of State.
4. *Export Administration Act*, 50 U.S.C. app. 2401. The act is implemented by the Export Administration Regulation, 15 C.F.R. 368 et seq., which includes the Commerce Control List administered by the Department of Commerce.
5. International Patent Cooperation Treaty, which is administered by the World Intellectual Property Organization, enables the U.S. applicant to file one application, "an international application," in English in the U.S. Receiving Office (U.S. Patent and Trademark Office) and have that application acknowledged as regular national filing in as many member countries to the treaty (there are ninety-one or so possibilities) as the applicant designates (http://www.wipo.int/treaties/en).
6. Department of Commerce, Patent and Trademark Office, *Manual of Patent Examining Procedure*, 6th ed. (Washington, D.C.: GPO, July 1997), Section 1801, pp. 1800–1–126.
7. 35 U.S.C. 112.
8. 37 C.F.R. 1.131, Code of Federal Regulations, Patent, Trademarks, and Copyrights, Rule 1.131.
9. Patent Disclosure Document, 37 C.F.R. 1.21(c).

10. Provisional Patent, 35 U.S.C.A. 111.
11. 447 U.S. 303, 206 U.S.P.Q. 193 (1980); *Thomas Jefferson: A Comprehensive, Annotated Bibliography of Writings about Him (1826–1980)*, vol. 5, ed. Frank Shuffelton (Washington ed., 1871) (New York: Garland, 1983), 75–76; *Graham v. John Deere Co.*, 383 U.S. 1, 7–10 (1969).
12. Inventions Patentable, 35 U.S.C. 101; Reduction to Practice 35 U.S.C. 112.
13. Conditions of Patentability, Novelty and Loss of Right to Patent, 35 U.S.C. 102; In Re: Glavas, 109 U.S. P.Q. 50, 52 (CCPA 1956).
14. Conditions for Patentability, Nonobvious Subject Matter, 35 U.S.C. 103; *Graham v. John Deere*, 383 U.S.1, 148 U.S.P.Q. 459 (1969).
15. *KSR International Co. v. Teleflex, Inc.*, U.S. Supreme Court, No.04–1350, April 30, 2007.
16. Rejections under 35 U.S.C. 102(a) or 102(b).
17. Inventions Patentable, Utility Patent, 35 U.S.C. 101.
18. Patents for Designs, 35 U.S.C. 171.
19. Best Mode of Specification, 37 C.F.R. 1.71.
20. Elements of U.S. Patent Application, 37 C.F.R. 1.77; 37 C.F.R. 1.51.
21. 37 C.F.R. 1.75, Claim(s); 35 U.S.C. 112.
22. Patents Rights—Retention by the Contractor (Short Form), FAR 52.227–11 (contractor is other than a small business or nonprofit organization).
23. Patents Rights—Retention by the Contractor (Long Form), FAR 52.227–12 (contractor is other than a small business or nonprofit organization or for the benefit of a foreign government under a treaty or executive agreement).
24. Patent Rights—Acquisition by the Government, FAR 52.227–13 (January 1997).
25. Rights in Data—General, FAR 52.227–14 (June 1987).
26. Authorization and Consent, FAR 52.227–1 (July 1995).
27. Policy, FAR 27.302, 302(a).
28. Contract Clauses, FAR 27.303.
29. Rights in Technical Data—Noncommercial Items, DFARS 252.227-7013, pars. (a) (3), (14).
30. Rights in Technical Data—Noncommercial Items, Unlimited Rights License, DFARS 252.227–7013, par. (a) (15).
31. Rights in Technical Data—Noncommercial Items, Limited Rights License, DFARS 252.227–7013, par. (a) (13).
32. Independent research and development and bid and proposal costs, FAR 31.205–18.
33. Bid and proposal costs, FAR 31.305–18.
34. DFARS 227.471 (1988); 48 C.F.R., Section 227.471; *Dowty Decoto, Inc., v. Department of Navy*, 883 F.2d.774 (9th Cir. 1989).
35. DFARS 252.227-7013 par. (a) (14); DFARS 252.227–7013 par. (a) (11).
36. Copyrights, 17 U.S.C. 101 with amendments; *Whelan, Inc. v. Jaslow Dental Laboratory*, 797 F.2d. 1222, 3d Cir. 1996.
37. DFARS 52.227–7013 Alt. II.
38. Computer Software, DFARS 27.480; DFARS 37.481.
39. *U.S. Trade Secrets Act*, 18 U.S.C. Section 1905 (1982).
40. *Freedom of Information Act*, 5 U.S.C. 552.
41. Rights in Noncommercial Computer Software and Noncommercial Computer

Software; documentation, DFARS 251.227-7014; DFARS 252.227–7014 par. (a) (11); DFARS 252.227–7013 par. (a) (14); DFARS 252.7013 par.(a) (11).

42. Patent Indemnity, FAR 52.227–3.

43. Waiver of Indemnity, FAR 52–227–5.

44. Deferred Delivery of Technical Data or Computer Software, DFARS 252.227–7026.

45. Deferred Ordering of Technical Data or Computer Software, DFARS 252.227–7027.

46. Web pages accessed April 22, 2008.

Chapter 10. Avoid Being Blacklisted

1. J. Lynn Lunsford and Anne Marie Squeo, "Boeing Dismisses Two Executives for Violating Ethical Standards," *Wall Street Journal*, November 25, 2003, A1, A8.

2. *Procurement Integrity Act*, 41 U.S.C. 423.

3. 10 U.S.C. 2397a, pars. (d)(1)(a).

4. Department of Defense Directive 5500.7D1f (2), D2d, F2c; FAR 3.104–3(b) & (e); FAR 3.104–4(g) and (h); FAR 3.104–6(a).

5. Robert Pear, "Health Industry Bids to Hire Medicare Chief," *New York Times*, December 3, 2003, A1, A28.

6. Department of Defense Directive 5500.7, FAR 3.104.

7. 18 U.S.C. Section 208; 5 C.F.R., Section 2635.603(b).

8. Procurement Integrity Restrictions, guidance produced by the DoD General Counsel's Office, Standards of Conduct (August 19, 2005).

9. The General Fraud Statutes used to prosecute procurement fraud by the Justice Department: U.S.C.A. Title 31, Section 5332 (bulk cash smuggling); Title 41 et seq. (the anti-Kickback Act); Title 18, Sections 1031 (major fraud against the United States), 1001 (false statements made in a matter within the jurisdiction of the United States, 1956 and 1957 (money laundering), 1341 (mail fraud), and 1343 (wire fraud), among others; House, Subcommittee on Crime, Terrorism, and Homeland Security, Statement of Barry M. Sabin, Deputy Assistant Attorney General, Department of Justice, June 19, 2007.

10. Standards of Conduct, 5 C.F.R. 2635.107; 41 U.S.C. 423.

11. Certificate of Competency and Determination of Responsibility, FAR Sup. 19.6; 15 U.S.C. 637.

12. General Standards for Responsibility Determinations, FAR 9.104–1.

13. False, fictitious or fraudulent claims, 18 U.S.C. 287; Monopolies and Combinations in Restraint of Trade, 15 U.S.C. 1, *Fraud and False Statements Act*, 18 U.S.C. 1001, chap. 47.

14. J. Lynn Lunsford and Anne Marie Squeo, *Wall Street Journal*, December 2, 2003, A1, A12.

15. Anti-Trust, Bid Suppression and Limiting, 15 U.S.C. 1.

16. *False Statements Act*, 18 U.S.C. 1001.

17. *The War Profiteering Prevention Act of 2007*, S. 119 and H.R. 400 (passed the House on October 9, 2007. Last major action was on October 17, 2007, when H.R. 400 was read twice and placed on the Senate legislative calendar under General Orders 423. Ref. Library of Congress, www.thomas.loc.gov. It calls for the following:

1. Amends the federal criminal code to impose a fine and/or prison term of up to twenty years for profiteering and fraud involving a contract or the provision of goods or services in connection with a war, military action, or relief or reconstruction activities within U.S jurisdiction.

2. Prohibits (a) executing or attempting to execute a scheme or artifice to defraud the United States, and (b) materially overvaluing any good or service with the specific intent to defraud and excessively profit from the war, military action, or relief or reconstruction activities.

3. Imposes a fine or prison term of up to ten years for (a) falsifying, concealing, or covering up by any trick, scheme, or device a material fact; (b) making any materially false, fictitious, or fraudulent statements; or (c) making or using any materially false writing or document knowing the same to be false, fictitious, or fraudulent.

4. Establishes the fine provided by this act as the greater of one million dollars or twice the gross profits or other proceeds derived by a person convicted of an offense under this act.

5. Expands venue rules for the prosecution of offenses under this act.

6. Grants extraterritorial federal jurisdiction over offenses under this act.

7. Subjects any property which constitutes or is derived from proceeds traceable to a violation of this act to civil and criminal forfeiture.

8. Makes the war profiteering and fraud offenses set forth by this act predicate crimes for racketeering and money-laundering offenses.

18. *2004 Federal Sentencing Guidelines Manual*, chap. 8, pt. B, sec. 8B2.1, "Effective Compliance and Ethics Programs," http://www.ussc.gov/2004guid/8b2_1.htm.

19. Contractor Code of Business Ethics and Conduct, FAR Subpart 3.10, FAR 52.203–13, 14 (December 2007). The subpart and clauses address the requirements for a contractor code of business ethics and conduct; an internal control, reporting, and disciplinary system; and the display of Office of the Inspector General Fraud Hotline posters within ninety days after the award of a contract having a value in excess of five million dollars and a performance period of more than 120 days. The requirements for a formal training program and internal control system are inapplicable for small businesses unless such a business is involved with a criminal or civil lawsuit or debarment or suspension.

20. Web pages accessed April 22, 2008.

Chapter 11. The Governance Game

1. Contract Administration, FAR Part 42.
2. Contract Modifications, FAR Part 43.
3. Inspection of Supplies—Fixed-Price, Cost-Reimbursement, FAR 52.246–2, 3.
4. Inspection of Services—Fixed-Price, Cost-Reimbursement, FAR 52.246–4, 5.
5. Inspection—Time-and-Material and Labor-Hour, FAR 52.246–6.
6. Higher-Level Contract Quality Requirement, FAR 52.246–11.
7. Warranties, FAR Subpart 46.7; Warranty of Supplies of a Noncomplex Nature, FAR 52.246–17.
8. Contract Administration, FAR Part 42.
9. Contract Modifications, FAR Part 43.

10. Government Contract Quality Assurance, FAR Subpart 46.4; Acceptance, FAR Subpart 46.5.
11. Inspection of Supplies—Fixed-Price, Cost-Reimbursement, FAR 52.246-2, 3.
12. Inspection of Services—Fixed-Price, Cost-Reimbursement, FAR 52.246-4, 5.
13. Inspection—Time-and-Material and Labor-Hour, FAR 52.246-6.
14. Higher-Level Contract Quality Requirement, FAR 52.246-11.
15. Inspections: Defense Supply Systems, Inc., ASBCA 54494, July 28, 2005.
16. Warranties, FAR Subpart 46.7.
17. Warranty of Supplies of a Noncomplex Nature, FAR 52.246–17.
18. Warranty of Supplies of a Complex Nature, FAR 52.246–18.
19. Warranty of Services, FAR 52.246–20.
20. Warranty of Construction, FAR 52.246–21.
21. Material and Workmanship, FAR 52.236–5.
22. Payments, FAR 52.232–1.
23. Advance Payments, FAR 52.232–12.
24. Assignment of Claims, FAR 52.232–23; *Assignment of Claims Act*, as amended, 31 U.S.C. 3727, 41 U.S.C. 15.
25. Progress Payments, FAR 52.232–16.
26. Prompt Payment, FAR 52.232–25.
27. Prompt Payment for Construction Contracts, FAR 52.232–27.
28. Performance-Based Payments, FAR 52.232–32.
29. Changes Clauses, FAR 52.243–1, 2, 3, 4 (Fixed-Price, Cost-Reimbursement, Time-and-Materials or Labor-Hours, Construction); Changes and Changed Conditions, FAR 52.243–5.
30. Cardinal change: *Krygoski Construction Co. Inc., v. United States*, 94 F.3d 1537, 1543 (Fed. Cir. 1965).
31. Information for Contractors, DCAAP 7641.90, DoD, Defense Contract Audit Agency (January 2004).
32. Equitable adjustment claims: *Wunderlich Contracting Co. v. United States*, 351F.2d 956, 968, 173 Ct. Cl. 180, 199 (1965); Precision Dynamics, ASBCA No. 50519, September 14, 2005; *Boyajian v. United States*, 423 F.2d 1231 (U.S. Ct. Claims, 1970).
33. Limitation of Cost, FAR 52.232-20.
34. Constructive change: *Ets-Hokin Corp. v. United States*, 420 F.2d 716, 720 (U.S. Ct. Claims 1970); *Miller Elevator Co. v. United States*, 30 Fed. Cl. 662, 678 (1994).
35. Government Delay of Work, FAR 52.242–17; *West v. All State Boiler Co., Inc.*, 146 F.3d 1368, 1372 (Fed. Cir. 1998).
36. Unabsorbed overhead (Eichleay formula): *P. J. Dick, Inc. v. Secretary of Veterans Affairs*, 324 F.3d 1364, 1370 (Fed. Cir. 2003); *Sauer, Inc. v. Danzig*, 224 F.3d 1340, 1347–48 (Fed. Cir. 2000).
37. Delays: *Wilner v. United States*, 24 F3d 1397, 1401 (Fed. Cir. 1994).
38. Excusable Delays, FAR 52.249–14.
39. Stop-Work Order, FAR 52.242–15; *Merritt-Chapman & Scott Corp. v. United States*, 429 F2d. 431, 443 (Ct. Cl. 1970).
40. Suspension of Work, FAR 52.242–14.
41. Termination for Convenience of Government, FAR 52.249–1 to 7 and cases: *Librach and Cutler v. United States*, 147 Ct. Cl. 605 (1959); *Kalvar Corp. v.*

United States, 543 F.2d 246, 1298 (Ct. Cl.1976); and *Colonial Metals Company v. United States*, 494 F.2d 1355 (Ct. Cl. 1974).

42. Default (Fixed-Price Supply and Service) clauses, FAR 52.249–8; Default (Fixed-Price Research and Development), FAR 52.249-9; Default (Fixed-Price Construction), FAR 52.249–10.

43. Default cases: *Radiation Technology, Inc. v. United States*, 366 F.2d 1003 (177 Ct. Cl. 227 1966); *DeVito v. United States*, 188 Ct. Cl. 979, 413 F.2d 1147 (1969); J. J. Seifert Machine Co., ASBCA No. 41,398, January 23, 1991, 91–2 BCA par. 23, 705; and KSC-TRI Systems U.S.A., Inc., ASBCA No. 54638, December 8, 2005.

44. Disputes, FAR 52.233–1; *Contract Disputes Act of 1978* (P.L. 95-563) as amended (41 U.S.C. 601–613).

45. *Certification of Claims under Disputes Act*, FAR 33.207.

46. Contractor Retention of Records, FAR Subpart 4.7; Audit and Records—Sealed Bidding, FAR 52.214–26; Audit and Records—Negotiation, FAR 52.215–2.

47. Earned Value Management System, FAR 34.2; Integrated Baseline Reviews, FAR 34.202; Notice of Earned Value Management System—Pre-Award IBR, FAR 52.234–2.

48. American National Standards Institute/Electronics Industries Alliance Standard–748.

49. Office of Management and Budget Circular A–11, Part 7.

50. Contract Data Requirements List, DD Form 1423: DI–MGMT–8004, Management Plan; 80227, Contractor's Progress Status and Management Report; 80269, Status of GFE Report; 81466, Cost Performance Report (Cost Management Report—Monthly Cost Report).

51. Web pages accessed April 22, 2008.

Index

About the Author

BILL C. GIALLOURAKIS is currently a lecturer and attorney consultant on federal contracting, including intellectual property. From 1982 through 2003, the author was in private practice in procurement law and intellectual property law in support of high-tech and construction companies whose primary market and customers came from the Department of Defense. He uses his military, engineering, and business backgrounds to solve contract problems during wartime and in peacetime.

He has provided counsel in bid protests before the Government Accountability Office, and he has extensive litigation experience involving contract terminations and claims at various boards of contract appeals, including the Department of Veterans Affairs, Armed Services, and Corps of Engineers, as well as federal courts. He has prosecuted patents and related oppositions and appeals before the U.S. Patent and Trademark.

During his more than twenty-two years of military service, during which he rose to the rank of colonel, he distinguished himself through service, being decorated as a field artillery officer in U.S. troop command assignments in South Vietnam and Germany. As assistant professor, he taught "electricity" to the cadets at the U.S. Military Academy. Mr. Giallourakis has served as the military assistant to the Army's chief scientist and served on the Army General Staff as missile R&D officer responsible for the improved HAWK Air Defense System. Later, he served as project officer for the SINCGARS-V Combat Net Radio and led the Army's Joint Interoperability Tactical Communications System (JINTACS) Task Force.

Mr. Giallourakis is a graduate of the United States Military Academy (BS), Fairleigh Dickinson University (MBA), Purdue University (MSEE), and Seton Hall University Law School (JD).

The Naval Institute Press is the book-publishing arm of the U.S. Naval Institute, a private, nonprofit, membership society for sea service professionals and others who share an interest in naval and maritime affairs. Established in 1873 at the U.S. Naval Academy in Annapolis, Maryland, where its offices remain today, the Naval Institute has members worldwide.

Members of the Naval Institute support the education programs of the society and receive the influential monthly magazine *Proceedings* or the colorful bimonthly magazine *Naval History* and discounts on fine nautical prints and on ship and aircraft photos. They also have access to the transcripts of the Institute's Oral History Program and get discounted admission to any of the Institute-sponsored seminars offered around the country.

The Naval Institute's book-publishing program, begun in 1898 with basic guides to naval practices, has broadened its scope to include books of more general interest. Now the Naval Institute Press publishes about seventy titles each year, ranging from how-to books on boating and navigation to battle histories, biographies, ship and aircraft guides, and novels. Institute members receive significant discounts on the Press more than eight hundred books in print.

Full-time students are eligible for special half-price membership rates. Life memberships are also available.

For a free catalog describing Naval Institute Press books currently available, and for further information about joining the U.S. Naval Institute, please write to:

Member Services
U.S. Naval Institute
291 Wood Road
Annapolis, MD 21402-5034
Telephone: (800) 233-8764
Fax: (410) 571-1703
Web address: www.usni.org